THE INTERNATIONAL
PSYCHO-ANALYTICAL
LIBRARY

EDITED BY ERNEST JONES

No. 16

THE INTERNATIONAL PSYCHO-ANALYTICAL LIBRARY
No. 16

THE
MEANING OF SACRIFICE

THESIS APPROVED FOR THE DEGREE OF DOCTOR
OF PHILOSOPHY IN THE UNIVERSITY OF LONDON

R. MONEY-KYRLE, M.A., Ph.D.

PUBLISHED BY LEONARD & VIRGINIA WOOLF AT THE
HOGARTH PRESS, 52 TAVISTOCK SQUARE, LONDON, W.C.
AND THE INSTITUTE OF PSYCHO-ANALYSIS
MCMXXX

Reprinted with the permission of The Hogarth Press Limited

JOHNSON REPRINT CORPORATION   JOHNSON REPRINT COMPANY LIMITED
111 Fifth Avenue, New York, N.Y. 10003   Berkeley Square House, London, W. 1

COPYRIGHT 1929

Landmarks in Anthropology, a series of reprints in cultural anthropology

General Editor: Weston La Barre

First reprinting, 1965, Johnson Reprint Corporation

Printed in the United States of America

PREFACE

THE author who wishes to acknowledge his indebtedness is not unlike the polyandrous mother who desires to cite a father for her child. She is prompted by natural gratitude, but also by the desire to share the responsibility with others. There are so many possible fathers that she hesitates to choose among them. She cannot even remember them all. She would like best to choose those who hold some high position. But she may fear that a relationship which to her is a source of pride may be indignantly repudiated. So, too, the author is grateful for the stimulus he has received, and, especially if his views are startling, he would like to share their guilt. But he cannot remember all his literary amours. And he may fear lest even those spiritual fathers he can remember and would like best to acknowledge would not acknowledge him.

For these reasons the majority of those who have influenced me indirectly or directly to write this book will remain unmentioned. Three names alone must be excepted: Prof. Freud and Dr. Ernest Jones, to whom I owe what acquaintance with psycho-analysis I possess; and Mr. J. C. Flügel, whose invaluable criticisms and suggestions I have constantly enjoyed.

I wish also to express my thanks to my wife for the preparation of the index and for assistance in the correction of the proofs.

CONTENTS

INTRODUCTION 9

PART I

THE OEDIPUS COMPLEX

CHAP.
I. The Unconscious 15
II. Incest and Parricide 20
III. The Origin and Maintenance of Repression . . 33
IV. Ambivalence and Inferiority 37
V. The Resolution of Ambivalence . . . 49
VI. The Return of the Oedipus Complex . . . 54

PART II

THE MEANING OF SACRIFICE

Introductory Remarks 71
I. The Distribution of Sacrifice 73
II. The Theories of Sacrifice 165
III. The Essence of Sacrifice 188
IV. The Modes of Sacrifice 212
V. The Overdetermination and Rationalization of Sacrifice 239
Abstract 257

INTRODUCTION

THE Subject.—The following investigation is an attempt, of which there are now many, to apply the findings of psycho-analysis in the social field. It deals with the origin and legacy of the Oedipus complex. Its main thesis is that part of this legacy consists in a variety of sacrificial rites.

In Part I. the origin and development of the Oedipus complex is discussed. I have tried to present the main findings of the Freudian School as plausibly as possible, to give biological reasons why some of these findings might have been expected, and to elaborate certain parts of the theory that still seem obscure. My excuse for thus diverging from the applied to the pure branch of psychology is that the theories that will be advanced depend largely upon the theories of analysts. And these have as yet found but limited acceptance. It is therefore necessary to defend what would otherwise have been presupposed. In Part II. I have applied the findings of Part I. to the elucidation of the meaning of certain varieties of sacrifice, that is, to the exposure of the unconscious impulses that evoked these rites. This part is therefore an elaboration of the theory of the origin of sacrifice given by Freud in his *Totem und Tabu.*

The Method.—Although I have tried not to overlook facts which do not fit my theory, the method of this essay is not inductive. I have not approached my material without bias, classified it by similarities, and allowed what uniformities there are to force themselves on my attention of their own accord. Such a method is theoretically the most reliable, but it is laborious not only for those who use it but for those who read their works. The deductive method is more economical of time. Miscellaneous reading in a certain field suggests the existence of some concealed uniformity, of some identity in difference. Henceforth new data are studied with a new purpose—to see whether they contain those characteristics which are now expected. And such a biassed investigation, even when unsuccessful, is not wholly sterile. If the parental solicitude which we may feel for our own productions has blinded us to the inadequacies of our views, we may take consolation in the assurance that others will be less tender-minded, and that a wrong turning in the maze that leads to truth may be permanently closed. At least discussion has been provoked and others saved from fruitless labour.

Having chosen to employ the deductive method in some research, its presentation raises a new problem. To destroy the scaffolding and expose the finished structure, first in its main outline, and then, in greater detail in the order in which each element logically presupposes those that follow, is more satisfying to the aesthetic sense, and kinder to those who have to read it. But it is harder to give and perhaps less honest than the fuller account of the origin of one's ideas and the doubts which have pursued their elaboration. I shall, then, while trying to present those parts of the theory which seem most certain as systematically as possible, not hesitate to deviate into obscurities which still seem incapable of reduction to a general principle.

This essay is not even intended to exhaust its field. In nature there are many independent variables which determine the conditions that we study. It is not possible to investigate them all at once, and we must be content to neglect the many and to abstract the influence of the few.

The Evidence.—Psycho-analysis has been applied not only to the discovery of the unconscious motives of recorded rites, but also to the reconstruction of their origin. It seems important that these two types of argument should be distinguished clearly, for they have a very different value.

Those analysts who endeavour to reconstruct the

past may be called psycho-analytical historians. The origins of the rites they study can no longer be observed. The archaeologist seeks them in the earth. But they have left few direct traces. The anthropologist seeks them among savages. But Primitive Man, whom we are apt to confound with Primeval Man, has a past as old as ours, and although he may have changed less than we have it is probable that he has changed considerably.

The reconstruction of the past is, however, still not hopeless, for this change which the civilized and the uncivilized have both suffered may have been external rather than internal, social rather than psychological. The size of the skull has not altered since long before the dawn of history, and, although the size is no sure measure of its efficiency, the conclusion that our intelligence has not progressed is supported by the consideration that social systems have seldom been eugenic. But even if we have progressed internally, and we may have changed without progressing, the new acquirements seem to have been superstructures added to, not substituted for, what was already there. If this is so, the recovery of the past is not impossible. We know some of the conditions under which our distant ancestors have lived. We can at least imagine how we should have reacted to these conditions, what effects these reactions would leave behind them, and how they would be modified with the alteration of the conditions that called them forth. If, finally, this train of thought leads us to anticipate institutions of which we already possess a record, our confidence in our reconstruction will be considerably strengthened.

Some psychologists believe that our position is even better, that there is a continuity between the generations which leaves something in the nature of a memory behind, and that to know the past it is only necessary to uncover the hidden recesses of our own unconscious minds. Biology does not, however, support this view. It is possible that the appearance of racial memory is delusive—that it is innate tendencies, not memories of their execution, that are inherited; and that if we sometimes react to these tendencies as if we had ourselves indulged them, our memory is not necessarily continuous with those who have.

But whichever view is taken, the past cannot be uncovered without first uncovering those tendencies which an adult environment allows to be neither executed nor expressed. Psycho-analysis can perform this task; but the facts which it reveals can be known only by acquaintance, not by description. Therefore the psycho-analytical historian must confess that the evidence which he can bring to support his theories is mainly psychological, and that it can be adequately judged only by those who in their own persons have experienced the correctness of Freud's teaching. If it were possible to convince others of the truth of psycho-analytical propositions by argument, analysts could dispense with the tedious process of psycho-analysis and recommend their pupils and patients to read books or attend lectures.

But though a psycho-analyst may sometimes push historical research beyond the limits of archaeology or anthropology, his results are unlikely to be certain. Many roads to a given goal are of equal psychological possibility, and he should be careful not to choose between them. For this reason I have generally confined myself to the psychological question of the unconscious motives which are satisfied by a given rite, and have avoided the historical question of its origin.

Truth and Utility.—The material prosperity and comfort of this generation is built on the physics and mechanics of the last. The social stability and welfare of the next may be founded on the psychology and anthropology of this. Perhaps scientific work should always be undertaken as an end in itself. But even that which is most disinterested is often discovered to have the most practical application. It is therefore legitimate to hope of one's work, firstly that it may be true, and then that it may be also useful.

PART I
THE OEDIPUS COMPLEX

CHAPTER I

THE UNCONSCIOUS

A WANT is at first a dim discomfort which compels the organism to act until, by accident or the assistance of other people, the need is stilled.[1] When, later, this need recurs, a memory of the situation which previously accompanied relief may be recalled. This memory converts the vague want into the conscious wish.[2] Thus a need must be, in a sense, unconscious until it evokes an image of the situation which would accompany its satisfaction.[3]

But if a need is incompatible with needs of greater moment it may remain, in this sense, unconscious; or, if it has already been discovered, it may be forgotten. The alteration of the environment which would satisfy such a want is not rehearsed in fantasy. The wish, that is, the image of the situation which is needed, does not consciously occur. It does not consciously accompany the want. Is it non-existent? Or does it exist in an unconscious state?

Metaphysicians have argued that the concept of an unconscious thought is self-contradictory, and, if they

---

[1] Freud, *Triebe und Triebeschicksale*, Sammlung kleiner Schriften, 4. Folge, 2. Aufl. 255. 'Das Nervensystem ist ein Apparat, dem die Funktion erteilt ist, die anlangenden Reize wieder zu beseitigen, auf möglichst niedriges Niveau herabzusetzen, oder der, wenn es nur möglich wäre, sich überhaupt reizlos erhalten wollte'.

[2] Freud, *Traumdeutung*, 7. Aufl. 420. 'Sobald das Bedürfnis ein nächstes Mal auftritt, wird sich, dank der hergestellten Verknüpfung, eine psychische Regung ergeben, welche das Erinnerungsbild jener Wahrnehmung wieder besetzen und die Wahrnehmung selbst wieder hervorrufen, also eigentlich die Situation der ersten Befriedigung wieder herstellen will. Eine solche Regung ist das, was wir einen Wunsch heissen; . . .'

[3] Freud, *Das Unbewusste*, Sammlung kleiner Schriften, 4. Folge, 2. Aufl. 307. 'Ich meine wirklich, der Gegensatz von bewusst und unbewusst hat auf den Trieb keine Anwendung. Ein Trieb kann nie Objekt des Bewusstseins werden, nur die Vorstellung, die ihn repräsentiert.'—Russell, *Analysis of Mind*, 32. 'A hungry animal is restless until it finds food; then it becomes quiescent. The thing which will bring a restless condition to an end is said to be what is desired. But only experience can show what will have this sedative effect, and it is easy to make mistakes.'

have previously defined a psychic process as something which is conscious, it is not difficult for them to show that the assertion that there are unconscious wishes contradicts an analytic proposition of apodeictic certainty.[1] But if the expression ' psychic process ' is not thus arbitrarily defined it is no less intelligible to talk about the unconscious wishes of ourselves than it is to talk about the conscious wishes of other people.[2] Both conceptions have the same logical status; and those who on metaphysical grounds cannot admit the significance of the word ' unconscious ' ought also to admit that the conception of other people's consciousness is equally devoid of meaning.

To the psycho-analytical layman the most convincing proof of the existence of unconscious thought is perhaps to be found in automatic writing. Janet remarks : ' Nous ne pénétrons jamais réellement la conscience d'une personne ; nous ne l'apprécions que d'après les signes extérieurs qu'elle nous en donne. Si je crois à la parole de Lucie, qui me déclare qu'elle ne sent pas, pourquoi ne dois-je croire à son écriture, qui me déclare qu'elle sent ? '.[3] The possibility remains, of course, that this writing is really automatic ; but so does the possibility that everyone in the world but me is a mere automaton.

The psychology of the adult, especially of the neurotic or pervert adult, is difficult to represent unless his mind is regarded as continuous with that of the

---

[1] Freud, *Das Unbewusste*, Sammlung kleiner Schriften, 4. Folge, 2. Aufl. 296. ' Diese Gleichstellung (des Bewussten mit dem Seelischen) ist entweder eine petitio principii, welche die Frage, ob alles Psychisches auch bewusst sein müsse, nicht zulasst, oder eine Sache der Konvention, der Nomenklatur. In letzterem Character ist sie natürlich wie jede Konvention unwiederlegbar. Es bleibt nur die Frage offen, ob sie sich als so zweckmässig erweist, dass man sich ihr anschliessen muss. Man darf antworten, die konventionelle Gleichstellung des Psychischen mit dem Bewussten ist durchaus unzweckmässig.'

[2] *Ib.* 298. ' Die Annahme des Unbewussten ist aber auch eine völlig *legitime*, insofern wir bei ihrer Aufstellung keinen Schritt von unserer gewohnten, für korrekt gehaltenen Denkweise abweichen. Das Bewusstsein vermittelt jedem einzelnen von uns nur die Kenntnis von eigenen Seelenzuständen ; dass auch ein anderer Mensch ein Bewusstsein hat, ist ein Schluss, der per analogiam auf Grund der wahrnehmbaren Äusserungen und Handlungen dieses anderen gezogen wird, um uns dieses Benehmen des anderen verständlich zu machen.'

[3] Janet, *L'Automatisme psychologique*, 9e éd. 298.

child he was. Thus a characteristic which develops in the adult is most easily explicable on the assumption that it is a result of a certain mental condition of the child. It is sometimes possible to verify this inference, but often only to verify that the child exhibited tendencies which, but for inhibitions, would have developed into this mental state. Analysts assume that it did develop even if it remained unconscious. In like manner a realist assumes that the mushroom he planted last night, and which he now sees fully grown, existed half grown this morning, even if it were locked in the cellar so that he could not see it. A subjectivist would modify this statement and say that it would have existed if someone had been there to see, and would regard the assertion of its existence as a convenient, if inaccurate, abbreviation for this proposition. For he knows with certainty only that some of the conditions for its reality are satisfied. Similarly, it is open to a philosophical analyst to modify the assertion that unconscious thoughts exist. He knows that some of the conditions for their reality are satisfied. He does not know whether the rest of the conditions are satisfied or not.

Again, a dream or a neurotic symptom can be explained, like the product of a code or a cypher, as the disguised expression of some thought which is incapable of becoming conscious. Analysts assume that this thought exists in the ' Unconscious ', and that it is represented in consciousness symbolically. A realist who found a footprint in the sand would regard this as evidence of the existence of an animal that made it ; and even a subjectivist would regard it as evidence that, to a suitable observer, an animal would occur. But for him another question will remain. Was there or was there not a suitable observer ? If so, and if he admits the existence of other people's minds, the animal existed as a constituent of such a mind. Similarly the psycho-analytical subjectivist will regard the unconscious first as that which in the absence of inhibitions would have been real to, or a part of, the ego. But he might proceed to ask : ' Was it real to some other observer ? ' If his knowledge of psycho-physical correlations was complete he could answer this question ; for then he could determine the thought from the cerebral process, or the process from the thought. If cerebral disturbances such as accompany conscious thoughts are found also to accompany ' unconscious' thoughts he would regard these unconscious thoughts as real. They would be real in the same sense that other people's minds, or the mushroom in the cellar to a suitable observer, are real. If, however, no such cerebral processes are found the subjectivist would regard unconscious thoughts as unreal. But they might still be spoken of as dispositions ; for they may correspond to cerebral paths of low resistance that are inhibited. The idea corresponding to such a path has a potential, or dispositional existence, but it is unreal in the sense that the plant whose seed was sown in ground too hard for it to pierce remains unreal in spite of all its efforts. To the subjectivist the mushroom that no one happens to have seen is unreal in exactly the same sense. Some only of the conditions of its reality were satisfied.[1]

But whatever may be the logical status of the unconscious thought or disposition, its symbolic expression remains real, and so, presumably, does the cerebral process concomitant with this expression. There are, then, two ways of interpreting the phenomenon of symbolic representation, and of describing the unobserved mental state which is the connecting link between two conscious states. We may assume that there are two cerebral processes, one correlated with the symbol and one, perhaps at a lower level, correlated with the thought symbolized. If we take this view, we shall assume that the unconscious thought

---

[1] I have discussed these questions more fully in ' Belief and Representation ', *Symposion*, i., and in ' The Psycho-Physical Apparatus ', *British Journal of Medical Psychology*, viii.

exists, but that it is dissociated from that consciousness which controls speech and is therefore incommunicable. We may, on the other hand, assume that there is only one cerebral process, that which is correlated with the conscious symbolic thought ; and that discharge along the associated path, which would have been accompanied by the thought symbolized, although of low resistance, is inhibited and shunted. If we believe this, we shall assume that the expression ' unconscious thought ' is an abbreviation of the description ' The thought that would have accompanied discharge in a neural path of low resistance if this discharge had not been inhibited '. The same alternative descriptions apply to unconscious thoughts that are intermediaries between two conscious thoughts. I do not know which of these descriptions is correct, and I shall use both of them indiscriminately throughout this paper. Psychoanalysis is fortunately unaffected by the problem, for ' unconscious thoughts ' can be defined as thoughts that would be conscious but for the presence of incompatible desires and they can be mentioned without the implication that they do or do not exist.

CHAPTER II

INCEST AND PARRICIDE

INCEST.—The greatest hostility to psycho-analysis has been evoked by two main contentions—that the affections of the child are sexual and that they are incestuous. Actual analysis and observation must remain the final arbiter of the truth of these assertions; but I think it can be shown that they are not incompatible with certain general biological and sociological considerations.

First, let us consider of what activities psycho-analysts predicate the adjective 'sexual'. They have been accused of unjustifiably extending the meaning of this word. In reality they have employed it in its accepted sense, but with greater consistency than other writers. Activities that, in the adult, precede, complicate, or, in perversions, replace, the act of coitus have always been regarded as sexual. Thus it has always been in accordance with common usage to describe normal oral-erotic activities, such as kissing, as well as pervert anal-erotic activities as sexual. Analysts have applied this name to such activities, not only when they are displayed by adults, but also when they appear in children.

Analysts, then, divide the erotic impulse into three parts—the oral, the anal, and the genital. These they trace to such activities as breast-feeding, defecation, urination, and masturbation, all of which are highly pleasurable to the young child. The impulses connected with these functions can be auto- or hetero-erotic, they can find their satisfaction within the body of their owner, or they may require an external object. When this external object is a member of the child's family, the impulse is said to be incestuous. It is maintained that not only the oral and the anal, but also an early form of the genital impulse invariably selects the mother as its object.

The young mammal at first loves its mother orally because she supplies its milk. Where, therefore, the genital impulse develops before this dependence ceases we should expect it to select the same object. But where this impulse only commences after the oral dependence on the mother is long over we should expect it to be unbiassed in its choice. The psychology of non-human animals appears to be in accordance with this last alternative. There is, as far as I know, little evidence of a genital impulse developing towards the mother at the oral stage, and, although when the later genital tendencies mature, the mother may be selected as the mate, there does not appear to be the obstinate predilection for incest that analysts have found in the unconscious life of man.

But man differs from animals in many ways. He is superior, not in that his innate reactions are better adapted to a hostile environment, but because his capacity to learn permits him to develop a unique command of nature. Hence individuals in which the infancy period was long would have further opportunities to learn by imitation than their more precocious brothers and would tend to be selected. And in this way natural selection may have increased the period of infancy until the child is dependent upon its mother at a time when formerly it would have had a family of its own. If so, we might expect that some relic of the earlier maturity characteristic of a bygone age would complicate the psychology of the child, and that an instinctual adolescence, a caricature of an adult genital impulse, would coincide with a physical and intellectual immaturity. And we might further expect, since the genital phase of development would begin before the dependence conditioned by the oral phase was over, that the objects of the two impulses would be the same, and that the boy child would display the genital affection for his mother that analysts assert that they detect.[1]

A social factor which may be in part responsible for this tendency has been described by Freud and Rank. This is the preference which mothers often display for their sons, and fathers for their daughters.[2] Such an attitude on the part of the parents must influence the children and promote in the son a demand for the undisputed possession of the mother.

But whatever may be the reason for the occurrence of incestuous tendencies, the fact remains that innumerable observers have detected them in children, neurotics, and normal people.

It might be thought that the truth of the assertion that these tendencies exist could be easily detected by direct observation of children. But anyone who tries to do so will find himself faced with the greatest difficulties. These difficulties are of two kinds—those that are determined by the character of the observer, and those that are determined by the character of the child he is trying to observe. If the observer has himself an Oedipus complex a great part of his energies are devoted to its repression, and it is astonishing how successful he may be in overlooking in children things that might remind him of his own repudiated childhood. If, for instance, he keeps a diary of his children he will find how readily he forgets, when he comes in the evening to write it up, to mention the most significant observations of the day. The other difficulties depend on the child. If the observer can remember anything of himself at the age of four he will find that, although his knowledge was extremely limited, his intelligence was far more acute than his parents generally supposed;

[1] Freud has pointed out that the long period of infancy in man must, at least in part, condition his incestuous predilections.

Rank, who lays great stress on the shock of birth, which he seems to regard as the only really important factor in the development of a subsequent neurosis (see *Das Trauma der Geburt*), considers that it is the desire to return to the womb which develops into the later incestuous wish. If so, the actual physical connection that once bound the child to his mother determines the selection of her as the object of his love.

[2] Rank, *Das Inzest-Motiv in Dichtung und Sage*, 2. Aufl. 36.

he was not as naïve as they assumed him to have been. His affections were intense and very private, and he was as ashamed of confessing them as he would now be of admitting any illicit or pervert love. If, when he remembers this, he listens to the conversation of his own children, he will realize how little of their thought he really knows. Again and again a child will seem on the verge of confirming his suspicions, only to 'change the conversation' with the obvious intention of keeping something back. If he trusts his inference and anticipates the child's confession he may get the confirmation he desires; but then its value as evidence is much weaker, because he may himself have suggested the thought he expects to find.[1]

But certain facts he will record. He will find that the child of two to five takes a great interest in his body and in its functions, and that this interest is soon extended to the bodies of other people. He will find that the child tries to monopolize those he cares for, resents rivals, and is extraordinarily sensitive to the least neglect. He will find that when the child is tired or disappointed he sucks his thumb or that this activity has been replaced by masturbation. Lastly, he will find a great curiosity about the facts of birth. Such observations are very general, but they are poor support for the assumption that the child has developed an illicit affection for his mother which will pursue him all his life.

Analysts, however, do not claim that the desires which they detect are fully conscious, but only that what is conscious is more than was previously suspected, and that what is unconscious is definitely sexual and incestuous. Hence it is not easily possible to demonstrate these incestuous tendencies to those who do not admit the validity of the analytic method.

[1] As an example of a spontaneous utterance of a boy of two and a half, which illustrate what analysts would call incestuous fantasies at a sadistic level of libidinal development, I may quote the following: 'Mummie, I should like to take your clothes off, and cut you up, and run over you with a steam roller, and eat you up for lunch. I would, I would.' This remark was made in tones of the greatest excitement, and obviously expressed the most agreeable fantasy.

The child's desires are in part unconscious. He has a limited vocabulary, and an aim can scarcely be regarded as the property of his ego until it can be expressed in words.[1] The adult, although he may not know the purpose of some urge he feels, is at least more favourably placed to find it out. He has a more adequate vocabulary, and the process through which he makes it 'conscious' is the process of its translation into words. But not only are the child's verbal instruments of discovery less efficient than the adult's, but the positive impediments are more formidable. The child is weak and helpless and even more terrified than the adult of the social consequences of his own desires. He represses them, prevents their discovery, or forgets them if they are already discovered. The analytic conception of the child, then, has been till lately[2] derived less from the analyses of children than from those of neurotic adults.

There is not space here to recapitulate the evidence which analyses of children and of adults have supplied for the conclusion that sexual and incestuous desires occur in children, and I must refer to the case histories which have been published. Indirect evidence, which may be more convincing to those who distrust the records of analyses which they have not themselves observed, is furnished in great quantity in such works as *Das Inzest-Motiv in Dichtung und Sage*, by Otto Rank. In the first section of chapter ii. he illustrates the incest motive in the dramas of Oedipus, Hamlet, and Don Carlos—which he treats in great detail in later chapters —and argues that they can only be explained as the distorted expression of infantile wishes that had become repressed. He compares these dramas to incest dreams, whose occurrence is accepted by the analytic school as convincing evidence of the presence of the wishes they fulfil.

---

[1] Freud, *Das Ich und das Es*, 20. ' Die Frage : Wie wird etwas bewusst ? lautet also zweckmässiger : Wie wird etwas vorbewusst ? Und die Antwort wäre : durch Verbindung mit den entsprechenden Wortvorstellungen.' See also : *Das Unbewusste*, Sammlung kleiner Schriften, 4. Folge, 2. Aufl. 334-5.
[2] Symposium on Child Analysis, *International Journal of Psycho-Analysis*, vol. viii. part 3.

But not only do the analyses of individuals and literary productions reveal the presence of incestuous tendencies which have survived from early childhood in a distorted form, but history presents examples in which they have come to direct expression. Rank quotes a number of poets who openly admit their incestuous inclinations,[1] cites accusations which were made against historic persons such as Nero and Agrippina,[2] Alkibiades,[3] and many others, and describes the prevalence of incest in Egypt, Persia, and Peru,[4] in Rome,[5] in Ireland, and in Arabia.[6] The gods, too, were persistent offenders,[7] and the myths which concern them can, like the dramas of the poets, be explained as the expression of wishes which had become repressed.

If, then, incestuous tendencies exist in children, find a distorted expression in neurotic symptoms, literary works, and systems of mythology, have been translated into action by isolated individuals in modern and mediaeval, and by whole nations in ancient, times, we might expect that they existed in a still more open form before the dawn of Ethics. If we find rites and customs which we can explain by the same assumption our confidence in it will be increased.

The study of backward peoples, whose culture is supposed to reflect an early stage of social evolution,

---

[1] Rank, *Das Inzest-Motiv*, 2. Aufl. 40. ' Stendhal, der tiefe Kenner aller menschlichen Leidenschaften, schreibt in seiner *Bekenntnissen eines Egoisten* : " Ich war immer in meine Mutter verliebt. Ich wollte meine Mutter immer küssen and wünschte, dass es keine Kleider gäbe. . . ." Ähnlich schreibt Baudelaire (*Briefe von 1841 bis 1866*, Verlag Bruns, Minden, S. 204) : "Was liebt das Kind so leidenschaftlich in seiner Mutter, in seiner Wärterin, in seiner Lieblingsschwester ? Ist es einfach nur das Wesen, das es nährt, kämmt, wäscht und wiegt ? Es ist auch die Zärtlichkeit und die sinnliche Wollust. Dem Kinde wird diese Zärtlichkeit ohne Wissen der Frau durch ihre ganze weibliche Anmut offenbar." Musset schreibt an George Sand : " Tu t'étais trompé, tu t'es crue ma maîtresse, tu n'étais que ma mère ; c'est un inceste que nous commettions ". George Sand antwortet : " Tu as raison ; notre embrassement était un inceste, mais nous ne le savions pas '."—*Rousseau en Savoie : extraits des ' Confessions ' par Fermale*, 120.
[2] Rank, *ib.* 82. [3] *Ib.* 392. [4] *Ib.* 388. [5] *Ib.* 393.
[6] *Ib.* 397.—Gerig, *Enc. Rel. and Eth.* v. 457 : ' Clotha, daughter of an Irish King, after having been the wife of her three brothers, married her son, Lugaid, supreme king of Ireland (Book of Leinster)'.
[7] Rank, *Ib.* ch. ix. ; see also, by the same author, *Der Mythus von der Geburt des Helden*.

seems at first to disappoint our expectation. For, in general, the more primitive the people, the more stringent is the incest taboo.

Sophisticated cultures, on the other hand, despising the morals of their less enlightened forebears, have often ridiculed such taboos as the decrees of man rather than of nature. The distinction which their sophists wished to formulate seems to have been that between laws designed to fulfil some useful purpose generally desired, such as the physical and material well-being of the community, and laws which, although supported by powerful affects, fulfilled no obvious purpose beyond their own observance. And, since the sophists of early Greece and Rococo France [1] perceived no evil effects from inbreeding, they regarded the incest taboo as the decree of man rather than of nature. Further, long before the sophists, kings and ruling families considered it their special privilege to be independent of the restraints of the vulgar. The Pharaohs of Egypt, the kings of Persia, and the Incas of Peru,[2] following the example of their gods, regularly transgressed the incest taboo, and set examples, in their turn, which their subjects were not slow to follow.[3]

If, then, it is true that high civilizations are often less restrained than their savage ancestors, ought we not to conclude that primeval man was more, rather than less, restrained than his primitive successor? Ought we not to see in the licence of cultured peoples a pervert pleasure in revolt against a 'natural' instinct rather than a proof that the instinct is not natural? Ought we not to see in the incest taboo an instinct evolved to protect the race from the evils of inbreeding?

Against this argument Rank quotes Rohleder, who considers that there is no evidence that inbreeding is detrimental to the race,[4] and Abraham, who suggests that inbreeding is the effect rather than the cause of an

---

[1] Rank, *Das Inzest-Motiv*, 2. Aufl. 403.   [2] *Ib.* 388-9.   [3] *Ib.* 388.
[4] *Ib.* 49. East and Jones: 'Inbreeding and Outbreeding', quoted by Flügel in *the Psycho-Analytic Study of the Family*, 203.

inherited neurotic character.[1] If taboos and punishments of great severity are necessary to support a 'natural' instinct, which is even then frequently infringed, its converse, the tendency to break taboo, is surely the more natural of the two,[2] even if it is dysgenic. If stealing is illegal and severely punished, we infer that stealing is the natural instinct and that respect for other people's goods is a late, and perhaps not even an inheritable acquirement, which must be fortified by law. We know that before the law existed stealing was a regular occupation of every honest man. Where there is a law the tendency which it restricts was once openly expressed. The law is the institution which proves the previous existence of the crime. May we not assume that the incest taboo is no exception to this general rule?[3] If so, the incest taboo of primitive people is a proof of the existence of the tendency it inhibits,[4] and the incest of sophisticated cultures is a rediscovery rather than an innovation.

That incest was openly desired in primeval times seems, therefore, certain; that it was preferred to other forms of mating is suggested by the results of analyses which with tireless monotony have all revealed it, by a study of literary and mythological productions, and by certain social and biological considerations.

Parricide.—If the facts of incestuous desires are once admitted, it is not hard to accept, as the probable corol-

[1] Rank, *ib.* 49. 'Dass in vielen Familien Inzucht und nervöse oder psychische Störungen zusammentreffen, kann keinem Zweifel unterliegen. Daraus folgt aber nicht ohneweiteres, dass beide Erscheinungen in dem einfachen Verhältnis von Ursache und Wirkung zueinander stehen müssen. Es fragt sich vielmehr, ob das Vorkommen von Verwandtenehen in gewissen Familien nicht seinerseits eine spezifische Ursache hat, ob nicht gerade in neuropathischen Familien eine eigentümliche Veranlagung dazu drängt, dass die Familien Mitglieder untereinander heiraten' (Abraham, *Die Stellung der Verwandtenehen in der Psychologie der Neurosen*).   [2] *Ib.* 405.

[3] *Ib.* 44. 'Wie bei den übrigen Tieren, gab es gewiss auch bei den Vorfahren der Menschen eine Zeit, in welcher Blutsverwandtschaft kein Hindernis des Geschlechtsverkehrs bildete' (Westermarch, *Sexualfragen*, Leipzig, 1909). This is not quite the view of Freud, who considers that at least an external 'Hindernis' always existed in the person of the primeval father, and that the later internal taboo is the introjection of the earlier external impediment.

[4] See Brenda Seligman, 'Incest and Descent: Their Influence on Social Organization', *Journal of the Royal Anthropological Institute*, lix.

lary, a third contention of analysis—that the boy child hates and is jealous of his father.

In families where the father regards his children, especially the boys, as an unmitigated nuisance,[1] or at least when this attitude alternates with more kindly feelings, it is not hard to observe in the sons a definite, though partially concealed, hostility to him. But even in sons of a patient and long-suffering father occasional outbursts of fury against his will occur. This amount of father hatred would be admitted by the ordinary observer, who, it must be remembered, can only see in others what he has not too successfully repressed himself. The analytically trained observer, however, will detect in occasional moodiness, in sudden fits of tears, in an irritability usually attributed to overtiredness, a more deep-seated, though concealed, hostility. At these times the child seems to demand a greater attention from his mother, and the effect of such behaviour, if not its object, is to monopolize his mother and keep her to himself. It will be noticed that these moods often arise when the child is disappointed with his mother because she does not fulfil his exorbitant demands, or when the other children or his father attract the attention which he claims himself. The child is angry with his mother for her infidelity and with his rivals. This jealousy is easier to observe when its object is his younger brother, whom he is not afraid to bully, but it also characterizes his attitude to his father. It alternates with periods of depression, for at the same time he loves his father. He would like to monopolize both his parents and live in a state of idyllic bliss in which they devoted their undivided love to himself. But he finds that the world is not made like this; his

---

[1] The father who, returning tired and harassed from his office, hopes for rest and peace in the society of his wife, only to find her whole evening monopolized by her children, does not always conceal his irritation with complete success. His small son perhaps feels a similar annoyance. 'Und wie die ersten feindseligen Impulse des Kindes sich gegen den gleichgeschlechtlichen Teil der Eltern richten, so ist es begreiflich, dass in diesem Elternteil eine Abneigung gegen das Kind erwachsen wird, welches ihn der Liebe des anderen Teiles zu berauben sucht' (Rank, *Das Inzest-Motiv*, 2. Aufl. 37).

parents reserve some of their affection for each other, and he feels that he must make a choice: one only he can keep; the other he must give up. Perhaps he feels he cannot dispose of his father, who is a 'bigger man' than himself,[1] and that he must give up his claim to be the sole owner of his mother; or perhaps he imagines a time when his father will be no more and he will be alone with his mother; but no sooner has he realized this dream in fantasy than he remembers all the games he played with his father and is sad. He also feels afraid. His father may discover what he has thought and hate him, he may never want to play with him again, or worse, he may do to him what he had wished to do to his father—separate him from his mother.

Such thoughts may not be fully conscious, but they may be reconstructed from the child's behaviour. A boy, aged four, told me that he would marry his mother when he grew up. When I asked him what would happen to his father he said that Daddy would marry one of the maids, or perhaps he would become a little boy again. When this child began to realize that fathers cannot be so easily disposed of, and are less accommodating than he hoped, the Oedipus complex began in earnest. But it was much harder to observe. At the age of four and three-quarters the same little boy asked innocently: 'Daddy, will you die when I get married?' and a little later: 'Little boys would cry if they killed their Daddies.' Here the unconscious wish is represented by a conscious fear. But the slightly less inhibited fratricidal desire was sometimes conscious. The same child attacked his little brother, half seriously, half in play. He was told to leave his brother alone. He said, while still holding him tightly: 'I want to kill him.' This child is as a rule a very gentle little boy, but I do not think that anyone who made systematic notes of these sort of remarks could remain in doubt of the

[1] This expression was used by a four-year-old boy who will often be mentioned.

actuality of the Oedipus complex. But it is astonishing how easily one overlooks or forgets such observations.

As with infantile incestuous desires the evidence of parricidal wishes has been till lately derived more from the analyses of adults than from the direct observation of children. I do not think than an analysis has ever been recorded in which these unconscious desires did not play the most important role. But the supposition of their existence is fortified by parallels from other fields.

To analysts, the most convincing evidence for the existence of the son's conflict with his father is to be found in the analysis of dreams.[1] Freud has shown in his *Traumdeutung*, with innumerable examples, that the dream is the distorted substitute for thoughts and wishes which are not allowed expression. As if an inhibited neural discharge had been shunted haphazard into those other paths whose disturbance is correlated with the visible or 'manifest' content of the dream, the conscious substitute or symbol is irrelevantly associated with the unconscious or 'latent' content that it is said to represent. Freud has classified these associations and succeeded in 'interpreting' the dream. It is not, however, easy to convince others of the presence of desires which it is their greatest achievement to have repressed, and evidence that is acceptable to those who have themselves been analysed is seldom effective in persuading those who have not. But not only dreams and symptoms but also literary productions can be analysed and distorted expressions of unconscious thoughts revealed. Rank, for example, shows how frequently conflict in the son between love for his father and love for his father's wife is the leading motive in the drama.[2] He shows how the child's jealousy for the mother may be replaced by jealousy for

---
[1] Freud, *Die Traumdeutung*, 2. Aufl. ch. v. ' Die Träume vom Tod teurer Personen '.
[2] Rank, *Das Inzest-Motiv*, 2. Aufl. ch. ii.—Ludwig, *Goethe*, i. 56. ' A thousand years are but half a night! ' cries Franz in Adeltheid's arms—the

the father's second wife,[1] or even by jealousy for his father's lands.[2] He has illustrated the same motives by examples of conflicts in ancient [3] and modern [4] times, and in the sagas of the heroes [5] and the legends of the gods.[6]

If, then, the motives of the Oedipus drama exist to-day in children and have found such frequent expression in dreams, in mythology, in history, and in literature, may we not expect to find them still more pronounced in primeval times?

In primitive times we find the parricidal taboo more strong than at present, and from this we may argue not that the desire was less but that the taboo was more necessary. Among the Celts, for instance, no child was allowed ' to approach his father armed; the result was that boys were brought up in strange families or by the Druids, a curious custom which persisted for a long time in Ireland; the English and French institution of boarding schools may be a survival of this practice '.[7] Anwyl, alluding to a similar custom, derives it ' from a judicious concealment by the mothers of the boys from the sight of their fathers, lest the head of the household should decide to reduce the number of his children '.[8] But the custom was surely as much to protect the fathers as the sons. Of primeval times we have no record, but, as with incest so with parricide we may regard the taboo as evidence of the former prevalence of the crime. And in the course of this investigation we shall meet with many examples of taboos of the killing of animals or persons who were clearly substitutes for fathers.

Atkinson supposed that parricide was the natural

Franz of the first Götz. ' How I hate the day. . . . Oh, that on thy breast I were one of the immortal gods, who lived self-centred in their passionate brooding ardour, and in a single moment engendered myriad teeming worlds, and felt the raptures of those myriad worlds in one swift instant touch themselves. . . . I would slay my father, if he disputed this place with me! "
[1] Rank, *ib*. ch. iv.   [2] *Ib*. 90.   [3] *Ib*. 206.
[4] *Ib*. ch. v. ' Zur Psychologie des Verwandtenmordes '.   [5] *Ib*. ch. v.
[6] *Ib*. ch. ix. ' Die Welteltternmythe '.
[7] Reinach, *Orpheus*, translated by Florence Simmonds, p. 116.
[8] Anwyl, *Encyclopedia of Religion and Ethics*, xi. 9.

termination of almost every primeval family.[1] As soon as the first signs of weakening age appeared, the sons banded together and killed their sire, each seizing as many of his sisters, aunts, or tribal mothers [2] as he could, to be in his turn destroyed by his own children. The behaviour of the higher apes supports this view [3] and archaeological research may ultimately find some traces of these tragedies, but for the present the strongest arguments are psychological. Jealousy has existed in all ages and is only precariously controlled by counter forces such as fear and love. Primitive man was more impulsive, less integrated, than ourselves. Emotions occurred singly, not all at once. Hate alternated rather than combined with fear, and whatever love there may have been was totally forgotten when jealousy awoke. Parricide would be likely among such people. Analysis has shown that the desire is there to-day; even in historic times it was not uncommon. Probably it was once the rule.

Looked at thus, it is not difficult to realize that what is now so deeply concealed that scarce a hint of it appears in consciousness was once openly expressed in thought and deed. The real problem is not to realize that our ancestors were habitually incestuous and parricidal, but to understand how they progressed beyond this stage. Man was to man a wolf, the most brutal of all the beasts, yet he is the only one that has become 'humane'. Something must have occurred to compel this change. Fear of the father cannot account for the repression of parricidal wishes, but only for the temporary suppression of their translation into action. Some affect towards the father which is incompatible with hate must have developed before the hatred became unconscious.

[1] Atkinson, *Primal Law*, 228.—Roheim, *Australian Totemism*, 37-8. Crawley, *Enc. Rel. and Eth.* iii. 447.
[2] All female members of the older generation were probably regarded as equivalent.
[3] Darwin, *Descent of Man*, vol. ii. ch. xx. p. 395.—Hermann, 'Modelle zu Ödipus und Kastrationskomplex bei Affen', *Imago*, Band xii. Heft 1.

CHAPTER III

THE ORIGIN AND MAINTENANCE OF REPRESSION

A BISMARCK or a Mussolini, if anxious to obliterate class conflicts, will stimulate hostility towards a foreign power. Such statesmen know that jealousies do not easily subside, but that they can be made to change their object. Internal peace is thus a by-product of external war, and it is unlikely that hatred of the primeval father would have subsided without the aid of external foes. Just as France was made a nation by the territorial claims of the early English kings,[1] so may concord have been forced upon the family by competition. An altered relation between population and food supply, or the clash with rival species, might have sufficed to knit the family together. Our ancestors seem to have displaced Homo Neanderthalensis, and it is tempting to speculate whether this heroic struggle may have been the influence which turned us into men.[2]

But whether in competition with other animals or with a kindred species, occasions must have arisen when the father was not the most conspicuous obstacle to life and pleasure. The impulses remained the same, but

[1] Duruy, *Histoire de France*, 22 éd. i. 518. ' Au contact de l'étranger, le sentiment de la nationalité s'éveilla en lui '.—Tylor, *Anthropology*, 1904, p. 432. ' The effects of war in consolidating a loosely formed society are described by travellers who have seen a barbaric tribe prepare to invade an enemy or defend their own borders. Provisions and property are brought into the common stock ; the warriors submit their unruly wills to a leader, and private quarrels are sunk in a larger patriotism.'

[2] Ferenczi has put forward the hypothesis that the privations of the ice age were responsible for the beginnings of repression. ' Nach einer Aussage von Prof. Freud ist der Rassencharacter der Niederschlag der Rassengeschichte. Haben wir uns aber einmal so weit über das sicher Wissbare hinausgewagt, so dürfen wir auch von der letzten Analogie nicht zurückscheuen und den grossen Verdrängungsschub des Individuums, die *Latenzzeit* mit der letzten und grössten Katastrophe, die unsere Stammvordern (schon zu einer Zeit, wo es sicher Menschen auf der Erde gegeben hat) traf, d.i. mit dem Elend der *Eiszeiten* in Konnex bringen, die wir in unserem Individualleben immer noch getreulich wiederholen ' (Ferenczi, *Bausteine zur Psycho-Analyse*, i. 83).

their objects changed. Some of the love for the mother was transferred to the threatened hunting ground,[1] a sense of property was developed, and hate diverted to those who disputed its possession. When they fought together against a common foe, the father became the companion of his sons; he became necessary to them and as such was loved. Gradually the ties became more permanent and less likely to break down at moments when external danger temporarily subsided. Incompatible desires, though they may alternate, cannot consciously occur together, and jealousy and the sexual wishes that produced it were checked by a growing love. The incestuous wishes towards the mother, which were thus repressed, were partially diverted to the father and helped to strengthen the love which originated from the need for a protector.[2] Thus the process was cumulative and every increase of affection for the father repressed still further that love of the mother which produced conflict with him, and tended to divert it to himself. In this way the concept of the father would be enriched with feminine attributes until it reached its climax in the God who created, nourished, and protected his children.

If external danger originated the repression of incestuous and parricidal tendencies, there remains the problem of the continuance of this repression in times of peace.

Those analysts who treat races as if they were individuals would perhaps attribute the original repression to the remorse resulting from the primeval parricide

[1] Ernest Jones, *Papers on Psycho-Analysis*, 2 ed. p. 153. ' . . . the conception of the earth as woman, and especially as mother, is universal and fundamental.' (See Dieterich, *Mutter Erde*, 2. Aufl., 1913.)

[2] Freud attributes the attachment to the father to the suppression and transference of the hetero-sexual impulse. But he suggests that the primal father's own intolerance was sufficient to produce this effect. He says: ' Der Urvater hatte seine Söhne an der Befriedigung ihrer direkten sexuellen Strebungen verhindert; er zwang sie zur Abstinenz und infolgedessen zu den Gefühlsbindungen an ihn und aneinander, die aus den Strebungen mit gehemmten Sexualziel hervorgehen konnten. Er zwang sie sozusagen in die Massenpsychologie. Seine sexuelle Eifersucht und Intoleranz sind in letzter Linie die Ursache der Massenpsychologie geworden' (*Massenpsychologie und Ich-Analyse*, 104).

III THE ORIGIN AND MAINTENANCE OF REPRESSION 35

and its continuation to the fact that the memory of this event is too painful to be recovered. But those who cannot so lightly accept the psychical continuity of races must seek some other explanation. Members of a group in which an inherent love of fathers was developed would better co-operate in war to destroy less-restrained societies; and if man has become innately less ferocious than his ancestors this is perhaps due rather to group selection than to the racial memory of a bygone crime. It seems probable, however, that our innate disposition has changed but little, that what change there is is due to changed surroundings, and that if one generation were to lose the civilization we have so slowly won, nothing would remain to distinguish the next from primeval man.

But so long as the cultured tradition remains unbroken there are social factors which tend to prolong repression, even after the conditions that originally inspired it have passed away. As Ernest Jones has pointed out, a son tends to regard his son as the reincarnation of his father. Hence sons who have once developed affection for their fathers readily transfer these feelings to their own sons,[1] who are thereby encouraged to reciprocate this love and to repress conflicting impulses. Thus filial devotion, once acquired, is an 'inductive' property. If it relates B to A it is likely to recur between C and B and so on *ad infinitum*.

As an additional precaution, the whole structure of society is directed to maintain the inhibitions on which its life depends. The taboos of the savage [2] and the morals of the cultured, the couvade to protect the young,[3] the initiation ceremonies to intimidate

[1] Ernest Jones, *Papers on Psycho-Analysis*, 2nd ed. 658-63.—Psalm xlv. 16. 'Instead of thy fathers shall be thy children. . . .'
[2] Freud, *Totem und Tabu*, 2. Aufl. 65. 'Heilend und schützend wirkt die Berührung, die vom König selbst in wohlwollender Absicht ausgeht; gefährlich ist nur die Berührung, die vom gemeinen Mann am König und am Königlichen verübt wird, wahrscheinlich, weil sie an aggressive Tendenzen mahnen kann.'
[3] Reik, *Probleme der Religionspsychologie*, i. 30-32. 'Wir werden nicht zögern, in allen diesen Verhaltungsmassregeln Schutzbauten zu erkennen,

them,[1] the elaborate matriarchal systems which avoid the conflicts between sons and fathers,[2] the influence of the nursery and of the school, of public opinion, of the law, and of religion, each in their separate way protects the social organism from the forces that still threaten to destroy it. If one generation omits these safeguards it is difficult to foresee what could save it from the next.

---

welche dem Impulse, dem Kinde zu schaden oder es zu töten, einen wirksamen Damm entgegensetzen sollen. . . . Es hat seine volle Berechtigung, wenn der Vater keine Waffen berühren, keine schweren Arbeiten verrichten, kein Tier töten und essen darf, denn diese Handlungen sind Ersatzhandlungen der verbotenen Realisierung seines Todeswunsches gegen das Kind. . . . Das Verbot wird beständig gefährdet durch das Andrängen unbewusster Impulse und ist genötigt, seine Grenzen zu verschieben und zu erweitern, da es auch Ersatzhandlungen der Triebbefriedigung nicht gestatten will.'

[1] *Ib.* 68. ' Das Benehmen der Männer gegen die Knaben hat in manchen Beobachten den Eindruck erwekt, als würden Einschüchterung und Erschrecken der Novizen zu den Hauptzwecken der Weihe gehören.'

[2] It has been stated by Malinowski that the Oedipus complex does not exist among the children of the Trobrianders who have a family organization unlike our own (*Psyche,* iv. 298). Reik has pointed out that the couvade may have as one of its functions the preservation of the child from its father (see note 3, p. 35). May not the Melanesian matriarchy serve a similar purpose as well as that of preserving the father from the hatred of his sons, a hatred that is dangerous to society ? This is the result which, according to Malinowski, has been achieved. May we not suppose that it was also the reason for the survival and development of such a social system ? See Ernest Jones' article, ' Mother-Right and the Sexual Ignorance of Savages ', and his review of Malinowski's book, ' Sex and Repression in Primitive Society ' (*International Journal of Psycho-Analysis,* vi. 123, and ix. 364-73).

CHAPTER IV

AMBIVALENCE AND INFERIORITY

THE repression of the Oedipus complex, which was perhaps the greatest cultural achievement of the race, is reacquired by each individual in his own childhood with varied success. In many, and probably in all at some stage of their development, the conscious alternation of love and hate is merely replaced by an unconscious ambivalence. Until one of these opposite impulses is diverted to other ends the victim of such a conflict is paralysed in action, like Hamlet 'sicklied o'er with the pale cast of thought,' unable either to serve or to destroy the father, reduced to impotence he knows not why. He is incapable of success in anything that demands effort, yet he is tormented with rage at his own failure. He feels a great energy within him, yet cannot apply it. He feels that he could rule the world, yet suffers acutely from his own inferiority. This seems to be a condition through which many men pass, once at the end of infancy and again at the end of adolescence, and in which some neurotics permanently remain.

Those whose ambivalence towards their fathers is the most acute are often the least aware of their hostile feeling. Yet the hostility breaks through in a certain gaucheness towards all who symbolize the father. The savage who kills and eats his god out of love, and the shy man whose embarrassment in the presence of his superiors is expressed as rudeness, are both examples of the external results of such ambivalence. The unconscious hate breaks through, while consciously there is only a strong desire to please and a feeling of inferiority and failure.

The Sense of Inferiority.—The sense of 'inferiority'

will perhaps be most easily investigated if it is first compared with its opposite—the sense of 'positive self-feeling'. This affect is characteristic of a stallion in the presence of a mare or of a stag in the rutting season, and seems to be originally the consciousness of sexual potency. It seems to be, in its purest form, the totality of bodily sensations which arise with that aggressive sexual excitation which is ready to defy all rivals. It is partially repeated in the subliminations of this condition.

Negative self-feeling, then, is perhaps the state which follows the inhibition of sexual potency or its subliminations. This view is in accordance with the findings of those analyses which, for example, detect the origin of excessive shyness in repressed masturbatory exhibitionism, but I will quote a pre-analytical psychologist who in his work of some 1400 pages devotes one small paragraph to the sexual instinct, and who, perhaps unconscious of the meaning of his words, gave a description of negative self-feeling that expresses its origin with unexampled clearness. James puts into the mouth of a believer in the Pure Ego the following account of shame: 'I feel . . . when I perceive my image in your mind to have changed for the worse, something in me to which that image belongs, and which a moment ago I felt inside of me, big and strong and lusty, but now weak, contracted, and collapsed. Is not this latter change the change I feel shame about? Is not the condition of this thing inside me the proper object of my egoistic concern, of my self-regard?"[1]

From the animal world the pride of the stag in the rutting season,[2] and the shame of the dog who, tail

[1] James, *Principles of Psychology*, i. 321-2.
[2] McDougall, *Social Psychology*, 13th ed. 62. 'The instinct of self-display is manifested by many of the higher social or gregarious animals, especially, perhaps, though not only, at the time of mating. Perhaps among mammals the horse displays it most clearly. The muscles of all parts are strongly innervated, the creature holds himself erect, his neck is arched, his tail lifted, his motions become superfluously vigorous and extensive, he lifts his hoofs high in the air, as he parades before the eyes of his fellows. . . . Such self-display is popularly recognized as implying pride; we say: "How proud he looks"! and the peacock has become the symbol of pride. . . . It is this primary

between his legs, is driven from a bitch, are good examples of the contrast of positive and negative self-feeling.

Inhibition due to Fear.—The feeling of being disapproved is not, I think, the primary cause of inferiority in animals or children.[1] But approval as the result of a ' nachträgliche Gehorsamkeit '[2] becomes a condition of potency and thus of self-esteem. Originally the child has no image of his image in other people's minds, but fears his father when he does something that might displease him, or when, in fantasy, he encroaches upon his father's own preserves. He begins to watch his father, and his mother if she is thought of as on his father's side, with anxiety to catch the first sign of a hostile movement. It is not his image in his father's mind that first concerns him, but his father's anger that he fears. Before every intended action he is anxious to ensure the absence of this anger and the presence of a positive approval. One small boy of three asked constantly : ' What would Daddy say then ? ' or ' What would you say, Daddy ? '—questions that seemed to be designed to relieve his mind of the dread of the possible consequences of his actions. Two years later the form of the question was sometimes varied to : ' What would the policeman say then ? '

The Castration Fear.—Analysts have found that the

---

emotion which may be called positive self-feeling or elation, and which might well be called pride, if this word were not required to denote the sentiment of pride. In the simple form in which it is expressed by self-display in animals, it does not necessarily imply self-consciousness.' This state in animals seems to perform three functions : it prepares the organism for the sexual act ; or for the duel with another male ; and it excites and attracts the female. It had originally, we may presume, the same functions in man.

[1] *Ib.* 65. 'It has been asked : " Can animals and young children that have not attained to self-consciousness feel shame ? " And the answer usually given is : " No ; shame implies self-consciousness ". Yet some animals, notably the dog, sometimes behave in a way which the popular mind interprets as expressing shame. The truth seems to be that while fully developed shame, shame in the full sense of the word, does imply self-consciousness and a self-regarding sentiment, yet in the emotion that accompanies this impulse to slink submissively we may see the rudiment of shame ; and, if we do not recognize this instinct, it is impossible to account for the genesis of shame or bashfulness.'

[2] ' Postponed obedience ', see Freud, *Jahrb. der Psycho-analyse*, 1919, i. 23.

fear of castration is an important motive for sexual inhibition, and support their views by a reference to modern dreams,[1] mediaeval superstitions,[2] and ancient sagas.[3] I do not know how far this fear is clearly formulated, but the actions of small boys are often such as would be determined by it. The same little boy was forbidden to play with matches, but told that he might play with them when he was grown up. He replied that he would not grow up, but would become like little Thomas, who on inquiry was discovered to have lost his hand through playing with a gun, an answer that is a complete *non sequitur* unless it is understood that playing with matches, or a gun, symbolize masturbation and the loss of the hand the castration which is thought of as its natural consequence. I do not think that this particular little boy was ever persecuted for his masturbation or threatened with castration, and it is difficult to understand how the fear can have developed. Those analysts who believe in a continuous racial mind might explain such fears as a memory surviving from the time when castration was a not uncommon punishment for the abuse of other people's wives,[4] but apart from the difficulty of understanding how those who have suffered this mutilation have transmitted the resulting trauma to their descendants, I am anxious to avoid additional hypotheses that are not yet unanimously supported by biologists.

[1] *E.g.* dreams of teeth extraction.
[2] Jones, *Der Alptraum in seiner Beziehung zu gewissen Formen des mittelalterlichen Aberglaubens*, 1912. S. 106-10.
[3] Rank, *Das Inzest-Motiv*, 2. Aufl. ch. ix. § 2 : Das Motiv der Kastration. Rank discusses the castration of Uranos by his son Cronos, and of Cronos by his son Zeus. One of the reasons why the son fears castration seems to be that he desires to castrate his own father and projects this desire.
[4] *Ib.* S. 279.—Gray, *Enc. Rel. and Eth.* v. 582. ' In Egypt castration was the penalty for adultery, while in India a Sūdra who committed adultery with the wife of an Ārya, or who insolently made water on a high-caste man, suffered amputation of the penis ; and a Brāhman who dishonoured the bed of his teacher had, as one of the three modes of death offered him, the option of himself amputating his penis and scrotum, and of then advancing, holding them in his hand, to the south-west (the direction of Nirrti, " Destruction ") until he should fall dead. Similarly, those who have sexual relations with women of other castes than their own (excepting, of course, lawful marriages with women of lower castes), who cause animals to be killed or who violate their teacher's wife, are punished, according to *Mahābhārata*, xiii. cxlv. 52 f.,

AMBIVALENCE AND INFERIORITY

Rank[1] derives all fears from the shock of birth, and regards those situations which later excite anxiety as repetitions of this trauma. Freud, although he was the first to regard the shock of birth as the prototype of all subsequent states of fear,[2] attaches a relatively greater importance to the situations of weaning,[3] of the education of the sphincters,[4] and to the first control of masturbation. All these periods in the life of the child involve the giving up of some object which is valued, or of some activity which is clung to with great determination. When he first realizes the opposition which he has to face he reacts with rage, anxiety, and sorrow, as anyone who frequents a nursery can easily

---

in their next incarnation by being born *kliba* (which means either " eunuch ", " impotent ", or even " hermaphrodite ").' We note that the penalty of castration is especially prevalent for adultery with the wife of anyone who stands in the same relation to the offender as the father. Thus offences against wives of teachers or high-caste men are punished with emasculation.

[1] Rank, *Das Trauma der Geburt*.
[2] Freud, *Vorlesungen*, 4. Aufl. 461. ' Wir sagen uns, es ist der *Geburtsakt*, bei welchem jene Gruppierung von Unlustempfindungen, Abfuhrregungen und Körpersensationen zu stande kommt, die das Vorbild für die Wirkung einer Lebensgefahr geworden ist und seither als Angstzustand von uns wiederholt wird. Die enorme Reizsteigerung durch die Unterbrechung der Bluterneurung (der inneren Atmung) war damals die Ursache des Angsterlebnisses, die erste Angst also eine toxische. Der Name Angst—angustiae, Enge— betont den Character der Beengung im Atmen, die damals als Folge der realen Situation vorhanden war und heute im Affekt fast regelmässig wiederhergestellt wird. Wir werden es auch als beziehungsreich erkennen, dass jener erste Angstzustand aus der Trennung von der Mutter hervorging. Natürlich sind wir der Überzeugung, die Disposition zur Wiederholung des ersten Angstzustandes sei durch die Reihe unzählbarer Generationen dem Organismus so gründlich einverleibt, dass ein einzelnes Individuum dem Angstaffekt nicht entgehen kann, auch wenn es wie dem sagenhafte *Macduff* " aus seiner Mutter Leib geschnitten wurde ", den Geburtsakt selbst also nicht erfahren hat. Was bei anderen als Säugetieren das Vorbild des Angstzustandes geworden ist, können wir nicht sagen. Dafür wissen wir auch nicht, welcher Empfindungskomplex bei diesen Geschöpfen unserer Angst äquivalent ist.'
[3] See also Alexander, *Psycho-analyse der Gesamt-persönlichkeit*, 140-1. ' In dem *Verlust eines lustspendenden Körperteils* (Kotstange, Brustwarze, die das Kind, wie Stäarcke es richtig bemerkt, zu dem eigenen Körper gehörend empfindet) und in dem *Nacheinander von Lust und Unlust* glaubte ich, die affektive Grundlage der Erwartung, den in der Onanie lustspendenden Penis zu verlieren, gefunden zu haben. Noch weiter in der frühesten Entwicklung suchend, nahm ich an, dass das Geburtserlebnis jene primitivste Verlustempfindung ist, die später in anderen Formen bei jedem Verlassen einer bereits eroberten Trieborganisations-stufe wiederholt wird und so als die früheste affective Wurzel der Kastrationsangst angesehen werden darf. Diese Auffassung entsprach Freuds Annahme, dass jedes spätere Angstgefühl mit dem Geburtserlebnis in irgend einem Zusammenhange steht.'
[4] Alexander, *International Journal of Psycho-Analysis*, iv. 23.

record. When these conflicts are not definitely ended they recur throughout life in all analogous situations.[1] Fear seems to be the anticipation of want, of pain, whether internal or external, of want that is unrelieved. It is generally accompanied by a memory of the situation which previously coincided with the dissipation of the want—a memory which is called a wish. That is, it is accompanied by the wish to avoid the pain. A fear, therefore, is often the thought of some object that stilled a need as unobtainable ; it is tinged with the memory of the pain which this object would have relieved. It includes the longing for this object. That which stilled a need is valued on its own account. That which was a means becomes an end. The child is dependent upon others and fears to be alone. All his needs were satisfied by his mother before his birth ; and when he is tired and thinks of his warm and comfortable bed he is wishing to return to the place from which he came ; and when he is hungry he remembers her who fed him first. Gradually he learns that much of what is lost returns ; that if he is left alone a few moments he is not permanently deserted, nor doomed to die of hunger if he is kept waiting for his food. The most important lesson of his education is to endure temporary loss,[2] especially when this causes no real pain, but only the thought that,

[1] Ernest Jones, *Papers on Psycho-Analysis*, ch. xl. ' The Anal-Erotic Character Traits '.
[2] Freud, *Hemmung, Symptom und Angst*, 82-3. ' Wenn der Säugling nach der Wahrnehmung der Mutter verlangt, so doch nur darum, weil er bereits aus Erfahrung weiss, dass sie alle seine Bedürfnisse ohne Verzug befriedigt. Die Situation, die er als " Gefahr " wertet, gegen die er versichert sein will, ist also die der Unbefriedigung, des *Anwachsens der Bedürfnisspannung*. . . .'
Mit der Erfahrung, dass ein äusseres, durch Wahrnehmung erfassbares Objekt der an die Geburt mahnenden gefährlichen Situation ein Ende machen kann, verschiebt sich nun der Inhalt der Gefahr von der ökonomischen Situation auf seine Bedingung, den Objektverlust. Das Vermissen der Mutter wird nun die Gefahr, bei deren Eintritt der Säugling das Angstsignal gibt, noch ehe die gefürchete ökonomische Situation eingetreten ist. Diese Wandlung bedeutet eine ersten grossen Fortschritt in der Fürsorge für die Selbsterhaltung, sie schliesst gleichzeitig den Übergang von der automatisch ungewollten Neuerstehung der Angst zu ihrer beabsichtigten Reproduktion als Signal der Gefahr ein.'
See also *Jenseits des Lustprinzips*, 12-17.

should it come, that which usually relieves it would be absent.[1]

Thus fear begins with the fear of the loss of the mother. But it is difficult to see how this dread can develop into the dread of castration.[2] What seems to happen is that the discovery of the penis is a compensation for the loss of the nipple. Children when they are disappointed at first suck their thumbs and then, if this activity has been given up, they masturbate. There is a continuity in development and new activities, or objects, are in reality modifications of old. Freud has suggested that an external object can only be abandoned when something that takes its place is found in the body of the self, that is, when the object is introjected. Perhaps the development from oral to genital eroticism is an example of this process. The nipple is given up and the penis is discovered. It is valued and its loss is feared because its attributes are in part transferred to it from the nipple. It is a substitute for the nipple, and masturbation is a substitute for sucking. But there is a further and still more speculative explanation for the fear of castration that we may consider.

The sensation of sucking may come to be valued on its own account, in the same way that the mother is valued on her own account, because it is a sensation that accompanies the dissipation of a want. Interference with the activity of sucking is, then, feared and resented, for the same reason that a temporary loss of the mother provokes anxiety and anger, because the child feels that its means of satisfying wants, should they arise, might not be there; and it cannot yet tolerate even momentary deprivation. Similarly, erotic sensations of the genital organs may be valued because

[1] Ernest Jones in his paper 'The Early Development of Female Sexuality' (*Int. Journal of P.-A.* vol. viii. part 4) uses the word *aphanisis* for complete deprivation. The idea of the loss of the mother in the oral, of the faeces in the anal, and of the penis in the genital stage are all examples of threats of partial aphanisis.

[2] For Alexander's account of the development of this threat, see note 3, p. 41.

they originally accompanied relief from the discomfort of pressure on the bladder. If so, the fear of castration is derived, in part, from the fear of the loss of the sensations which are the concomitants of urinal relief. A child learns to suck by trial and error, although its inherited physical and neural structure is such that the correct reaction is likely to be soon found. It is possible that it has also to learn to urinate, and that this capacity too is not perfected without trial and error. If so, the child, from time to time, may have to repeat the sensations of this act to ensure that he still has the power to relieve his wants, and to avoid the anxiety characteristic of the random reactions of the learning stage.[1] Thus the penis may be first known as the seat of the sensations which accompany the removal of a want, and the power over these sensations may be the guarantee that the want can always be relieved. If the sensation is lost the fear of an unsatisfiable want occurs. The ideal representation of the fear must then be, at first, the idea of this sensation as unobtainable, that is, the idea of the sense of effort which usually leads to the sensations accompanying the removal of the want but without the memory of these sensations; and later, when visual images have become associated with tactual sensa, the idea of the loss of the urinary or sexual organ.

Thus the fear of the loss of the mother is perhaps originally the visual representation of the fear of the loss of the capacity to take nourishment, and the fear of castration that of the fear of the loss of the capacity to urinate. But since the penis is also a substitute for the nipple, its inherent value and the dread of its loss is correspondingly increased.[2]

[1] Freud, *Jenseits des Lustprinzips*, 13 ff.
[2] A further reason for the development of castration fears was mentioned in note 3, p. 40. It is found that children envy their father's penis. This envy is regularly discovered in analysis, and may be observed in its symbolic expression in the child's desire to possess his father's knife or walking-stick. This envy, combined with jealousy and hatred, seems to lead to the desire to castrate the father—a desire that is often realized in mythology. This idea is now repressed and cannot find direct expression. But it can sometimes appear as a projection. The idea and the wish occur, but they are disowned, and attributed to someone else. Thus the child may avoid the conscious wish to

Relation of the Castration Fear to the Oedipus Complex.

—After this digression we may return to collect the threads of the topic of this chapter. It was argued that the sense of inferiority is due to the inhibition of sexual potency, and that this inhibition is, at least partly, due to fear of castration. How is this fear related to the Oedipus complex?

In the analysis of the little boy's remarks about little Thomas we concluded that he was unconsciously afraid of castration as the result of his masturbation, and we attempted to explain how the fear of castration could be developed. We concluded that the penis was valued because it was a substitute for the nipple, and that masturbation was pleasurable because it was a substitute for thumb-sucking. We further concluded that the child was already familiar with the idea of loss since he had already lost the nipple and had his bodily freedom interfered with by his nurse in various ways. He therefore would be ready to believe that his masturbation would be similarly interfered with, and that like the nipple, the faeces, and his other toys, this too might be taken from him.

But what has all this to do with the Oedipus complex? We know from numerous analyses that the castration threat does in fact come from the father, but we have still to explain why this is so. The answer is, I think, firstly, that masturbation is accompanied by erotic fantasies concerning the women of the child's environment and more especially about his mother, and that these fantasies are very naturally thought to encroach upon his father's rights. Hence the person who would be most likely to disturb his newly acquired genital activities and fantasies would be his father. Secondly, the fear of the father is partly the fear of the projection of the child's own unconscious hostility to his father. Intermediate between complete repres-

---

castrate his father only by replacing it by the fear that his father desires to castrate him. There is the same wish, but in the fantasy that conveys it the rôles are reversed.

sion of desire and its conscious acceptance is the consciousness of the desire as unowned, projected, and attributed to someone else. Thus those who have only partially repressed their sadism, project their cruelty, rediscover it in others, and join societies for the prevention of cruelty to animals or children. Similarly, the child attributes his own hate and envy to his father. And this is perhaps the chief motive for his fear. It is, therefore, ultimately the fear of the father, and of being castrated by him, that is mainly responsible for the inhibition of genital sexual impulses and for the resulting sense of inferiority.

Inhibition due to Love.—But I do not think that the content of this fear is often fully conscious, even in children who are in the midst of their Oedipus complex ; nor that fear of the father is the first cause of repression. In an earlier section it was argued that if the attitude towards paternal authority had been purely hostile, jealousy and hate, and the envy that inspired them, would not have remained, or become, unconscious. Their overt expression would have been suppressed until the child was strong enough to follow the example of his ancestors in the primeval horde. But this suppression would have been external rather than internal, and would have produced a sly timidity rather than a sense of inferiority. It is comprehensible that the fear of castration might inhibit a sense of potency, or of positive self-feeling, in the child, but that this inhibition should continue when the child is full grown is more difficult to understand.

The continuance of this inhibition may be due partly to the automatic action of inhibitions that have become unconscious. But I think that it is also due to the fact that the neurotic is paralysed by love as well as fear ; and that this love is both the main cause of his fear and of his defencelessness against it. For love causes, first, the repression of those hostile wishes that reappear as projections to form the main object of the fear, and then renders its victim defenceless against them. This point will perhaps become clearer if we pass on to consider the sense of failure, which, together with the sense of inferiority, seem to make up the conscious expression of unconscious ambivalence.

The Sense of Failure.—The sense of failure is associated with, but is distinct from, the sense of inferiority. Analyses have shown it to be often the conscious affect evoked by the inhibition of the unconscious desire to kill the father. Thus whereas inferiority is due ultimately to the inhibition of incest through fear, the sense of failure is due to the inhibition of parricide through love. Inferiority alone would perhaps dissolve with the passing years as the fear on which it was founded became more and more inappropriate to the relative strengths of the son and his father; for the son would feel that he was a match for his father and that he could kill him if he were threatened. But the unconscious struggle between love and hate and the guilt and remorse that this entails keeps the son defenceless before his father, and in consequence unable to outgrow the castration threat on which his inferiority is based. The affect of neurotic failure is the affect of a Hamlet who is unable to kill his uncle, the uncle who is at once the symbol of his father and of his father's murderer, that is, himself.[1] There is in victims of such a sense of failure an unconscious conflict of love and hate. One side desires to destroy the father, to kill him, to castrate him, or simply to forget him; the other side loves him, protects him, and keeps him ever present in unconscious thought, where he remains a barrier to the mother and to all that symbolizes her possession.

In literature this conflict is often portrayed on a more conscious level. The son is estranged from, yet dominated by, the image of his father. This image hangs like a dark cloud about him and foredooms his efforts in love and war to failure. Sometimes he shakes

---

[1] See Ernest Jones' essay on Hamlet in his *Essays in Applied Psycho-Analysis*.

it off for a short time and attacks some work with a frenzied zeal ; but it is all to no avail, and in the end he perishes a victim of his own impulse to destroy that can find no outlet and that is turned at last against himself.[1]

The Concept of the Father.—Thus the ambivalence towards the father, which is due to the Oedipus complex, is manifest in a sense of inferiority and of failure. But what happens to the sexual and aggressive impulses that are repressed ? A great part of them are projected, as we have already seen. They are projected to form the concept of the father, who may be thought of as a sort of superman, potent, fearless, and dangerous. There will be formed, therefore, two concepts : one of the self as inferior and impotent, the other of the father as superior and mighty. And this opposition between the ideas of the self and of the father serves but to aggravate the psychic tension, until it discharges in one of two directions.

[1] For a good example of this sort of literature, see *Midas and Son*, by Stephen McKenna.

CHAPTER V

THE RESOLUTION OF AMBIVALENCE

THE crippling ambivalence of the Oedipus complex may be relieved in two ways known to analysts as direct and inverted solutions. In the first the love for the father, and in the second the hate for him, is given up or diverted.[1]

The Direct Solution of the Oedipus Complex.—The direct solution in its purest form is the solution of primeval man at a time when repression was still weak. Then the son killed his father and ruled and courted in his place. But we have assumed that even at this epoch fathers were loved as well as hated. Would not the son fall into depression at his loss and would not the ghost of his loved father haunt his thoughts so that his last state was worse than his first?

We know that loved objects are sometimes forgotten and do sometimes lose their spell, and Freud has made a suggestion as to how this comes about. The Unconscious, he thinks, though faithful to its first love, may be deceived and accept a symbol for the reality. Father substitutes may be found which the Unconscious will accept and love, and among these objects is the son himself. He has taken the place of his father, he acts in all things as his father acted before him, and his Unconscious may come to believe that he really is his father; or at least to act as if it did. He ' introjects ' his father and thus compensates himself for his loss.[2]

But not only is the loss of an object made good by

[1] Freud, *Das Ich und das Es*, 37. ' Bei der Zertrümmerung des Ödipuskomplexes muss die Objektbesetzung der Mutter aufgegeben werden. An ihre Stelle kann zweierlei treten, entweder eine Identifizierung mit der Mutter oder eine Verstärkung der Vateridentifizirung. . . .'

[2] *Ib.* 34. ' Wenn das Ich die Züge des Objekts annimmt, drängt es sich sozusagen selbst dem Es als Liebesobjekt auf, sucht ihm seinen Verlust zu ersetzen, indem es sagt: " Sieh, du kannst auch mich lieben, ich bin dem Objekt so änlich ".'

introjection. The qualities of the object are also introjected, and the negative self-feeling replaced by the sense of superiority. When the primeval parricide was a boy and dominated by his father, the sense of inferiority arose, as we have seen, through the inhibition of certain tendencies—an inhibition for which the father was primarily responsible. When the boy thought of his brothers, or his sisters, in situations which would excite these tendencies, his own sense of inhibition was associatively aroused; because these persons occupied the same relation to his father as he did himself. That is, he attributed the same sense of inferiority to the lesser members of his family. But there was one person whom he could not conceive of as subject to restraint, the person to whom his own inhibitions were due—his father. He could not conceive his father in situations which would excite fear and inferiority, because his very idea of his father was composed of the projections of his own inhibited, aggressive and sexual, desires. When, therefore, his father was thought of as excited by what were for him forbidden tendencies it was not the sense of inhibition, but the sense of power which he would have felt were it not for the existence of his father that was associatively evoked. He built a picture of his father as a sort of superman free from doubt, insecurity, and fear, and longed to think of himself as equally courageous, and to identify himself with this ' Imago '. And now that he has become a man and has killed his father and occupies his father's place, he feels that this wish has been fulfilled and that he has become his father. For he has reintrojected to form the concept of himself what he once projected to form the concept of his father. He now stands, in his own estimation, as much above the rest of the world as formerly he stood below it, and with no more reason; for he was not less in sexual potency than his fellows, though he believed so unconsciously, and he is now not superior to them. But the fact that he thinks so tends to give him a real superiority in all sexual sublimations. Thus buoyed up with the conviction of his own apotheosis, he becomes the great and mighty ruler of the clan that his father was before him.

The stability of this solution depends upon his Unconscious. If this other personality within him, like his subjects, accepts him as his father all is well; but if it holds to its original Imago, and sees in him but a weak and criminal impostor, the shadow of this Imago will remain a separate entity within him and the conflict with it will inhibit him in all his actions.

The Inverted Solution of the Oedipus Complex.—Fortunately for fathers the archaic solution of the Oedipus complex rarely occurs to-day. At the opposite extreme there is the inverted solution.[1] The son has two loved objects, his father and his mother; for a little while he can enjoy both, but the time may come when the presence of the one limits his enjoyment of the other. If, at this mental stage, he were not a child, but a grown man, he might behave as his primeval ancestors behaved before him. In a moment of irritation he might kill and eat his father. He might give him up as an external loved object and introject him. To the child, however, such a solution of his difficulties is physically impossible even if the moral inhibitions of a softer age allowed it. But if he cannot destroy and introject his father, if he cannot give up and become his father, he may give up and become his mother. He can adopt a feminine or inverted solution of his Oedipus complex, project his original masculine desires and enjoy them by proxy.

In so far as he adopts this inverted solution he will become a feminine homosexual. His masculine and aggressive tendencies will remain projected upon his

---

[1] In *Triebe und Triebschicksale* (Sammlung kleiner Schriften iv.) Freud describes the inversion of an impulse, the conversion of sadism into masochism, of curiosity into exhibitionism, of active into passive. The active impulse seems to be disowned, attributed to, and enjoyed in the person of another. The affect remains the same, but there is a rearrangement of the parts of the image that accompanies or evokes it; the original subject, the self, has taken the place of the original object. Even masochism is sadism by proxy.

father. But he will no longer fear them, nor feel them as an indignity. He will accept his own feminine rôle and will find in it the compensation for what he has given up. And even the projected impulses he will enjoy by proxy, by identification with his father.[1] He will co-operate with his father, and in doing so will reflect his father's strength. Thus there is a certain opposition between introjection and identification. After introjection the object is given up. But identification requires the continued existence of the object. A soldier can identify himself with his commander and a woman with her husband; both will thereby regain some of the masculinity that they have projected; but neither may be able to dispense with the object of their love and admiration. This is clearly shown by the panic which may befall the best armies on the death of their commanders. In the inverted solution of the Oedipus complex the son loses his inferiority through identification with an external object that is conceived to be superior. Only in the positive solution is this object introjected.

The Mixed Solution of the Oedipus Complex.—But neither the pure masculine nor the pure feminine solutions of the male Oedipus complex are now normal. Most often a compromise is formed and the son exhibits characteristics of both. By changing the object of his original sexual desire he can remain heterosexual without conflict with his father.

This renunciation may produce the partial introjection of the mother, and some degree of inversion in the sublimates of the original desires. Since, however, the son abandons his father as an erotic object, he introjects his father's heterosexuality and many of its derivatives. But, unlike the primeval parricide, he does not become his father in all things; for he also introjects his father's prohibitions, including the incest

[1] The word 'identification' is sometimes used as equivalent to 'introjection'. It seems better, however, to reserve it for that process by which someone else's character is enjoyed by proxy as if it were our own—a process which is distinct from introjection and for which there is no other single word.

taboo.[1] His ego thus derives from his mother those feminine sublimations which give him a certain docility to authority, and from his father a certain combination of manliness and morality which leave him heterosexual but ' exogamous '. In this way that first moral ego is formed, which survives throughout life as an automatic or unconscious conscience, and which is known to the devout as the voice of God and to analysts as the Super-Ego.

Thus, even if extreme solutions are avoided, the Oedipus complex leaves a curtailed potency, a certain amenity to the discipline of superiors, and a morality derived from the introjection of a father's prohibitions. Without these qualities no society could have arisen. They have given stability at the expense of progress. But some day it may be possible to maintain a culture at a lesser cost.

[1] Freud, *Das Ich und das Es*. 40. ' So kann man als allgemeinstes Ergebnis der vom Ödipuskomplex beherrschten Sexualphase einen Niederschlag im Ich annehmen, welcher in der Herstellung dieser beiden, irgendwie miteinander vereinbarten Identifizierungen besteht. Diese Ichveränderung behält ihre Sonderstellung, sie tritt dem anderen Inhalt des Ichs als Ichideal oder Über-Ich entgegen.

' Das Über-Ich ist aber nicht einfach ein Residuum der ersten Objektwahlen des Es, sondern es hat auch die Bedeutung einer energischen Reaktionsbildung gegen dieselben. Seine Beziehung zum Ich erschöpft sich nicht in der Mahnung : So (wie der Vater) sollst du sein, sie umfasst auch das Verbot : So (wie der Vater) *darfst* du nicht sein, d.h. nicht alles tun, was er tut; manches bleibt ihm vorbehalten.'

CHAPTER VI

THE RETURN OF THE OEDIPUS COMPLEX

REAL and Psychological Loss of Father.—Neither the inverted nor semi-inverted solution of the Oedipus complex is necessarily stable; the same conflict may return with new actors. In so far as the incestuous desires and their sublimations are unsatisfied, they remain to revolt against their repressor whether this is the real father or the super-ego who has adopted his prohibitions. In so far as they were satisfied by inversion, they demand the empathetic enjoyment of the father's love as a compensation for what is given up. And this consolation is precarious and likely to be of short duration; for the son may lose his father either psychologically while he is still alive, or actually through death.

If the father is a Pharaoh ruling Egypt with despotic power and convinced of his own divinity he may in truth resemble the man he is thought to be. But the less sublime his confidence and his temporal power, the greater is the gulf between the concept and the real, the sooner it will be disclosed. If the father is seen to be subject to authority, to hesitate, perhaps to fear, the whole psychological structure which has been built about him tumbles to the ground as surely as if he had been removed by death.

Freud in his *Massenpsychologie und Ich-Analyse*[1] has described the panic in a battle which may occur if the leader is killed or loses the confidence of his men; that is, if either of the events occur which correspond

---

[1] Freud, *Massenpsychologie und Ich-Analyse*, 54. ' Der typische Anlass für den Ausbruch einer Panik ist so ähnlich, wie er in der *Nestroy*schen parodie des *Hebbel*schen Dramas von Judith und Holofernes dargestellt wird. Da schreit ein Krieger: "Der Feldherr hat den Kopf verloren", und darauf ergreifen alle Assyrer die Flucht. Der Verlust des Führers in irgend einem Sinne, das Irrewerden an ihm bringt die Panik bei gleichbleibender Gefahr zum Ausbruck. . . .'

within the family to the two ways by which the father may be lost. Such a panic is, therefore, a neurosis in miniature which recapitulates the disturbance which may follow the death of, or the loss of confidence in, a father. Freud first derived such anxiety from a general principle by which libido thwarted of its object was converted into fear; but in a later work [1] he regards it as the conscious reaction to an unconscious desire. Such a desire may be projected in a disguised form and feared as an external danger. Thus the paranoiac's fear of his pursuer is the fear of his own repressed, distorted, and projected homosexual wishes. Similarly, the army whose sublimated homosexual attachment to its leader is suddenly destroyed may be paralysed by fear of the libido that is thereby freed, distorted, and projected. In like manner the real or moral loss of a father may produce an anxiety neurosis.

Father Substitutes.—We saw earlier that a loved object which is lost may be introjected, and, in fact, the normal man does recover from the loss of his father in this way. Thus in Dostoevsky's novel *The Brothers Karamazoff*, Alyosha, at the death of his father-substitute Zossima, after weeping bitterly, stands up, no longer as a boy but as a man. But in the neurotic this introjection is prevented by the super-ego; for, though the super-ego is itself a father introjection, it consists more of prohibitions than of masculinity. And it remains to hinder all subsequent introjection of manly qualities. Thus the loss of the father leaves an aching void, and the son hunts everywhere for substitutes who will fill his place, for someone by whom he will be loved, and in whose strength he can feel strong. With such he repeats his first drama. In their presence he is at first inferior, uncertain, and ill at ease. Then if they treat him kindly he is happy in the sunshine of their approval, and if, by assisting in some enterprise he can identify himself with one of them, he regains the peace that he had before. An understanding teacher or older

[1] Freud, *Hemmung, Symptom und Angst*, S. 118 f.

boy, a considerate and courageous commanding officer, or a sympathetic and distinguished chief may serve the purpose, and as long as the son can retain these substitutes he may regain his mental equilibrium. But his condition is dependent on someone outside himself and subject to the same dangers as the original relation of which this is the copy.

Fictitious Father Substitutes.—There is a way, however, in which a more independent dependence may be won. If a substitute for the father must be found, he may be like Nietsche's Zarathustra, a friend in need but a friend created.

An American questionnaire [1] revealed that an astonishing percentage of adults remember fantasying, that they were foundlings, the real children of kings or queens or of socially distinguished individuals; there must be many more who have forgotten similar theories of their origin. The little boy I have often quoted, who was impressed by the imposing size of a neighbour's establishment, once said that Lord X was his daddy. He, like the socialists, was very shocked that Lord X's mansion was larger than the house of his own father, and used often to ask why this was. Folk-tales and novels habitually employ this motive, and the readiness with which some accept the authenticity of doubtful, but patrician, pedigrees is surely a sublimated variety of the desire to prove their parentage other than it is.[2]

---

[1] Conklin, *American Journal of Psychology*, xxxi. 59.

[2] This desire to prove one's parentage other than it is can sometimes be detected in the latent content of a dream. I will quote an example in which the dreamer seems to take part in the ceremony of his own conception. ' A family wedding, a very important affair. I had to go down steps into the church, which was underground. I got lost and found the way blocked. . . . The organist pointed out the way. I went on, through a hole, and down the pendulum of an enormous clock. Half-way down I noticed to my surprise my own heraldic arms on the pendulum. They were much larger than my father's arms which were on his book plate, and I imagined that they must have belonged to a great-uncle, or to some remote and famous member of the family. During the marriage ceremony I sat by myself in a soft arm-chair at the top of the church. Rather to my surprise and mortification I was not asked to take any part in the service.' In this dream the dreamer seems to have believed that some remote and distinguished ancestor was his father, and to have represented this belief most explicitly.

Supernatural Father Substitutes. — In these last examples new fathers have been invented to take the place of old, who had died or been discarded as unworthy and unlike the ideal which had been formed. Those who build their confidence on them are no longer dependent upon the existence of an individual ; but their position is not yet inviolate, for it is founded upon a false belief, and such beliefs, though of astonishing longevity, are not immortal. There are, however, other types of ideal father which are progressively more immune from the ravages of knowledge, and whose genealogy is the pedigree of God. But we will first consider two collateral ancestors of the deity—the ghost and the totem.

Ghosts.—It may be believed that the father is not really dead, but that his soul is still alive and potent, ready to work for the good or evil of his children. How does this belief arise ?

There is a strong desire to believe that those we love are not really dead, removed from our lives never to return, and the asylums provide examples of persons who have escaped the pain of such a loss through a delusion. And where the super-ego is an impediment to introjection this desire is especially potent. The belief in ghosts has been derived from dreams which members of a tribe may have after the death of their chief. Freud has shown that dreams are wish-fulfil- ments, and, if the dreams of savages are like those of children and express their wishes openly, the dream of the departed chief must be derived from the wish that he were still alive. He was the protector and defender of his tribe, he was invested with all those characters which the members once attributed to their fathers, and they were dependent upon him in no small degree. They refuse to give him up, dream of him, and thereby are convinced of the reality of his ghost.

The realization of another's death may be still more easily prevented if the body is not seen to fall into decay. Ancestors who were not seen to die, and whose tombs were consequently empty, seem often to have been regarded as spirits of unusual power. The body of Osiris was hidden from Isis, and, if this legend is founded upon fact, the belief in the powers of this king may have been partially determined by the fact that he was not seen to die. Nyakang, the founder of the Shilluk dynasty, with whom Frazer compares Osiris,[1] also died mysteriously. Grecian heroes were sometimes translated without dying either to the depths of the earth [2] or to the Island of the Blessed,[3] and in the Middle Ages there were many tales of kings who were not dead but who would return to save their people in the hour of need. Even in our own time similar legends were current about Kitchener and the Czar.

Totems.—A firm belief in the immortality of the soul, however it arises, may enable the son to survive the death of his father without a crisis. He can retain the old Imago and need not find a substitute. If he has been reconciled to his father, his dependence upon him may be undisturbed by guilt and he may enjoy the support he cannot do without. The dead were worshipped and believed to help their people throughout the world in ancient and in modern times.[4] Even the most sophisticated are often unable to repress uneasiness when alone at night they pass a graveyard; for they fear what they unconsciously desire. And the spiritualists still profess to communicate with, and sometimes to recall, the spirits of the departed. Those whose imagination is unchecked by the scepticism of knowledge and who desire to recover their dead relations will see them in many forms. Thus primitive peoples often recognize their ancestors in the form of animals or plants. Among the Shilluks, a pastoral and partially agricultural people of the White Nile, the spirits of the departed monarchs appear from time to time in the form of certain insects, of white birds or of giraffes.[5]

---

[1] Frazer, *Golden Bough*, 3rd ed. vi. 167. 'Both died violent and mysterious deaths: the graves of both were pointed out in many parts of the country. . . .'   [2] Rhode, *Psyche*, 7. and 8. Aufl. i. 113 ff.
[3] *Ib.* i. 69.   [4] Frazer, *Golden Bough*, 3rd ed. vi. ch. xi.   [5] *Ib.* p. 162.

Nyakang, the traditional founder of their dynasty, manifests himself to his people in the form of an animal. 'Any creature of regal port or surpassing beauty may serve as his temporary incarnation. Such among wild animals are lions, crocodiles, little yellow snakes that crawl about men's houses, the finest sorts of antelopes, flamingoes with their rose-pink and scarlet plumage, and butterflies of all sorts with their brilliant and varied hues.'[1]

It is certain that similar beliefs have often led to the worship of animals[2] or plants, and perhaps all such beliefs are so derived. In particular, it is likely that totemists first regarded the animals they revere as reincarnations of their parents. At present, however, the totemist looks on his totem less as a parent than as a cousin or brother[3] who is descended from the same ancestor as himself. But even the present members of the totem species are treated with extraordinary respect, for each incarnates the common ancestor of man and beast. Thus a totem is still consciously identified with an ancestor. Sometimes it is still consciously believed to be a parent. Probably the primitive unconscious always so regards it.

Such unconscious beliefs are not confined to savages. Thus a certain man was puzzled by the peculiar emotion with which he was affected by the discovery of seedling oaks, until he remembered that twenty years before his father had died under an oak, and that acorns from this tree had been planted in his memory.

Gods.—There are at least two types of father god, and both are substitutes for fathers. One is a humanized totem, the other a deified king. It is difficult, if not impossible, to trace the origin of most deities with certainty to either of these alternatives to the exclusion of the other, and often they seem to be eclectic structures—half-man, half-beast—perhaps derived from kings who were later identified with totems. Javeh seems to have been at first a bull and then a ram, and to owe his

---

[1] *Ib.* p. 163-4.   [2] Spencer, *Principles of Sociology*, 1893, i. ch. xxii.
[3] Roheim, *Australian Totemism*, 77-8.

later humanity more to the philosophy of his prophets than to his imitation by horned priests.[1] The gods of Egypt, with the possible exception of Osiris,[2] would seem to be almost wholly totemic ; but the apotheosis of the Pharaohs and the Roman emperors suggests that some of the earlier gods may have been the deified rulers of their people.[3]

Phallic Attributes of Gods.—We have seen that the concept of the father, or of a father substitute, is composed largely of the projection of the masculine potency that in the Oedipus complex is repressed ; that, when envy is replaced by femininity in the invert solution to this complex, this projected potency is enjoyed by proxy ; and that, in the contemplation of the Imago's omnipotence, the lost sense of superiority is emphatically regained. Thus we should expect the earliest gods to display their phallic attributes explicitly.

The worship of mother goddesses of fertility, such as Aphrodite and Astarte, included rites concerned with sacred stones. According to Frazer, ' the precise significance of such an emblem remains as obscure as it was in the time of Tacitus ' ;[4] but their shape and their association with goddesses of fertility leaves little doubt that they were phallic emblems, though it is not clear to whom they originally belonged. They may have been the last remnant of a father god in an earlier trinity, of which only the mother and the son have survived. They may have belonged to the son or human lover, *e.g.* Attis or Adonis, or they may have been always the property of the creator and mother goddess who in her own person combined both the male and the female organs of procreation. If so, the pregnant snake which occurs sometimes in dreams would be her fitting symbol.

[1] Reik, *Probleme der Religionspsychologie*, 1919 ; Das Schofar.
[2] Frazer, *Golden Bough*, 3rd. ed. vi. 159-60.
[3] *Ib.* 167. ' The examples of Nyakang seems to show that under favourable circumstances the worship of a dead king may develop into the dominant religion of a people.' Tammuz and Gilganiesh are also thought to have been once real kings. Hopkins, *Origin and Evolution of Religion*, 74-5.
[4] Frazer, *Ib.* v. 35-6.

Phalli and phallic symbols are a common, if not a universal, attribute of early deities. Isis is depicted weeping for the lost member of Osiris. Heliogabalus dances and sacrifices before the black stone of Emesa.[1] On the walls of the Egyptian temples certain gods are portrayed with erect phalli. Priapus, a typically phallic deity, was a late introduction into Greece, perhaps from Lampsacus or the Hellespont, where, according to Pausanias, he was esteemed above all other gods.[2] The same author ' observes that at Cyllene "the image of Hermes, which the people of the place revere exceedingly, is nothing but the male organ of generation erect on a pedestal"'.[3] In the East Indian Archipelago ithyphallic statues are frequently found. ' The people of Nias, an island off the coast of Sumatra, are in the habit of representing their *adu*, or supernatural beings, by means of wooden images. In many of these the male sex is emphasized in the usual way. When a man dies, such an image is carved in his honour, and is called an *adu zatua*. Offerings are made to it ; and the Niasese are accustomed to implore it for a numerous offspring. When a child is born, a thank-offering is presented. Before the dwellings of chiefs and persons of rank, stones are erected in honour of deceased members of the family. They are called *gowe salawa*, and are sometimes in human form, sometimes in that of a phallus.'[4] Again, in the Barbar Archipelago at the festival of Upu-Cero, 'An emblem of the generative and creative force of the sun, in whose honour the feast is held, is erected, in the form of a standard flying a pennant of white cotton, almost five feet long. The pennant is cut in the form of a man bearing, fastened to it, a stuffed phallus and testicles —an apt suggestion of the orgies enacted below.'[5]

' Certain of the Shinto gods of Japan are ithyphallic. They are represented in wood and stone and are the

[1] There is a vivid and probably fairly accurate reconstruction of these rites in Couperus' novel *Heliogabal*.
[2] Hartland, *Encyclopaedia of Religion and Ethics*, 1917, ix. 816.
[3] *Ib*. 818.   [4] *Ib*. 817.   [5] *Ib*. 817.

object of offerings and worship. Whether similar deities were honoured by the ancient Gauls we do not know. It is certain that in the Middle Ages, and since, in various parts of France and Belgium, ithyphallic saints have been worshipped for the purpose of obtaining offspring or curing impotence and sexual disease. Perhaps the most famous of these was St. Foutin (whose name is variously spelt), by tradition the first bishop of Lyons. His cult was widespread in the south of France. When, in 1585, the Protestants took the town of Embrun, they found among the sacred relics of the principal church an object said to have been his phallus. The extremity was reddened by the libations of wine offered to it by women in need of his help.'[1]

Again, the serpent, which is a well-known phallic symbol, was often worshipped as a god. ' In order to obtain offspring women used to resort to the great sanctuary of Aesculapius, situated in a beautiful upland valley, to which a path, winding through a long wooded gorge, leads from the bay of Epidaurus. Here the women slept in the holy place and were visited in dreams by a serpent ; and the children to whom they afterwards gave birth were believed to have been gotten by the reptile. That the serpent was supposed to be the god himself seems certain ; for Aesculapius repeatedly appeared in the form of a serpent, and live serpents were kept and fed in his sanctuaries for the healing of the sick, being no doubt regarded as his incarnations. . . . Again, the mother of Augustus is said to have got him by intercourse with a serpent in a temple of Apollo ; hence the emperor was reputed to be the son of that god. Similarly, tales were told of the Messenian hero Aristomenes, Alexander the Great, and the elder Scipio : all of them were reported to have been begotten by snakes. In the time of Herod a serpent, according to Aelian, in like manner made love to a Judean maid. Can the story be a distorted rumour of the parentage of

[1] Hartland, *Encyclopaedia of Religion and Ethics*, 1917, ix. 817.

Christ?'[1] 'In India even stone serpents are credited with power of bestowing offspring on women.'[2]

The reason, according to Frazer, ' why snakes were so often supposed to be the fathers of human beings is probably to be found in the common belief that the dead come to life and revisit their old homes in the shape of serpents. This notion is widely spread in Africa, especially among tribes of the Bantu stock.'[3] Thus the ancestor or god is often represented solely by a phallic symbol.

Such phallic attributes of father substitutes may be compared with the phallic symbols that occur in dreams.

There is a common type in which the dreamer knows that there is some dangerous snake, or perhaps a homunculus, hiding somewhere about the house. It is a danger to himself and his wife and children. He tries to find and to destroy it. Analysis will show that this dangerous being is a penis. It is generally his father's; but sometimes, since as a child the dreamer did not know, or refused to accept, the difference between the sexes, it may turn out to be his mother's, as in dreams where the snake is pregnant and looks like a cross between a serpent and a swan. But if the analysis is pushed still further, the penis is usually discovered to be the dreamer's, which had those designs upon his mother that he attributes to his father. He has repressed his incestuous desires, projected them, and rediscovered them elsewhere. Thus, on analogy, we may suppose that the phallic and dangerous attributes of gods were also ultimately projections of attributes of the self.

If the feminine, or inverted, attitude to the divine phallus or its symbol has been consciously acquired it

---

[1] Frazer, *Golden Bough*, 3rd ed. v. 80-81. [2] *Ib.* 81.
[3] *Ib.* 82. See also pp. 82-6. The belief that the dead are reincarnated in snakes is also held ' by the Zulus, the Thonga, and other Caffre tribes of South Africa ; by the Ngoni of British Central Africa ; by the Wabondei, the Masai, the Suk, the Nandi, and the Akikuyu of German and British East Africa ; and by the Dinkas of the Upper Nile (pp. 82-3) '. ' The Romans and Greeks appear to have also believed that the souls of the dead were incarnate in the bodies of serpents (86).'

is no longer feared, but welcomed. Through the sense of union with the loved and admired object, the positive self-feeling which was lost in projection is regained. And this source of the unconscious pleasure in the love of a god is revealed even in the English prayer-book, when marriage is said to have been ordained to symbolize Christ's union with his Church.

The Belief in Gods.—A god, like a king, is a substitute ✓ for a father. He is invented to still a need. The real romances of life are in the past, not in the future ; we shall not love again as we did in infancy, nor be loved as we then imagined that we were. That these relationships are over never to return, that our own wilfulness contributed not a little to their imperfection, and that we were disillusioned in proportion to the intensity of our demands, are facts which are hard to face. The memory of them is obliterated, and they are regarded as unreal. But since they are too important to be given up, something as perfect but more enduring is expected in the future. The belief that somewhere and sometime, either in this world or in the next, we shall experience the perfect love is a fantasy that none escape. The romances of youth, the belief in the soul or in God, and the delusions of insanity are refusals to renounce the past. They differ in the strength of this refusal and in the fixation which they project. So in religion, whether it is naïve anthropomorphic superstition or subtle metaphysic, the disappointments of the world of sense are redeemed in a world that transcends sense, and a lost or defective mother or father is rediscovered more perfect in the person of a goddess or god.

But the attitude towards a father substitute is, like ✓ the attitude towards the original, highly ambivalent. He is loved and hated, propitiated and feared, sought and avoided. Motives for belief in his existence, and for doubt, subsist together. The advance of knowledge renders the world of faith ever more difficult to believe, ever easier to doubt. Something more scientific must be substituted for ' Nature's cure for neurasthenia '.

THE RETURN OF THE OEDIPUS COMPLEX

Aknaton, king of Egypt (B.C. 1375-1358 ?), if Weigall's reconstruction of his life and character is correct, seems to have been the first to reconcile the love of God with a belief in his non-existence, and this king's conception was the prototype of all mystical apology. He found it difficult to believe that a Being worthy of adoration could possess the defects which distinguished the gods of his age, and he came eventually to strip his Aton of almost every material attribute. But *nihil est in intellectu quod non prius fuerit in sensu*, and had he been successful there would have been nothing left for him to love. As happens in such cases, his emotion compromised with his intelligence and he accepted as the symbol of the object of his adoration that which his reason told him was not a Person. He became a nature lover, and worshipped as nature's most perfect element the ' Heat that is in the Sun.' His attitude was not consistent ; for he could love only what he could personify, and yet he was convinced that his God transcended anything which by analogy with things around him he could conceive.[1]

The conflict between love and hate for the father is fought out again in the schools of the philosophers as a conflict between love and intellectual doubt. God is not manifest to the senses, and the old wish for the death of the father finds an easy expression in doubt of the existence of his substitute. Yet this doubt can bring no satisfaction, for the son has become dependent upon his father, his strength is no longer in himself but in the object of his inverted love, and when this object is lost he feels inferior, dejected and utterly alone. His pride and arrogance is centred no longer in himself but in his God. He is no longer self-sufficient but feminine, at least in the sublimate of potency, dependent upon the existence and the love of another.

Spinoza rejected the crude beliefs of the religion of his fathers, and was cast out from the synagogue. But,

[1] This account of Aknaton is based on Weigall's book *Aknaton*, which is admittedly rather a speculative reconstruction of his life. See also Abraham, *Amenhotep* iv., *Imago* i.

since he could not live without God, he invented a new God of his own. Lewis, summing up his teaching, says: 'God is existence. He alone truly exists. Whatever else may be conceived as existing exists in and through him; it is a manifestation of his being. This also is the language of St. Paul, which is chosen by Spinoza as his epigraph. "In Him we live and move and have our being." '[1]

But was there perhaps after all some truth in the allegation of his Jewish biographer Philipson that it was his wish to marry a Christian 'which led him to meditate on Judaism, Christianity, and Religion in the abstract, whence he rose through love to Philosophy'?[2] It is possible that his earthly love revived the Oedipus situation, awoke an unconscious hate of God, which was satisfied in the loss of the old faith, and atoned for in the construction of the new.

He attained to reconciliation with God, to unity with the pantheistic Substance, only through renunciation of the flesh. 'For those things which most frequently occur in life, and in which men, judging from their acts, think supreme happiness consists, may be reduced to three—*riches, honours,* and *pleasures of the senses* (*Divitias, honorem, atque libidinem*). By these three the mind is so occupied it is scarcely able to think of any other good. Pleasures of sense, especially, so absorb the mind that it reposes in them, and thus is prevented from thinking of anything else. But after fruition follows sadness, which, if it does not absorb the mind, at least disturbs and deadens it. . . . But after meditation thereupon, I found, first, that in giving up the ordinary advantages I really renounced only an uncertain good for another equally uncertain, the latter, however, being only uncertain as to the possibility of my attaining it. After assiduous meditation I found that I was only quitting certain evils for a certain good.'[3] Thus Spinoza found the compensation for the

---

[1] Lewis, *History of Philosophy*, 1880, 5th ed. ii. 195.
[2] *Ib.* 173. [3] *Ib.* 174-5.

loss of the direct libidinous desires, which led to 'sadness', the result of conflict, in an inversion, and developed his ' Intellectual Love of God.'

The *Meditations* of Descartes are a classical example of the desire to believe in God warring against an almost equally strong will to destroy Him. Each fresh proof awakens a new doubt which must in turn be stilled, until at last the conscientious philosopher, like Paley, has contributed more to the cause of scepticism than he has to that of faith.

Immanuel Kant was one of the first Europeans to dispense with God. He therefore saw clearly the necessary frivolity of every symbol and the impossibility of speculation beyond experience. Yet he was aware of a Super-Ego which he called the ' Kategorische Imperative', and was mistaken only in supposing it to be objective. Perhaps in his attempt to find a logical justification for morality we may see a last endeavour to construct a God, who would be at once the projection of, and the compensation for, his repressed desires. This attempt seems to have been satisfactory to himself, but it is in reality unsound. Logical justification of morality is impossible, for logic is concerned with tautologies—not with facts which are the accidents of nature. If the Good were first objectively defined, it would be possible with logic to analyse this concept, and to determine the individual things and actions which deserve this predicate. Then moral judgments would possess a universal truth ; but the definition would remain arbitrary and its consequences worthless. If, on the other hand, the Good is subjectively defined as that which evokes moral approbation, moral judgments would be true only to those who made them, and as varied as there are people in the world.

Conclusion.—Enough has perhaps been said to illustrate the return of the Oedipus complex in new forms. The first solution left a super-ego formed of the introjection of parental inhibitions, and an ego which was inverted in the sublimates of sexuality. Thus, as a woman can sometimes only feel sexual pride empathetically in the person of her lover, so can the repressed man only feel the sublimates of this pride in the person of his God. Just as the woman often feels incomplete and inferior without a man, so does the partially inverted man feel incomplete and inferior without a hero, a leader, or a God. This Imago is the projection of his own repressed power and arrogance. In His strength he regains his own strength, and in His love he regains the love of his mother that his super-ego forces him to give up. But the super-ego represses more than is regained and the envy and hostility are ever ready to return. They are repressed and give rise to inferiority and guilt, so that their victim must turn yet more humbly to his God for forgiveness, love, and strength. In psycho-analysis this result is obtained, with less strain on the credulity, by the reconstruction of the super-ego.

PART II
THE MEANING OF SACRIFICE

INTRODUCTORY REMARKS

WHEN a psycho-analyst talks about the 'meaning' of a symptom he does not refer to the connotation of the symptom's Latin name, but to the unconscious *purpose* which has provoked it. It is primarily in this sense that I have called my essay 'The Meaning of Sacrifice', for I regard sacrifice as a neurotic symptom and have sought to disclose the unconscious purpose that it expresses. But there is also some logical justification for the title.

Any theory, if it is correct, can be used as a definition without altering the denotation of what it defines. And, in fact, the definitions of most general terms were once synthetic propositions that predicated of a set of things some common property. The word sacrifice popularly denotes a variety of rites—The *Encyclopaedia Britannica* (9th ed.) mentions six—that seem, at first sight, to have little in common except the name. Hence to define this term we must either enumerate these rites, or we must discover some hidden purpose which underlies them all. We cannot, at once, adopt this latter method, for our theory would then become a *petitio principii*. It would be unassailable, for we should have excluded *a priori* all the facts that did not fit. It would be also valueless, for there would be no guarantee that our concept corresponded to what is usually understood by sacrifice, nor, indeed, that it corresponded to anything at all. But if we commence with a definition by enumeration, and then discover common characters, these can be subsequently used in a new definition which will possess the same denotation as the old. And for this reason the discovery of the unconscious purpose of sacrifice would provide us with the 'meaning' of this term.

In this essay, then, we shall start with a discursive account of sacrifice in many lands which will itself form a rough definition of our subject. Then, after some account of the past and present theories, we will develop that which seems most plausible. If it is correct, it should give the ' meaning ' of sacrifice both in the psycho-analytical and in the logical sense ; the unconscious purpose and the genetic character.

In the account of the distribution of sacrifice, which forms the preliminary definition of the subject, I have been content to resort to the standard works,[1] and have not returned to the original sources, for whose study I am not qualified. But this is no great evil for my purpose, which is to show why certain rites are psychologically satisfying rather than to reconstruct their detailed history.

There is, I think, a legitimate threefold division of labour in anthropology. First, there are the field workers who collect the raw material. Next, the library workers who classify, and entrapolate to some extent from the historic to the prehistoric. Lastly, there are the psychologists who interpret the rites which the library workers have collected in an easy and accessible form. Their theories are a challenge to the field workers to confirm or to reject. Thus Anthropology progresses spiralwise from the field worker to the library worker, from the library worker to the psychologist, and from the psychologist back to the field worker, who starts the cycle all over again.

[1] The works that I have chiefly consulted are Frazer's *Golden Bough*, 3rd ed., Loisy's *Essai sur le Sacrifice*, and de la Saussaye's *Lehrbuch der Religionsgeschichte*, 4. Aufl.

CHAPTER I

THE DISTRIBUTION OF SACRIFICE

I. *Sacrifice in China*

ACCORDING to the *Lehrbuch der Religionsgeschichte*, Chinese religion has three foundations—the cult of nature deities, the cult of ancestors, and the cult of the heavenly bodies.[1] To the psycho-analyst, such gods, ghosts, and spirits are all reproductions on a grander scale of infantile parental Imagos. But the real parents still enjoyed an authority only second to that of the divinities that were created in their image. ' The father of the family was the absolute monarch in his family circle on their common land and at the same time their only priest. He offered to the ancestors whose tablets stood in a shrine on the south side of the house, and to the Earth-god, whose holy place was, in the earliest times, under an opening in the roof in the middle of the house where the sun could shine down on to the earth. Certain genii who protected the family home also enjoyed offerings; such were the spirit of the hearth, of the spring, of the house-door and of the door of the court. The ancestors belonged to the family; they were simply its invisible part, who lived elsewhere. But they took their part in the lives of their successors, they received their nourishment from the younger generation, and were informed of important events which happened in the family. They were considered to be present at its councils. The earth-god extended his dominion when sibs and families combined into larger groups; he had his place—perhaps because the housing improvements no longer permitted the opening in the roof—outside the house on the common land. It consisted of an altar made

[1] Franke, *Lehrbuch der Religionsgeschichte*, 4. Aufl. i. 195-6.

out of earth, a simple hillock, which might not be roofed over lest the union of the gods with the forces of the air should be hindered, and out of a tree planted on the hillock. . . . Probably the tree was a sign of fertility, of the living activity of the god.'[1]

On analogy with themselves, everything for these primitive people had a sex and a reproductive function. Everything was either masculine or feminine, yang or yin. In everything they saw a conjugal pair, in Sun and Moon, Heaven and Earth, Light and Darkness, Warm and Cold, Dry and Wet, High and Deep, Prince and Retainer, Summer and Winter.[2] And in these couples may perhaps be recognized the indefinite multiplication of the divine pair, the creators of the world, that appear in so many mythologies, and who are, to psycho-analysts, the projections of the child's own father and mother.

As among primitive peoples all over the world, there seem once to have been spring festivals in which the young men and women imitated the union of nature; but the later official morality disapproved of these customs and suppressed them, and removed their traces from the literature.[3] Analogy suggests that such rites would have been accompanied by sacrifice, a trace of which may still linger in the fire festivals described by Frazer. In these 'the essential feature of the ceremony seems to be the passage of the image of the deity across the fire'.[4] Perhaps originally the deity himself, or his human representative, was burnt.

Gradually as the state became more centralized, it monopolized the control of religion. The temple of the ancestor of the prince and the temple of the earth-god became the symbol of the state itself, the one as the masculine, or yang, principle, the other as the feminine, or yin, principle. The prince or emperor was the priest who officiated at the sacrifice. He was psycho-analytically a father symbol, and it was fitting that he should

---
[1] Franke, *Lehrbuch der Religionsgeschichte*, 4. Aufl. i. 196-7.
[2] *Ib.* i. 197.   [3] *Ib.* i. 198.   [4] Frazer, *Golden Bough*, 3rd ed., xi. 5.

perform for the state what the father performed for the family. 'From now on the seat of the ancestors of all dynasties of the Chinese emperors is the sky, indeed the ruler of Heaven or Heaven itself is the original ancestor of the ruling family. The emperor is the 'Son of Heaven' (it is not certain if this expression was introduced in the text before the Tschou time), his power is of divine origin, his position demands divine honours'.[1] Such were the foundations of Chinese religion which survived and penetrated alike the metaphysical Taoism, the Confucian revival, and the Buddhist invasion.

Of the three elements—ancestor worship, nature worship, and the worship of the celestial bodies—that made up this religion, ancestor worship was the most important. After the death of a relation there was a fixed period of mourning which varied with the importance of the departed. The mourning for the Son of Heaven, like that for a father or mother of a family, was three years. During this time many of the ordinary sacrifices, which were times of rejoicing, were superseded. Immediately after death there was a rite to recall the ghost.[2] The tablet that bore the name of the deceased stood on the outer covering of the coffin. The sons of the dead, for the last time, invoked him to return. Then the spirit entered into the tablet; henceforth it was kept at the altar of the house, and the name of the deceased was spoken no more.[3] There was a careful preparation of the corpse; a peg was inserted between the teeth so that rice and precious stones could be placed in its mouth; the legs were tied, probably to keep the spirit quiet, and perhaps, as so often among primitive people, to keep it from molesting the living. Food was placed near the corpse and near the coffin and in the grave. On the return from the funeral the tablet was placed near the place where the coffin had lain, and the offering of 'rest' was laid here every day of the mourning. After the end of the mourning, or the time

[1] Franke, *Lehrbuch der Religionsgeschichte*, i. 200.
[2] Loisy, *Le Sacrifice*, 146-7.   [3] *Ib.* 171.

of 'perpetual tears', the offerings were changed, and henceforth the dead received the ordinary gifts of the 'manes' of the dead.[1]

Although this mourning was no doubt consciously sincere enough, there are perhaps still traces of the ambivalence of primitive man to his dead. We may be suspicious of the real purpose of the tieing of the legs and of the taboo of the name which may have been unconsciously intended respectively to prevent the voluntary return, and to avoid the magical evocation or recall, of the departed. Again, the expression 'perpetual tears' looks like an over-compensation for a deficiency of real sorrow. Such considerations strengthened by the analogy of similar rites among other peoples make us more ready to believe that the offerings too were not intended solely for the good of the dead.

Even in modern China there are feasts for the dead. At Emoui, on the fourth or fifth of April, after piling up various meats before the ancestral tablets, the family assemble at the family tomb carrying meat and vegetables and strips of white and coloured paper. These are placed on the funeral mound. Similar offerings are laid at the altar of the god of the country which stands on each tomb. Coloured paper is burnt before the tomb of the ancestor and the altar of the god, and crackers are pulled to drive away the hungry demons who might wish to participate in the ceremony. Finally, the offerings are collected and eaten by the family. 'It is believed that the dead return on the night before the beginning of the seventh month, and on this night and on the following nights for the whole month there are tables at the doors of the houses with plates of offerings, candles and sticks of lighted incense; paper raiment is also burned to clothe the spirits; a small part of the offerings are also burnt, but it is mainly consumed by the family.'[2] It is probable that, as in many places, such attention was originally enjoyed only by rulers and princes, and that it only later became universal.[3]

[1] Loisy, *Le Sacrifice*, 146-7.   [2] *Ib.* 173.   [3] *Ib.* 171-2.

But mortuary sacrifice was not the only sacrifice known to China. In olden times, when there was a plague, many animals were sacrificed at the gates of the towns, and after the victims had been sacrificed they were dismembered and scattered.[1] In times of war, the tablets of the imperial ancestors were anointed with the blood of victims, and carried with the army on its campaigns.[2]

There are also traces of human sacrifice of well-known types, such as the sacrifice of a king, of a young girl to a river, and of first-born sons. 'We are told by the great historian Ssŭ-ma Ch'ien and by others that, as in the land of Egypt in the time of Joseph, seven years of drought prevailed in the Empire, leading to a terrible famine. To such extremities did matters come that it was suggested that a human victim should be offered as a sacrifice to appease Heaven and bring down the shower of much-needed rain. The emperor T'ang said: "If a man must be a victim, I will be he", and prepared himself for the sacrifice. Ere the prayer he offered was finished, the rain fell in heavy showers on the parched land for hundreds of miles.'[3] There is further an account of the sacrifice of a bride to a river and of the eating of first-born sons, which I will quote from Frazer. ' It is said that under the Tang dynasty the Chinese used to marry a young girl to the Yellow River once a year by drowning her in the water. For this purpose the witches chose the fairest damsel they could find, and themselves superintended the fatal marriage.'[4] In the state of Khai-muh, to the east of Yueh, it is recorded that ' it was customary to devour first-born sons, and further, that to the west of Kiao-chi or Tonquin, "there was a realm of man-eaters, where the first-born was, as a rule, chopped into pieces and eaten, and his younger brothers were nevertheless regarded to have fulfilled their fraternal duties towards him. And if he proved to be appetizing food, they sent

---

[1] Ib. 84. [2] Ib. 172.
[3] Dyer Ball, ' Human Sacrifice,' Encyclopaedia of Religion and Ethics, vi. 845. [4] Frazer, Golden Bough, 3rd ed., ii. 151-2.

some of his flesh to their chieftains, who, exhilarated, gave the father a reward"'" (de Groot).[1]

The official ancestor cult was associated with that of nature spirits. The imperial ancestors enjoyed, for example, four big sacrifices a year, one for each season. There were six victims—a bull, a horse, a sheep, a dog, a pig, and a pheasant—and six sorts of grain which were brought by the ladies of the imperial harem. The Son of Heaven himself took the lead and brought in the principal victim, the bull. Such rites ensured good crops.[2] Certain spirits, the descendants of the nature spirits of the plebs, received state offerings and official recognition. Such were the four (or five) holy mountains, the four rivers, the four cardinal points, the Sun, the Moon and the five planets, the spirits of the wind, of the clouds, of the rain and of the fire, of the walls and of the hollows (Gräben).[3]

Offerings were also made to evil spirits. But afterwards they were driven away with great noise of guns and cannons, and overwhelmed with curses for their evil actions. A similar sacrifice was made for men condemned to death before the execution.[4] If this was to propitiate his ghost, the custom in some countries of allowing criminals their wishes on their last night may be partially dictated by a similar motive.

Sometimes sacrifice seems to have been received by proxy. Nature spirits were represented by men who took the offerings on their behalf; and dead ancestors seem also to have been represented by some surviving member of the family, if possible the grandson, who issued their commands, and received offerings.[5]

There were also sacrifices at solemn contracts. When the feudatory princes took their oaths to the Son of Heaven at the time of the Tcheou dynasty, an ox was killed and bled into a bowl ornamented with pearls. Each prince took of the blood and touched his lips.

---

[1] Frazer, *Golden Bough*, 3rd ed., iv. 180.   [2] Loisy, *Le Sacrifice*, 172-3.
[3] Franke, *Lehrbuch der Religionsgeschichte*, i. 201.
[4] Loisy, *Le Sacrifice*, 310.
[5] *Ib.* 94.—Moore, *History of Religion*, i. 15-17.

The ox was then buried together with a copy of the contract. According to Loisy, the participants in this rite believed that they would suffer the same fate as the victim if they broke their oaths.[1]

Temples, and the utensils necessary to their cults, and the royal ornaments were consecrated with the blood of animal victims.[2] Finally, there was a special form of mortuary offering which occurred in ancient China, as in other places. Retainers were killed or killed themselves at the death of their lord to follow him into the next world; and even until recent times widows who committed suicide were especially honoured.[3]

2. *Sacrifice in Japan*

The Japanese are composed mainly of three elements—the Aino aborigines, the Korean or Mongolian emigrants, and the Malayan conquerors. Their religion is largely derived from a mixture of the earlier Korean or Mongolian and the later Malayan cultures.[4] Of their gods, most live on the earth, as gods of the mountains, rivers, and trees, some rule in the underworld of the dead, and others, such as the Sun-goddess and the Moon-god, though born on earth, live in heaven.[5]

There were sacrifices of various kinds. These seem sometimes to have been considered as a sort of exchange of commodities with the gods. Thus in the ceremonial recitation of the offerings the words occur: 'If you, great Gods, grant so and so then will the princes and the common people bring rich offerings'.[6] There are also purifications where the sins of the people are written down, transferred to a paper model of a man, and cast into the sea.[7] At the larger shrines offerings of clothing material, weapons, and live animals were made.[8] In every Shintoist house is a shelf, on which usually there stands a little shrine for the god that is specially

---

[1] Loisy, *Le Sacrifice*, 302-3.   [2] *Ib.* 372-3.   [3] *Ib.* 486.
[4] Florenz, *Lehrbuch der Religionsgeschichte*, 4. Aufl. i. 269.
[5] *Ib.* i. 274.   [6] *Ib.* i. 329.   [7] *Ib.* i. 330.   [8] *Ib.* i. 330-1.

honoured in the house. Every morning, or at least three times a month, a lamp is lighted before it, and wine and flowers are offered.[1]

The official Shintoism does not recognize human sacrifice, but in earlier times men were offered to the gods of the rivers, of the waters, and of the trees. Men were buried under bridges and fortresses as offerings, according to Florenz, to the Earth-goddess. And at important funerals the necessary retinue for the next world were buried alive. Later images took the place of men, but voluntary suicide of retainers continued until recently.[2] Food, arms, ornaments, and earthen vases were also placed in the important tombs.[3]

The ancient Shinto did not, however, associate the cult of the dead with the cult of spirits as in China. Everything connected with the dead was impure for the service of the god.[4] Although offerings seem always to have been made to the dead in Japan, their regular cult is probably due to Chinese influence.[5]

There was an annual feast of first-fruits of the harvest; the offerings were chiefly of rice and rice-beer. The Mikado himself placed the rice before the cushion prepared for the god, as a 'divine nourishment'.[6]

Not all the offerings seem to have been designed to placate, or gain the favour of the gods. Some seem to have magically strengthened him and increased his divine force. Such may have been the intention of the offerings of mirrors to the Sun-goddess, and of the sacrifice of a black horse or dog to procure rain, or a white horse to bring fine weather, offerings which may have represented respectively a rain spirit and a fine weather god.[7]

There were also sacrifices of divination and of purification. For divination, the shoulder blade of a stag was taken and exposed to the fire. The cracks which were caused by the heat were then interpreted as if they were the writings of the gods.[8] For the purification of

---

[1] Florenz, *Lehrbuch der Religionsgeschichte*, 4. Aufl. i. 332.   [2] *Ib.* i. 331.
[3] Loisy, *Le Sacrifice*, 148.   [4] *Ib.*   [5] *Ib.* 174.   [6] *Ib.* 224.   [7] *Ib.* 486.   [8] *Ib.* 266

the Mikado clothes were made as if for him to wear. He then blew on them. After which they were cast into the water.[1] With them, presumably, perished all spiritual impurity.

Like the Emperor of China, the Emperor of Japan, the Mikado, is divine, but he is the incarnation of a female deity, the Sun-goddess, who is the ruler of the universe. 'Once a year all the gods wait upon him, and spend a month at his court. During that month, the name of which means "without gods", no one frequents the temples, for they are believed to be deserted.'[2] Human sacrifices were formerly offered at the graves of the Mikados, 'the personal attendants of the deceased being buried alive within the precincts of the tomb. But a humane emperor ordered that clay images should henceforth be substituted for live men and women.'[3]

Frazer has described the sacrifice of a black dog for rain in detail. 'Among the high mountains of Japan there is a district in which, if rain has not fallen for a long time, a party of villagers goes in procession to the bed of a mountain torrent, headed by a priest, who leads a black dog. At the chosen spot they tether the beast to a stone, and make it a target for their bullets and arrows. When its life-blood bespatters the rocks, the peasants throw down their weapons and lift up their voices in supplication to the dragon divinity of the stream, exhorting him to send down forthwith a shower to cleanse the spot from its defilement.'[4] In many similar rites in other parts of the world such a victim would be itself regarded as divine. And here, too, the black or white dog may have personated, or incarnated, the rain or the fine weather god. If so, this sacrifice would only present one more example of the slaughter of a divinity—a form of sacrifice from which all other sacrifices may have been derived.

In Japan deities were sometimes openly ill-treated if

[1] *Ib.* 312.   [2] Frazer, *Golden Bough*, 3rd ed., i. 417.
[3] *Ib.* iv. 218.   [4] *Ib.* i. 291-2.

they refused to provide rain. 'In a Japanese village, when the guardian divinity had long been deaf to the peasants' prayers for rain, they threw down his image and, with curses loud and long, hurled it head foremost into the stinking rice-field. "There", they said, "you may stay yourself for a while, to see how *you* will feel after a few days' scorching in this broiling sun that is burning the life from our cracking fields."'[1]

Again, in spite of all their piety to the souls of the departed, the Japanese sometimes treat these also in a manner lacking in respect. After the feast of all souls the people fear 'that some poor souls may have lagged behind, or even concealed themselves in a nook or corner, loth to part from the scenes of their former life and from those they love. Accordingly steps are taken to hunt out these laggards and send them packing after their fellow-ghosts. With this intention the people throw stones on the roofs of their houses in great profusion; and going through every room armed with sticks, they deal swashing blows all about them in the empty air to chase away the lingering souls. This they do, we are told, out of a regard for their own comfort quite as much as from the affection they bear to the dead; for they fear to be disturbed by unseasonable apparitions if they suffered the airy visitors to remain in the house.'[2] The whole process is more reminiscent of the common methods of driving away demons than of the otherwise pious treatment which the Japanese bestow upon their dead. But there is a very general tendency among all primitive peoples to promote their relations on their death to the rank of evil demons. Perhaps the Japanese, to some extent, share this tendency.

In the sacrifice of the bear by the Ainos, the aboriginal people of Japan, that combination of friendly gesture and hostile action which so often characterizes the attitude of savages to their supernatural friends is still clearly expressed. The bear among them has many

[1] Frazer, *Golden Bough*, i. 297.   [2] *Ib.* ix. 152.

characteristics of a totem, for the Ainos worship it when dead, speak of it as a divinity when alive, and sometimes claim it as ancestor. But the bear is nevertheless freely hunted, and not spared as among true totemists. The bear which is to be sacrificed is caught young, brought up in the family, and often suckled by a woman. When it is grown up it is ritualistically killed amid lamentations and apologies. It is reminded, in a long oration, of all the kindness that has been showered upon it and entreated to give a favourable report of its murderers to the gods. Sometimes it is strangled to avoid bloodshed, and sometimes it is shot with an arrow. Before it is killed it is offered libations, and after it is dead its flesh is eaten and sometimes its blood is drunk, so that its worshippers may acquire its virtue. Its corpse may also be given part of its own flesh as its portion of the communal meal. As in all communal feasts, everyone is forced to participate, so that everyone may share the divine virtue and, perhaps, so that no one shall escape the guilt.[1]

In this sacrifice we may have an example, almost unaltered, of some of the most primitive religious practices of mankind. As so often in such ceremonies, the intention of the libations given to the victim is probably to appease its wrath at being slain. Where, in later cults, offerings are made to a god by worshippers who declare themselves to be miserable sinners, we may suspect that the crime for which they thus atone was once the murder of this same god. The god is no longer the victim, but he still receives the propitiatory offerings of a former deicide.

3. *Sacrifice in Egypt*

The Egyptian pantheon—a menagerie of sacred beasts and animal-headed gods—was formed by fusing and relating the various local gods whose districts

[1] Frazer gives a full account of the Ainos bear sacrifice. See *Ib.* viii. 180-90.

combined to form the Egypt of the Pharaohs. The Pharaoh was, even during his life, the divine son of heaven, and after his death he was assimilated to the god Osiris, whose resurrection was imitated at every funeral.

According to tradition, Osiris, the good and beloved king of Egypt who introduced the cultivation of the corn and of the vine, was lured to his destruction by his brother Set. Isis, his sister and wife, searched for the body, found it, hovered over it in the form of a hawk, and so conceived Horus the younger. A favourite design of the temple reliefs shows her thus hovering over the erect phallus of her fallen lord. After this the body was again found by Set, who rent it in fourteen pieces and scattered it abroad. But Isis sailed up and down the marshes looking for the pieces, and found them all but the genital member, which had been eaten by the fishes. Finally, with the help of the gods she pieced the body together and mummified it, performing all the rites which the Egyptians perform over the bodies of their dead. Henceforth Osiris reigned in the Underworld, Lord of Eternity, Ruler of the Dead.[1]

The burial rites, first of the Pharaohs, and later of the chief officials, and finally of almost everyone, were modelled on the alleged burial of Osiris. The corpse was embalmed and immense care taken to preserve it from decay. Through these rites the deceased became Osiris. In early tombs his servants were buried with him, though soon these were replaced by models. So too his whole equipment was provided, furniture and utensils, food and drink. And here again reliefs and paintings supplemented, if they did not replace, the objects they represented.

Not only were offerings of food and drink made for the dead, but sacrifices to them to propitiate them seem to have occurred. ' Geese and gazelles were also sacrificed by being decapitated; they were supposed to represent the enemies of Osiris, who after the murder

---

[1] Frazer, *Golden Bough*, 3rd ed., vi. 3-23.

of the divine man had sought to evade the righteous punishment of their crime but had been detected and beheaded.'[1]

The gods, as well as men, were assimilated to the dead Osiris, and their cults were like those to the human departed.[2] In ancient times prisoners of war were sometimes slaughtered in the cult of the gods, or strangled and then burnt in the cult of the dead.

The Pharaoh himself presided at the cults of all the gods and all the dead. 'To this concentration of the religion in the person of the king corresponds the unification of ritual, which one can say is common for the dead and for the gods. The common ritual at the service of the gods and the deceased seems to have been first conceived to reanimate the remains of the dead king by virtue of sacrifice; applied to Osiris, it made of this dead god—originally doubtless a god of vegetation—a risen god; applied to all the gods, it resuscitated them each day to perform their cosmic tasks and to protect their worshippers; applied to all the dead, it set them on the road to immortality. Chief of this funerary service, a minister of general and perpetual resurrection, the Pharaoh, the god-king, plays the rôle of a supreme mediator between the divine and human worlds.'[3]

Thus the fundamental rites from which the Egyptian official religion was derived seems to have been the mummification and apotheosis of the dead king in the character of Osiris. But there is evidence that this apotheosis did not originally follow the natural death of the king, but that it was the last rite in his sacrifice. This earlier custom may be reconstructed from the myth of Osiris, from certain survivals in the cult, and from the comparison of these with the practices of other peoples.

A great festival called the Sed was celebrated every thirty years. This festival seems to have been designed to renew the divine life of the king, by identifying him

[1] *Ib.* vi. 15. [2] Loisy, *Le Sacrifice*, 431, 487. [3] *Ib.* 487.

while yet alive with Osiris.[1] It is therefore reminiscent of the funeral rites. Its origin has been reconstructed by Petrie and quoted by Frazer as follows : 'In the savage age of prehistoric times, the Egyptians, like many other African and Indian peoples, killed their priest-king at stated intervals, in order that the ruler should, with unimpaired life and health, be enabled to maintain the kingdom in its highest condition. The royal daughters were present in order that they might be married to his successor. The jackal-god went before him to open the way to the unseen world ; and the ostrich feather received and bore away the king's soul in the breeze that blew it out of sight. This was the celebration of the " end ", the *sed* feast. The king thus became the dead king, patron of all of those who had died in his reign, who were his subjects here and hereafter. He was thus one with Osiris, the king of the dead. This fierce custom became changed, as in other lands, by appointing a deputy king to die in his stead, which idea survived in the Coptic Abu Nerūs, with his tall crown of Upper Egypt, false beard, and sceptre. After the death of the deputy, the real king renewed his life and reign. Henceforth this became the greatest of the royal festivals, the apotheosis of the king during his life, after which he became Osiris upon earth and the patron of the dead in the underworld.'[2]

Three other customs that suggest that Osiris was originally sacrificed may be mentioned. The ancient Egyptians used to burn red-haired men and scatter their ashes with winnowing fans, ' and it is highly significant that this barbarous sacrifice was offered by the kings at the grave of Osiris. We may conjecture that the victims represented Osiris himself, who was annually slain, dismembered, and buried in their persons that he might quicken the seed in the earth.'[3] The fact that in the myth of Osiris the god was divided and scattered over the ground lends further weight to

---
[1] Frazer, *Golden Bough*, vi. 153.
[2] Petrie, *Researches in Sinai*, 185, quoted by Frazer, *Golden Bough*, vi. 154-5.
[3] Frazer, *Golden Bough*, vi. 97-8.

this conclusion. In a 'sacrifice of a bull in the great rites of Isis all the worshippers beat their breasts and mourned',[1] which is reminiscent of the mourning for Osiris. Bulls also seem to have been sacrificed as scapegoats. Again, 'red oxen sacrificed by the Egyptians were said to be offered on the ground of their resemblance to Typhon (Set), though it is more likely that originally they were slain on the ground of their resemblance to the corn-spirit Osiris.'[2] Men too were sacrificed to Osiris with the head of an animal fastened to them.[3]

From these and similar customs, and from their comparison with similar customs among other peoples, we may conclude, with Frazer, that victims were once slain, dismembered, and scattered abroad in the character of Osiris; and that bulls and oxen, red-haired men, and the kings of Egypt themselves have all died in this rôle. But the motive given by Petrie and Frazer that such rites were intended to preserve the divine king from decay, and by Frazer that they were ultimately to increase the fertility of the soil, seem not wholly adequate to explain this ritual slaughter.

Further, it is not yet clear what part in the ceremony was played by Isis, the divine sister and wife of the slain Osiris. We are told that she wept for him, pieced him together, and bore his son Horus to avenge him. But certain features in the rites suggest that she was once a more formidable goddess. Behind the gods and goddesses of antiquity we seem always to see the dim and terrible figure of a Great Mother who herself devoured her lovers and her children. The Sed festival was connected with Sirius, the star of Isis.[4] She was often represented by a cow, and the bulls, who, as we have seen, may have stood for Osiris, were sacrificed to her. Her priest seems to have worn a jackal's mask.[5] Was she associated with the jackal-god who led Osiris to the underworld? She stole the name of the sun-god Ra,

---

[1] *Ib.* vi. 117.   [2] *Ib.* viii. 34.   [3] *Ib.* vii. 260-1.
[4] *Ib.* vi. 153.   [5] *Ib.* vi. 85, n.

and for this purpose she made a serpent of his spittle, which bit him so that he told her his name that she might cure him.[1] Does this myth also record a cult? In one story she is said to have been decapitated by her son Horus.[2] Perhaps behind this story is a myth like that of Perseus and the Gorgon, and behind that a cult in which Isis too was slain.

But although the rôle of Isis remains a mystery it seems certain that Osiris was the name of a god-victim who was slain, dismembered, scattered, mourned, propitiated, and pieced together. The historic burial rites are at once the repetition and the denial of the earlier cult. The mourning, the propitiation, and the piecing together is retained, but the slaughtering, dismembering, and scattering is repudiated in the whole purpose of the later cult. Immense care was taken to preserve the corpse from destruction. And indeed the fear lest the body should be injured after death seems to have been the main preoccupation of the Egyptians. King Kufu (Cheops), the builder of the Great Pyramid of Giza, employed 100,000 men for twenty years to preserve his mummy from destruction. And the changes in the construction of the pyramids, and the later rock tombs, has been described as a series of stages of defence and attack. The corpse was embalmed with the greatest skill and it was concealed either in the depths of the earth, as in the tombs of the Valley of the Kings, or under mountains of stone, like the pyramids of Giza. In these defences may perhaps be seen the reaction against the older custom of the ritual destruction of the divine victim in the person of the king—a danger that remained from the ravages of tomb-robbers, who mutilated as well as robbed. But the rites still contained traces of the earlier ceremony in the mourning and propitiation, and perhaps also in the strange custom by which the 'man whose duty it was to slit open the corpse for the purpose of embalming it fled as soon as he had done his part, pursued by all the persons present, who pelted him

[1] Frazer, *Golden Bough*, iii. 387.   [2] *Ib.* vi. 88, n.

with stones and cursed him '.[1] Such ritual flights, of which we shall find other examples, are very characteristic of those sacrifices in which a divine victim was slain.

Thus the myth of Osiris probably preserves a record of the earliest form of the cult, which it was supposed to account for, but from which it was in reality derived. The first kings who were mummified may have been themselves the victims of a sacrifice in which they died in the character of Osiris as the Mexicans died in the characters of their gods. They may have been the priest-consorts of queen-goddesses, the embodiments of Isis, who were periodically dismembered, scattered abroad, re-collected, pieced together, and mummified to rise in the persons of their successors.[2] But there are many elements in the records that do not fit into so simple a scheme. Why, for instance, did the earlier kings boast on their pyramids that they feasted on gods?[3] For this boast looks as if the kings were once the priests and sole participants of a sacrifice in which the divine animal was eaten; not that they were themselves the victims. Perhaps they performed both rôles; one at their inauguration, one at their apotheosis.

There were also other types of sacrifice that seem to have had little relation to the state Osirian cult. Before or at the time of the cutting of the dam at Cairo to irrigate the fields, a young virgin decked in gay apparel was thrown into the river as a sacrifice and as a bride for the river spirit. We have already come across a similar custom in China. The Wajagga of German East Africa threw an uncircumcized child of unblemished body into the river before irrigating their fields. 'They imagine', says Frazer, 'that the spirits of their forefathers dwell in the rocky basins of these rushing streams, and that they would resent the withdrawal of the water to irrigate the fields if compensation were not offered them.'[4] Some similar idea perhaps underlay the Chinese and Egyptian customs.

---
[1] *Ib.* ii. 309, n. [2] *Ib.* vi. 18, 201-18; Loisy, *Le Sacrifice*, 175.
[3] Brearsted, *Development of Religion and Thought in Ancient Egypt*, 127-9.
[4] Frazer, *Golden Bough*, vi. 38.

The offering of hair is a common form of sacrifice, a variant of which occurred in Egypt. After boys or girls recovered from sickness, 'their parents used to shave the children's heads, weigh the hair against gold or silver, and give the precious metal to the keepers of the sacred beasts, who bought food with it for the animals according to their tastes'.[1]

Lastly, I will quote from Frazer the account of the ceremony to help the Sun-god. 'Every night when the sun-god Ra sank down to his home in the glowing west he was assailed by hosts of demons under the leadership of the arch-fiend Apepi. All night long he fought them, and sometimes by day the powers of darkness sent up clouds even into the blue Egyptian sky to obscure his light and weaken his power. To aid the sun-god in his daily struggle, a ceremony was daily performed in his temple at Thebes. A figure of his foe Apepi, represented as a crocodile with a hideous face or a serpent with many coils, was made of wax, and on it the demon's name was written in green ink. Wrapt in a papyrus case, on which another likeness of Apepi had been drawn in green ink, the figure was then tied up with black hair, spat upon, hacked with a stone knife, and cast on the ground. There the priest trod on it with his left foot again and again, and then burned it in a fire made of a certain plant or grass. When Apepi himself had thus been effectually disposed of, waxen effigies of each of his principal demons, and of their fathers, mothers, and children, were made and burnt in the same way. The service, accompanied by the recitation of certain prescribed spells, was repeated not merely morning, noon, and night, but whenever a storm was raging, or heavy rain had set in, or black clouds were stealing across the sky to hide the sun's bright disc. The fiends of darkness, clouds, and rain felt the injuries inflicted on their images as if they had been done to themselves; they passed away at least for a time, and the beneficent Sun-god shone out triumphant once more.'[2]

[1] Frazer, *Golden Bough*, i. 29.   [2] *Ib.* i. 67-8.

Demons are often degraded gods or the gods of other peoples.[1] It is therefore not impossible that the bad Apepi may have been once a beneficent god—a view which the name of the early Pharaoh Pepi helps to support. If so the rite of destroying the image of Apepi may be a degenerate form of an earlier sacrifice of him. In the later rite the hate of Apepi was clearly admitted. In the earlier form it would have been denied, and the god would have perished amid protestations of piety and regret. But the ceremony of the destruction of Apepi is paralleled by similar customs all the world over, and it is hard to believe that they are all degenerate sacrifices. It is, however, not unlikely that the magical destruction of demons and the religious destruction of gods have related origins. A psycho-analyst would see in both the same motives, though in the religious rite the motive would be unconscious.

4. *Sacrifice among the Semites*

A baffling variety of sacrificial rites characterizes the religion of the Semites. But perhaps the most important were those concerned with the cults of the Great Mother and her slain Son, who, under such names as Astarte and Adonis, or Cybele and Attis, are a constantly recurring theme reminiscent of the Egyptian Isis and Osiris. And there can be little doubt that even the Virgin Mary and her crucified Son Jesus were accepted, at least by some of their contemporaries, as a new edition of these old divinities.[2] In the legends the slain god was sometimes the son, sometimes the lover of the great goddess. Often he was both at once. He was slain by an enemy or died as the result of a self-inflicted castration, and rose again from the dead.

[1] Reik, *Der eigene und der fremde Gott*, 136.
[2] Frazer, *Golden Bough*, 3rd ed., ix. 412-23.—Reik, *Der eigene und der fremde Gott*, 17. 'Noch in der Apokalypse Johannis heisst die Himmelskönigin die Mutter des Siegers (12, 1) und dessen Braut (21, 9).'

From these myths, and from the records of the cults, Frazer in the fifth volume of his *Golden Bough* (3rd ed.) has reconstructed the original rites with great plausibility. As I understand him, his theory is as follows : The early Sumerian and Semitic dynasties, like the dynasties of Egypt, descended theoretically in the female line, that is, in the only line in which originally descent could be surely traced. But male descent was in practice secured by royal incest. The king and queen personated the god and goddess whose union was believed magically to secure the fertility of the soil. And the king, the human god, was sacrificed periodically to rise from the dead in the person of his successor. He thus acted the drama of the dying and returning vegetation. But, in process of time, the kings, loth so soon to terminate their rule, succeeded in delegating their fatal office to their sons. Thus the main scheme, which varied within limits, included a divine queen, her brother, the priestly or divine king, and her son, the divine victim.

The goddess seems to have been personated not only by the queen, but also by temple prostitutes,[1] of which there were a great many, and a son of any one of these would probably suffice to play the part of the slain or emasculated god. In later times the part of the victim was taken by an image ; though in the ritual of Attis the novices still castrated themselves, and the priests who were already eunuchs gashed their arms, in imitation of their saviour.[2]

Two other types of sacrifice may perhaps be in part derived from Frazer's fundamental scheme of the dread goddess and the dying god. These are the sacrifice of children, especially of first-born children, and the

---

[1] These were perhaps the historical ancestresses of the nuns of the Christian Church.

[2] Frazer suggests that this mutilation was designed to assist the resurrection of Attis (*Golden Bough*, v. 268). It has also been suggested that the purpose of such self-mutilation was to identify the self with the goddess. Hercules is supposed to have worn female attire for a similar purpose. It seems most likely, however, that the rite was the repetition of the death of Attis, and that the novices identified themselves with him.

sacrifice of chastity, or of hair, by women at the temple of the goddess.

If the sacrifice of the king's son was substituted for the sacrifice of the king himself, it seems likely that the sons of common people might have come to be substituted for the royal children. And once the quality of the victims had been debased it is natural that the balance should have been redressed by increasing their quantity. Thus might arise the custom of sacrificing the first-born sons of all the people, as was done probably in the earliest form of the Passover,[1] or of the nobles in time of stress, as in the sacrifice to Moloch in the siege of Carthage.[2] Thus the king would evolve from the hapless victim to the ferocious god who never tired of demanding the blood of others. In his first form he appears as Attis or Adonis, in his last as Moloch.[3]

[1] Frazer believes that originally at the Passover the first-born children of the Israelites were slain ; ' that in fact the slaughter of the first-born children was formerly what the slaughter of the first-born cattle always continued to be, not an isolated butchery, but a regular custom, which with the growth of more humane sentiments was afterwards softened into the vicarious sacrifice of a lamb and the payment of a ransom for each child ' (*Golden Bough*, iv. 176-7).

[2] Frazer, *Golden Bough*, iv. 167-8. 'When the Carthaginians were defeated and besieged by Agathocles, they ascribed their disasters to the wrath of Baal ; for whereas in former times they had been wont to sacrifice to him their own offspring, they had latterly fallen into the habit of buying children to be reared as victims. So, to appease the angry god, two hundred children of the noblest families were picked out for sacrifice, and the tale of the victims was swelled by not less than three hundred more who volunteered to die for the fatherland. They were sacrificed by being placed, one by one, on the sloping hands of the brazen image, from which they rolled into a pit of fire. . . . But all the place in front of the image was filled with a tumultuous music of pipes and drums to drown the shrieks of the victims.' Similar rites were practised by the Israelites in the valley of Hinnom outside Jerusalem (*ib.* 169). Here again it seems to have been the first-born that thus suffered in the flames. ' The Prophet represents God as saying, '' I gave them statutes that were not good, and judgments wherein they should not live ; and I polluted them in their own gifts, in that they caused to pass through the fire all that openeth the womb, that I might make them desolate "' (*Ib.* 172).

[3] The Massacre of the Innocents by Herod at the time of the birth of Jesus and by Pharaoh at the time of the birth of Moses is perhaps a story that attributes to these rulers traditional actions of the gods they represented. It is conceivable that the order of development that we have suggested must be reversed and that the sacrifice of first-born children preceded the sacrifice of god-kings. It may have been simply considered unlucky to keep the first-born child. And this custom may have lived on longer in the royal house than among common people. If the period to which the king's first-born son was allowed to live was gradually increased, the sacrifice of heirs would develop into the sacrifice of old rulers.

But if the fiction had to be preserved that the victim was the son of the goddess, the mothers, first of the king's less important sons, and then of all the people from whom victims were drawn, might be required to serve at the temple of the goddess and thus identify themselves with her. In this way the fiction that the king's whole harem were incarnations of the goddess, the custom of prostituting the inmates, and finally the custom of requiring every woman to prostitute herself to a stranger once in her life at the temple, may have arisen. And it is not impossible that the sacrifice of hair which was sometimes accepted in lieu of chastity was a vicarious sacrifice for the child which would have resulted from the divine union.

Thus the conception of the Great Mother and her slain Son, and of the modifications of her cult, which is due to Frazer, can perhaps be extended to explain some features in a variety of sacrificial rites. But there remain other practices that do not so easily fit into this scheme.

It seems that the personification of the great queen-goddess could also on occasion be sacrificed. But nothing in our reconstruction of the original religion suggests an explanation for this custom. Was it an essential element in the earliest form of the cult? Or was it only a late development? Both Dido and Semiramis, about whom doubtless accumulated the legends of the goddesses they incarnated, are said to have perished upon a pyre. 'At Carthage, the greatest of the Tyrian colonies, a reminiscence of the custom of burning a deity in effigy seems to linger in the story that Dido or Elissa, the foundress and queen of the city, stabbed herself to death upon a pyre, or leaped from her palace into the blazing pile, to escape the fond importunities of one lover or in despair at the cruel desertion of another. We are told that Dido was worshipped as a goddess. . . . The two apparently contradictory views of her character as a queen and a goddess may be reconciled if we suppose that she was both the one and the other; that in fact the queen of Carthage in early days, like the queen of Egypt down to historic times, was regarded as divine, and had, like human deities elsewhere, to die a violent death either at the end of a fixed period or whenever her bodily and mental powers began to fail. In later ages the stern old custom might be softened down into a pretence by substituting an effigy for the queen or by allowing her to pass through the fire unscathed.[1] With Dido Frazer compares Semiramis, who destroyed her lovers, and who for this and other reasons he identifies with the Babylonian goddess Istar or Astarte.[2] 'Semiramis herself, the legendary queen of Assyria, is said to have burnt herself on a pyre out of grief at the death of a favourite horse. Since there are strong grounds for regarding the queen in her mythical aspect as a form of Istar or Astarte, the legend that Semiramis died for love in the flames furnishes a remarkable parallel to the traditionary death of the love-lorn Dido, who herself appears to be simply an avatar of the same great Asiatic goddess. When we compare these stories of the burning of Semiramis and Dido with each other and with the historical cases of the burning of Oriental monarchs, we may perhaps conclude that there was a time when queens as well as kings were expected under certain circumstances, perhaps on the death of their consort, to perish in the fire. The conclusion can hardly be deemed extravagant when we remember that the practice of burning widows to death survived in India under English rule down to a time within living memory.'[3]

Thus Frazer offers two explanations for the burning of a queen-goddess. One that she, like her consort, died in the flame when her bodily and mental vigour declined; and one that she was expected to die at his death and was not permitted to outlive him. Both explanations may be true of different epochs.

But the origin and history of the Great Mother is wrapt in mystery. She must have arisen at a time

[1] Frazer, *Golden Bough*, v. 113-4.   [2] *Ib.* ix. 371-2.   [3] *Ib.* v. 76-7.

when the dynastic descent passed only in the female line, so that the man who married her human incarnation acquired a kingdom for her dowry. Through her alone could pass the sceptre of royal power. She married, as a rule, her own brother, and sometimes her son, so that the new king in practice inherited his father's might, not directly as in patriarchal systems, but only through his union with his sister or his mother. Partly for this reason the queen may have come to usurp many of the attributes of male rulers, and to have transmitted them to the goddess who was built in her image and whose human incarnation she was believed to be. The most common emblem of the goddess was the conical stone which has been interpreted by many anthropologists, and by all psycho-analysts, as a phallic symbol.[1] Was this originally the symbol of her slain or castrated lover ? Or was she herself thought of as equipped with the male organ ? Freud, in his paper on 'Fetishism', has argued that a fetish is the symbol of the mother's penis which the fetishist unconsciously believes that she possesses.[2] Psycho-analyses have often shown that a great reverence and awe of women may be due to a similar belief. It is not improbable that the Great Mother Goddess of fertility owed her power to the same cause. But why she was sometimes required to die, and why her lovers perished regularly, remains a problem. Though it is easier to understand that as they grew in power they and the gods they represented should have first delegated their fatal office and have finally appeared as angry deities who demanded victims on the least provocation.

[1] Another favourite symbol of the goddess was the snake. This is perhaps the most universal phallic symbol of all. The snake-goddess spread from the East into the classical West. ' M. S. Reinach has rightly seen that the tradition of such a snake-goddess survives alike in the Furies of Aeschylean Tragedy with the snakes "that hiss in their hair", and in the Artemis of the Arcadian Lycosura, who was represented as carrying a torch in one hand and two serpents in another. In classical Crete itself the symbolism of the old religion is probably to be seen in the Medusa-like heads found at Praesos and Palaikastro, where snakes are held in either hand, or spring from head or shoulders ' (Burrows, *Discoveries in Crete*, 138).

[2] Freud, ' Fetishism,' *International Journal of Psycho-Analysis*, ix. part 2.

Besides the rites concerned in the cults of the great mother or earth goddess and her son, various other types of sacrifice were known to the Semitic peoples. The ancient Sumerians or Semites of Mesopotamia buried or burnt their dead. Food and clothing were placed with their remains.[1] When Ashurbanipal took Babylon and suppressed the revolt of his brother he executed a certain number of rebels as an offering to his grandfather Sennacherib. Such a sacrifice may have been intended to provide servitors. But two other explanations are possible : the intention may have been to propitiate the dead or to resuscitate him.[2]

The Babylonians practised divinatory sacrifices in which they read the oracle from the liver of sheep.[3] Purification and expiation, that is, the elimination of an impurity or a malady, were widely practised. The victim was either killed or driven away. Loisy thinks that the victim was not offered as a vicarious sacrifice but that it was there to entice away the animistically conceived malady.[4]

5. Sacrifice in India

In India there were many sacrifices performed with an exact and complicated ritual. The householder on small occasions, the king on great ones, presided at the rite. He and his wife underwent a lengthy dedication which included bathing, fasting, and sexual continence. This dedication was supposed to represent a new birth. The gods enjoyed their portion at the banquet to which they were invited. Originally it seems to have been laid on the grass, but later it was burnt.[5]

But there were also practices that are reminiscent of the rites of Adonis, Attis, and Osiris. ' The Gonds of India, a Dravidian race ' (*i.e.* Pre-Aryan) ' kidnapped Brahman boys, and kept them as victims to be sacrificed on various occasions. At sowing and reaping, after

[1] Loisy, *Le Sacrifice*, 148-9.   [2] See *ib.* 149.   [3] *Ib.* 267-8.
[4] *Ib.* 325.   [5] Konow, *Lehrbuch der Religionsgeschichte*, ii. 47-9.

a triumphal procession, one of the lads was slain by being punctured with a poisoned arrow. His blood was then sprinkled over the ploughed field or the ripe corn, and his flesh was devoured. The Oraons or Uraons of Chota Nagpur worship a goddess called Anna Kurari, who can give good crops and make a man rich; but to induce her to do so it is necessary to offer human sacrifices. In spite of the vigilance of the British Government these sacrifices are said to be still secretly perpetrated.'[1] Perhaps these victims, like Osiris, Adonis, and Attis, provided the blood which the goddess of fertility required before she could properly perform her functions.

A still closer resemblance to the Semitic and Egyptian deities is shown by the Meriahs of the Khonds of Bengal, another Dravidian race. The Meriah was the victim offered to the earth goddess Tari Pennu or Bera Pennu. He seems to have been originally a god. Like Osiris he was dismembered and scattered over the fields.[2] But Westermarck, disagreeing with Frazer, seems to regard the Meriah as a substituted victim, not as a corn-spirit.[3] If, however, as in Semitic sacrifice, the king's son was first substituted for the king, and then the sons of ordinary mortals for the king's son, the two views can perhaps be reconciled. The earlier form of the sacrifice seems to have survived in the practice of killing the king after a certain period of years. Thus in some parts of India the king ruled twelve years; and at the end of this time he cut his own throat at a public ceremony especially instituted for the purpose.[4] Sometimes, however, a retainer seems to have sacrificed himself in the place of his master.[5] The custom which was common in the India of the Middle Ages for men voluntarily to cut off their own heads as a sacrifice to their gods may have been likewise due to the substitution of a common for a royal or divine victim.[6]

[1] Frazer, *Golden Bough*, vii. 244. [2] *Ib.* vii. 245-51.
[3] Westermarck, *Origin of Moral Ideas*, i. 445 *sq.*
[4] Frazer, *Golden Bough*, iv. 46-51. [5] *Ib.* iv. 52-4.
[6] See *ib.* iv. 54-5.

The goddess Kali seems to have been another variant of the Dread Mother of Asia. 'Sacrifices to Kālī or Chandikā were formerly common. They were freely offered in the days of Mārāthā rule; and in Western India there are many temples at which such sacrifices were common only a century ago. The victim was taken to the temple in the evening and shut up; and in the morning he was found dead, the Dread Goddess having "shown her power by coming in the night and sucking his blood".[1] In the great Saiva temple at Tanjou there is a shrine of Kali where a male child, purchased for the purpose, 'was sacrificed every Friday evening, until the advent of British rule led to the substitution of a sheep'.[2] The implication that the victim was originally the divine consort of the goddess is strengthened by the special privileges allowed the victims. 'It appears from the *Haft Iqlīm* that in Koch Bihār persons, called *bhogīs*, sometimes offered themselves as victims. From the time when they announced that the goddess had called them, they were treated as privileged persons. They were allowed to do whatever they liked, and every woman was at their command until the annual festival came round, when they were sacrificed to the goddess.'[3] It is further recorded that 'In the Jaintia *parganas*, human sacrifices to Kālī were offered annually. As in Koch Bihār, persons frequently volunteered themselves as victims. . . . On the *Navami* day of the *Durgā Pujā*, the victim, after bathing and purifying himself, was dressed in new attire, daubed with red sandal wood and vermilion, and bedecked with garlands. Thus arrayed he sat on a raised dais in front of the goddess, and spent some time in meditation and the repetition of *mantras*. He then made a sign with his finger, whereupon the executioner, after uttering the prescribed sacrificial *mantras*, cut off his head, which was placed before the goddess on a golden plate. The lungs were cooked and eaten by

---

[1] Gait, *Encyclopaedia of Religion and Ethics*, vi. 850.
[2] *Ib.* [3] *Ib.*

such *Kandrā Yogīs* as were present, and the royal family partook of a small quantity of rice cooked in the blood.'[1] Similar customs were practised by the Chuliyāa in the service of the goddess Kesāi Khāti (eater of raw human flesh), who is now identified with Kali.

It is interesting to note that, in this last rite, the victim was anointed with the same ointment as at his birth.[2] Thus, though the sacrifice to Kali is similar, on the one hand, to the sacrifice of divine kings or of their divine sons in the rites of the great Asiatic mother-goddess of fertility, it is also reminiscent, on the other hand, of the puberty rites and ordeals of savage peoples. These puberty rites submitted the youths to a painful ordeal that symbolized their death and rebirth, and it is not unthinkable that the sacrifices to mother-goddesses may have been derived from them. The two types of rite have much in common. They are probably related in origin. But it is difficult to decide which came first.[3]

An interpretation of the religion of Kali has been given from the psycho-analytical standpoint by Daly.[4] He mentions that she is said to have killed her husband Siva, and that she is often depicted dancing on his prostrate form, holding the head of a decapitated giant in one hand, brandishing a sword in another, adorned with the heads and forearms of her victims, and sticking out her tongue at the terrified observer of her picture. He points out that she is almost completely decked with phallic symbols,[5] so that there can be little doubt

---

[1] Gait, *Encyclopaedia of Religion and Ethics*, vi. 850.   [2] *Ib.* vi. 851.
[3] In the sacrifices of the cult of the Great Mother three elements stand out: the killing of the victim, his dismemberment or emasculation, and his rebirth. In the puberty rites of primitive peoples these same three elements are symbolically expressed. A pretence is made of killing the novice, he is circumcised or a tooth is knocked out, and he is symbolically reborn. Obviously there is a psychological connection between these two sorts of rite. Probably there is a historical one as well. For a psycho-analytical interpretation of puberty rites see Reik, 'Die Pubertätestiten der Wilden', in *Probleme der Religionspsychologie*.
[4] Daly, 'Hindu-Mythologie und Kastrationskomplex', *Imago*, xiii.
[5] *Ib.* xiii. 173-4. That the heads that form the pearls of the necklace of Kali are the heads of her sons is disclosed in Bengal poetry quoted by Daly (*ib.* xiii. 190-1).

that her worshippers, like Freud's fetishists, believed, unconsciously at least, that she possessed the male organ. But Daly extends his interpretation beyond the current analytic theory and supposes that the form of Kali resulted from what he calls the 'menstruation complex'. Of this, at least, we can be fairly confident, that Kali was a phallic goddess and that she castrated and destroyed her consort. No psycho-analysts could question this interpretation, and the parallel with the Semitic goddess and her castrated and slain son Adonis [1] should make it probable to anthropologists of other schools.

As in many cults the original custom of sacrificing the king seems to have developed into the vicarious sacrifice of other victims. But though in some forms of these cults the god, who was originally the victim, became the being to whom sacrifice was offered, so that he eclipsed his consort, Kali seems to have retained her dominant position as the recipient of sacrifices. At a still later epoch piacular offerings in times of crisis seem to become votive offerings after deliverance. Thus we learn ' That when a husband or a son is dangerously ill, a vow is made that, on the recovery of the patient, the goddess will be propitiated with human blood. The vow is fulfilled either at the next *Durgā Pujā*, or at once in some temple of Kālī. The wife or mother, after performing certain ceremonies, draws a few drops of blood from her breast with a nail cutter, and offers them to the goddess.' [2]

Among other forms of Indian sacrifice the following miscellaneous collection may be mentioned. To purify a village of cholera the Mallan and the Kurmi tie a yellow sack full of grain, cloves, and minium to a black she-goat or cow and drive it to the next village: the disease is believed to be transferred with the scapegoat.[3] At the foundation of buildings children, especially first-born children, were sometimes buried under the walls.[4]

[1] Frazer, *Golden Bough*, v. 264.
[2] Gait, *Encyclopaedia of Religion and Ethics*, vi. 853.
[3] Loisy, *Le Sacrifice*, 314.   [4] *Ib.* 367.

If a Brahman novice fails in continence, an ass, which is supposed to be an especially licentious animal, is sacrificed to repair the fault. The novice's portion in the sacrificial meal is cut from the genital organ.[1] Reminiscent of the sacrifice of virility at the altar of Cybele was the practice in India to dedicate men who were born eunuchs to the goddess Huligamma.[2]

6. *Sacrifice in Persia*

The ancient religion of the Persians was similar to the Vedic religion. 'According to Herodotus, the Persians when they sacrificed to their supreme God, to the sun, to the moon, to the earth or the fire, to the water, the winds or to Anakita, take the victim to a hallowed spot; for they have no altars. They pray for the prosperity of the Persians, and of the king, since the sacrificer has no right to demand celestial favours for himself alone. The flesh of the victim, after it is boiled, is deposited in small pieces on a bed of fine herbs as a meal for the god, as in the Vedic sacrifice. . . . After waiting some time the sacrificer takes up the meats and uses them as he chooses.'[3] But sacrifices were also made to Ahriman, Prince of Darkness. The juice of an haoma plant was mixed with the blood of a wolf, an animal sacred to Ahriman, and cast into a place where the sun never shone.[4] Sometimes human sacrifices were offered to this power of evil.[5]

As an example of purificatory sacrifice Loisy mentions the execution by Xerxes of the son of Pythios.

---

[1] Loisy, *Le Sacrifice*, 40. [2] Frazer, *Golden Bough*, v. 271, n.
[3] Loisy, *Le Sacrifice*, 494. [4] *Ib.*
[5] *Ib.*—Reinach interpreting the legend of Mithra discovers a former condition of totemism and totem sacrifice. *Orpheus*, translated by Florence Symons, 68-9. 'Mithra sprang from a rock; he causes a spring to gush from it by striking it with an arrow, concludes an alliance with the Sun and engages in combat with a bull, which he overcomes and sacrifices. . . . The sacrifice of the bull seems to indicate that the worship of Mithra under the most ancient form was that of a sacred bull, assimilated to the sun, which was immolated as a god, its flesh and blood being consumed in a communal meal. Mithra, the slayer of the bull, was the result of a duplication common to all the religions which have passed from totemism to anthropomorphism.'

When the great king was about to leave Sardis to pass into Europe, the Lydian Pythios asked him to leave the eldest of his five sons behind. Xerxes instead took the son of Pythios, cut him in two, and put one half on each side of the road through which the army had to pass.[1] Such a sacrifice is reminiscent of rites in which an individual to be purified is made to pass through the carcase of a victim, perhaps to symbolize rebirth.

Persian burial customs are interesting and unusual among civilized peoples. The magian priests exposed their dead to the dogs and the birds till the bones were picked clean, and they enforced this custom generally.[2] At their festival of 'All Souls' food and drink was left about for the spirits of the departed.[3]

Frazer has also detected traces of the sacrifice of divine kings as in so many other places. There was a rite called the 'Ride of the Beardless One' which took place both in Persia and Babylonia at the beginning of spring. 'On the first day of the first month, which in the most ancient Persian calendar corresponded to March, . . . a beardless and, if possible, one-eyed buffoon was set naked on an ass, a horse, or a mule, and conducted in a sort of mock triumph through the streets of the city. . . . If a shopkeeper hesitated a moment to respond to his demands, the importunate beggar had the right to confiscate all the goods in the shop; so the tradesman who saw him bearing down on them, not unnaturally hastened to anticipate his wants by contributing of their substance before he could board them. Everything that he thus collected, from break of day to the time of morning prayers, belonged to the king or governor of the city; but everything that he laid hands on between the first and the second hour of prayer he kept for himself. After the second prayer he disappeared, and if the people caught him later in the day they might beat him to their heart's content.'[4] Frazer argues that the Beardless One was originally a

---

[1] *Ib.* 334. [2] *Ib.* 152. [3] Frazer, *Golden Bough*, vi. 68.
[4] *Ib.* ix. 402-3.

king who died in the character of the dead vegetation of the old year and revived and rose in the character of the new vegetation of the new year. In Haman and Vashti he sees an example of the dying god and his consort, and in Mordecai and Esther, whom he equates with the Babylonian deities Marduk and Istar, an example of the same god and goddess at their birth. Originally, he thinks, the human god ruled for a whole year, and that the later ' curtailment of his reign on earth was probably introduced at the time when the old hereditary divinities or deified kings contrived to shift the most painful part of their duties to a substitute, whether that substitute was a son or a slave or a malefactor. Having to die as a king, it was necessary that the substitute should also live as a king for a season; but the real monarch would naturally restrict within the narrowest limits both of time and of power a reign which, so long as it lasted, necessarily encroached upon and indeed superseded his own.' [1]

There is little evidence to show what happened to the divine consort of the slain god. But the legend of Semiramis, who burned herself on a pyre in Babylon at the loss of a favourite horse, suggests that the goddess Istar, like her consort, was expected to die by violence. For Semiramis almost certainly incarnated Istar, one of whose lovers was also a horse.[2]

In a long note at the end of the ninth volume of the *Golden Bough* Frazer further suggests, very plausibly, that the rapid spread of Christianity may have been due to the fact that Christ may have been put to death in the character of Haman.

Finally, it is worth noting that the Beardless One was, if possible, one-eyed. Since the loss of an eye is known often to symbolize castration, and since the slain god was sometimes also the castrated god, it is perhaps not overbold to assume that the Beardless One was once emasculated as well as slain.

---

[1] Frazer, *Golden Bough*, ix. 407.   [2] *Ib.* ix. 407, n.

7. Sacrifice in Greece

In ancient Greece religion was never organized into a single state cult as in Egypt or China. Centralized political authority and centralized religion usually accompanied each other, and to the absence of both in the Grecian world was due at once its political insecurity and its intellectual wealth.[1] Progress in the past has resulted from the alternation of social stability and freedom of thought. It is perhaps the main unsolved problem of practical sociology to combine the two.

To the anthropologist the variety of Grecian cults and the absence of a single Greek religion renders his work at once more difficult and more promising. More difficult because he hardly knows where to begin; more promising because he is likely to find more traces of primeval rites than in the great empire religions which discarded what they could not distort into a single system.

To the same absence of system is due an immense amount of borrowing from neighbours which complicates the task of the historian bent on tracing cults to their sources. But this difficulty does not embarrass the psychologist who is concerned in discovering why certain practices are satisfying rather than whence they came.

Since it is difficult to give any account of Greek religion as a whole, we will consider some of the deities in turn, and try to reconstruct their cults from their myths and legends.

Cronus.—Like many ancient deities Cronus is said to have castrated his father and to have been in turn castrated by his son. He also married his sister Rhea,

---

[1] This combination of independence and lack of unity is attributed by Gomperz to Geography. 'So viele Bergkantone, so viele mögliche Stätten eigenartiger Bildung, so viele Sitze eines stark ausgeprägten Sonderlebens, welches für die reiche, vielgestaltige Gesittung Griechenlands so erspriesslich wie für die staatliche Zusammenfassung seiner Kräfte verhängnisvoll werden sollte' (*Griechische Denker*, 4. Aufl. i. 3-4).

and swallowed his own children. Zeus only escaped and grew up to castrate his father and to rule in his stead.

If we translate this myth into the cult that is probably behind it we arrive at the same sort of condition of affairs that Frazer has supposed for the Semitic divine kings. But probably the story combines a record of two epochs. In one Cronus was the title of a king who sacrificed or ate his sons. In another he was a king who succeeded his father by marrying his sister,[1] and who was in due time sacrificed or castrated by his son. And perhaps between these epochs the sons were driven out, as in so many legends, to marry the daughter and to win the throne of some other monarch.[2]

That at some stage the king's sons were sacrificed, and that this practice is recorded in the story that Cronus ate his children, as well as in the legends that identify him with Moloch, seems probable.[3] But did this ritual filicide historically succeed the sacrifice of the king himself? Was the sacrifice of the son the substitute of the sacrifice of the father as Frazer suggests of the Semitic kings? Or must we invert the order? That both kinds of sacrifice occurred seems certain. But the evidence is insufficient to determine their temporal relation to each other.

The theory that regicidal sacrifices were the older and that they later gave place to the vicarious sacrifice of the king's son has already been considered. It is supported by all the learning of the author of the *Golden Bough*. But it may be as well to consider the alternative. There are many legends in which kings are warned of danger from their sons, and in consequence kill them or drive them out. It seems likely that the ancient ruler had just cause to fear his sons, for they were above all others envious of him, and frequently succeeded in deposing him and taking his place. For this reason he may have killed them all,

---

[1] Frazer, *Golden Bough*, iv. 194.—For arguments against the supposition of matrilineal descent in ancient Greece, see Rose, 'Prehistoric Greece and Mother-Right', *Folk-lore*, xxxvii.   [2] Frazer, *Golden Bough*, ii. 278-9.
[3] Farnell, *Cults of the Greek States*, i. 27-8.

or the eldest, or submitted them to some ordeal to break their wills, or have driven them out. This practice might explain the passage of the kingdom in the female line ; for if the king drove out, or killed, all his own sons, there would be no one left to succeed him. He who won the hand of the queen would, in such cases, be most likely to procure at the same time the kingdom.

In primitive societies the initiation rites, which Reik has interpreted as including, as one of their main functions, the symbolic castration and killing of the young to teach them a due respect for the old,[1] we may see a variant of the custom of kings to drive out or kill their sons, or submit them to some ordeal to check their revolutionary ardour. Such practices of primitive peoples are often combined with a matrilineal system that has as its effect, if not as its ' final cause ', the abolition of most sources of conflict between sons and father.[2]

The killing of the royal princes that was ultimately intended to remove possible rivals for the kingdom may have come to be regarded as a magical rite to prolong the life of the king, and so have developed into a ritual sacrifice. If so, such a custom is an instructive example of the development of magic. Conscious only is the fact that the sacrifice secures the life of the king. The reason for this—namely, that otherwise the son might usurp the place of his father—is repressed. What was formerly the rational means to a desired end is now thought of as the supernatural means. It may even be performed only symbolically. It is therefore no longer rational, but magical. Later, as the meaning of the rite came to be still more completely forgotten, vicarious sacrifices, instead of the killing of the princes, may have been considered sufficient magically to prolong the life of the king. But we must suppose that the

---

[1] Reik, *Probleme der Religionspsychologie*, ' Pubertätesriten der Wilden '.
[2] Ernest Jones, in his article ' Mother-Right and Sexual Ignorance of Savages ' (*International Journal of Psycho-Analysis*, vi.), points out that the conflict with the father is only displaced on to the maternal uncle who symbolizes him.

renunciation of the princes of all aspirations to their father's throne was at first a condition of their survival, and that inheritance remained matrilineal. A relic of the first period may be found in the legend of the Swedish king who sacrificed his sons in turn to prolong his life,[1] and of the second in the myths of king's sons who were banished because it was prophesied that their fathers should die at their hands. Finally, the matriarchal inheritance, which may have been originally but the consequence of the banishment or slaughter of the princes, may have come to be regarded as an end in itself, and rationalized as the only sure method of tracing descent. By this time we must suppose that the relations between sons and fathers had improved and that the king could look with greater equanimity at the prospect of his son's succession. And this was then secured by the marriage of the prince with his sister. In Egypt, where kings frequently associated their sons with their rule even before their death, the original hostility must have reached its lowest level.

But where in this scheme are we to place the sacrifices of king-consorts that undoubtedly occurred? Such kingly victims ruled not in their own right, but as consorts of their divine mothers or sisters. They were essentially the products of a matriarchal age. If, therefore, matriarchy was originally the consequence of the slaughter or banishment of the princes, the slaying of the king-consort must have succeeded, rather than preceded, the slaying of the sons. It can only have occurred after the sons had been allowed to live long enough to marry their sisters and to succeed. Possibly the original practice of killing the royal princes may have been first mitigated by lengthening their span of life until they died after, rather than before, their fathers. If so, the practice of killing them, which was originally intended to prevent them from threatening the state with all the evils of civil war, would have completely lost its first purpose and would have been

---

[1] Frazer, *Golden Bough*, iv. 57 *sq.*

continued only as a magical rite to preserve the state from famine. Remembered only would be the fact that killing the princes prevented famine. Forgotten would be the reason that famine is the result of civil war, and civil war the result of allowing the princes to live. The killing would be continued, but at a time when it lost its original purpose. Superstitions connecting the king with vegetation, which probably had an independent origin, would be quoted as the real purpose of the rite.

No doubt other equally coherent theories of the order of the development of sacrifices of kings and princes could be given. I shall be quite ready to discard this one as soon as something more plausible is suggested. If it is true, the earlier members of the dynasty who identified themselves with Cronus destroyed their children, and the later members were themselves destroyed. The story that Cronus ate his children would correspond to the period in which the princes were slain, and the story that he married his sister and was emasculated by his son to the period at which princes succeeded by marrying their sisters but were still expected to die for a reason that had been long forgotten. A similar interpretation could probably be given to the similar myths that we have considered. From the frequency with which emasculation accompanied, or was substituted for, the killing of a god in myths we may infer that castration was also a common feature of the sacrifice.

There appears further to have been a Semitic Cronus who sacrificed his sons; for according to the statement of Philo of Byblus that ' Cronus, whom the Poenicians call Israel, being king of the land and having an only-begotten son called Jeoud (for in the Phoenician tongue Jeoud signifies ' only-begotten '), dressed him in royal robes and sacrificed him upon an altar in a time of war, when the country was in great danger from the enemy '.[1]

Zeus.—In the historic period Zeus was the king of Heaven. He is said to have been the son of Cronus by

[1] *Ib.* iv. 166.

Rhea and to have castrated his father and usurped his place. It is possible that this connection with Cronus was due to an attempt to relate all the gods, whatever their origin, to one Pantheon, and that in earlier times Zeus was an independent deity. Kings seem to have borne the title of Zeus,[1] and it is likely that this deity was once incarnate in the head of many a royal house. In later times local gods frequently enjoyed his name.

On Mount Lycaeun human sacrifice to Zeus Lycaeus continued to the time of Pausanias. And there are legends of King Lycaeon which seem to record such sacrifices in earlier times. It is said that this king offered a human child at the altar, that he set human flesh before Zeus when feasting him unawares at his table, and that he was changed into a wolf, or that someone present at the sacrifice always turned into a wolf, but could recover his human form if he abstained from human flesh for nine years.[2] These myths seem therefore to record a rite in which a king sacrificed, and ate, a child, which was possibly his son.

The part of the myth that relates the king's metamorphosis into a wolf is reminiscent of totemism. In totemic sacrifice a member of the totem species, which represents the totemic ancestor of the clan, is sometimes killed and eaten by the whole community. Most of the deities that we have considered have animal attributes; they had the heads of animals or animals were sacred to them, and it is very possible that they may all have been originally totems. If so, there is a hiatus between the sacrifice of totems and the sacrifice of divine kings or of divine princes that is hard to fill. Perhaps the simplest hypothesis is that the sacrifice of divine kings, or of their sons, had two independent origins, one in totemic sacrifice, the other in the precautionary exposure of children. It is as well to keep before us many possibilities, and to test them in the

---

[1] Frazer, *Golden Bough*, ii. 177, 361.
[2] Farnell, *Cults*, i. 41; Frazer, *Golden Bough*, ix. 353-4.

light of the new material. We shall then be less likely to overlook facts which are significant.

Still more reminiscent of totemic sacrifice was the ceremony of Zeus Polieus at Athens, called the *Bouphonia*, or ox murder. 'It took place about the end of June or beginning of July, that is, about the time when the threshing is nearly over in Attica. According to tradition the sacrifice was instituted to procure a cessation of drought and dearth which had afflicted the land. The ritual was as follows. Barley mixed with wheat, or cakes made of them, were laid upon the bronze altar of Zeus Polieus on the Acropolis. Oxen were driven round the altar, and the ox which went up to the altar and ate the offering on it was sacrificed. The axe and knife with which the beast was slain had been previously wetted with water brought by maidens called "water-carriers". The weapons were then sharpened and handed to the butchers, one of whom felled the ox with the axe and another cut its throat with the knife. As soon as he had felled the ox, the former threw the axe from him and fled ; and the man who cut the beast's throat apparently imitated his example. Meantime the ox was skinned and all present partook of its flesh. Then the hide was stuffed with straw and sewed up ; next the stuffed animal was set on its feet and yoked to a plough as if it were ploughing. A trial then took place in an ancient law-court presided over by the King (as he was called) to determine who had murdered the ox. The maidens who had brought the water accused the men who had sharpened the axe and knife ; the men who had sharpened the axe and knife blamed the men who had handed these implements to the butchers ; the men who had handed these implements to the butchers blamed the butchers ; and the butchers laid the blame on the axe and knife, which were accordingly found guilty, and condemned and cast into the sea.'[1] The guilt that the participants in this sacrifice displayed and the name of the rite seems to prove, as Frazer

---

[1] Frazer, *Golden Bough*, viii. 4-5.

suggests, that the ox incarnated the god. The sacrificers at once shared, disowned, and avoided the guilt. They 'all tasted the flesh of the dead and refrained not ',[1] that is, they were all forced to share the guilt as well as the benefit of the sacrifice. But at the same time they disowned guilt and brought the axe to judgement. Finally they avoided guilt and stuffed the ox and pretended that it was still alive, ready to perform its useful and magical functions perhaps, as Frazer thinks, as a corn-spirit.

But what are we to think of the origin of such a rite ? Did the king, or his son, once play the part of the ox-god ? Or is the rite preserved in its original form ? The flight of the man who struck the blow reminds us of the scapegoats that were driven out to bear away the sins of the community. He may once have escaped less lightly. If so, in his fate we may find the origin at once of the scapegoat and of the piaculum.

Frazer cites evidence to prove 'that in Thessaly and probably in Boeotia there reigned of old a dynasty of which kings were liable to be sacrificed for the good of the country to the god called Laphystian Zeus, but that they contrived to shift the fatal responsibility to their offspring, of whom the eldest son was regularly destined for the altar'.[2] It appears that later a ram was substituted for the princes as in the story of Abraham and Isaac. But this later development may have been a return to the original form of totemic sacrifice.

Hera.—Hera was the sister of Zeus and his bride. Her cult at Corinth was perhaps not of pure Greek origin. She was associated with Medea, and the sacrifice of children seems to have been part of her primitive sacrifice. Sometimes the people, sometimes the goddess, were believed to be responsible for the slaughter. There was a ritual of mourning and sorrow, of shaven head and dark robe which is reminiscent of the worship of the oriental Aphrodite.[3] There is little evidence that

---

[1] Farnell, *Cults*, i. 57.   [2] Frazer, *Golden Bough*, iv. 164-5.
[3] Farnell, *Cults*, i. 203.

the pure Greek Hera was ever a very terrible person; she was known only as the wife of Zeus, and as the goddess who encouraged marriage and aided childbirth.[1] But in spite of her later benevolence it is possible that she was once another example of the dread mother.

Artemis.—Artemis had affinities both with the Asiatic goddesses and with totems. She seems, like the Dread Mother elsewhere, to have been associated with a lover who came to a bad end.[2] Like Astarte and Cybele she was served at Ephesus with eunuch priests.[3] She was also especially a goddess of wild animals. 'The hare, the wolf, the hind, the wild boar, and the bear are consecrated to her by sacrifice or legend.'[4] Her rites seem to have included 'a great holocaust of stags and fawns, wolves and bears, and birds which were all thrown or driven into the flames of a great fire'.[5] She was supposed to partake of the flesh of a wild boar offered to her.[6] 'At Agrae in Attica . . . five hundred she-goats were offered annually by the polemarch to Artemis *Agrotera* as a thanksgiving for the victory of Marathon. . . .'[7]

The older religion seems to have seen in her more the protectress of animals, especially those with young, than as the huntress and destroyer of later times.[8] But she also participated in rites that were very similar to the sacrifice of totems.

It seems to have been once 'the custom for young maidens, clothed in a saffron robe, to dance in the Brauronian ceremonies of Artemis, and that in this dance they, as well as the priestess, were called " bears "; the saffron robe was possibly worn in order to imitate the tawny skin of the bear, and probably in the earliest times of the rite an actual bearskin was worn by the dancers'.[9] It is therefore likely that the goddess was originally a bear totem and that 'the maidens dressed up as bears assist at the sacrifice to the

---

[1] *Ib.* i. 195.　　[2] Frazer, *Golden Bough*, i. 39.　　[3] *Ib.* v. 269.
[4] Farnell, *Cults*, ii. 431.　　[5] *Ib.* ii. 431-2.　　[6] *Ib.* ii. 432.
[7] *Ib.* ii. 434.　　[8] *Ib.* ii. 434.　　[9] *Ib.* ii. 436.

bear-goddess of an animal akin to her and to themselves, and thus, if the sacrificial meal followed upon the act of oblation they would be recruiting their physical life and reviving the communion between themselves and their divinity. At the same time the feeling of kinship with the bear would easily lead to the belief at a later time that the goddess was angry because her animal was killed.'[1] Or perhaps, as in the suggested derivation of at least one form of the sacrifice of Zeus, the sacrifice was originally the totem feast of the therianthropic goddess which the sense of guilt that increases with civilization turned into a piaculum.

There are traces of this piaculum in the holocaust of the animals and, less surely, in certain other rites. At Athens two *katharmata*, ' probably criminals, were sacrificed in a sort of religious execution ; but though Artemis, from her connection with Apollo, came to obtain a place in that festal worship, yet it does not appear that the *katharmata* were devoted to her'.[2] There was further a flagellation of Spartan ephebi before the altar of Artemis which has been regarded as a modification of an earlier act of religious oblation. But Farnell, following Robertson Smith, thinks that this is more naturally explained ' as a ceremony of initiation, in which the youth is admitted into the full status of tribesman, and in which the altar or sacred idol must be touched with blood in order that the physical bond between him and his divinity may be

[1] Farnell, *Cults*, ii. 437.—Reinach is a strong believer in the totemic origin of the Greek gods. ' The primitive sacrifice of the god, generally accompanied by eating his flesh (communion), was perpetuated in ritual, and becoming incomprehensible, gave rise to numerous legends. To understand their genesis it is essential to bear in mind two essential elements of the totemic rites ; *masquerade* and *adoption of a name*. As the object of the sacrifice of the totem was to deify the faithful who took part in it, and to assimilate them to the god as closely as possible, the faithful sought to embrace this resemblance by taking the name of the god and covering themselves with the skins of animals of the same kind. Thus the Athenian maidens who celebrated the worship of the Bear-Artemis, dressed as, and called themselves, she-bears. The Maenads, who sacrificed the faun Pentheus, dressed themselves in the skins of fauns. Even in later forms of worship, we found the devotees of Bakkhos taking the name of Bakkhoi' (Reinach, *Orpheus*, translated by Florence Simmonds, 83).

[2] Farnell, *Cults*, ii. 439.

strengthened'.[1] Be this as it may the flagellation surely has some connection with expiation. The blood bond may be established as it is in the totem feast, or as in initiation ceremonies, but it is established in a manner that is more painful to the youths than to the goddess. Perhaps initiation ceremonies always contained ordeals which were, in some sense, expiatory.

The piacular element in the sacrifice of Artemis is again suggested by the legend of the sacrifice of Iphigenia, the priestess of Artemis, and in the condition of Orestes' life ' that in the yearly sacrifice there (at Halae) the sword should be held to a man's throat and some blood drawn, "for the sake of righteousness and that the goddess might have honour"'.[2] Further, at Phocaea a human victim seems to have been burnt alive to Artemis.[3]

The legend of Iphigenia is particularly interesting, as it seems to represent the substitution of the priestess for the goddess; for it is more likely ' that Iphigenia was a substitute for a doe than that the doe was a substitute for Iphigenia'.[4] There may have been first the communal sacrifice of the totem-goddess, by which the divine power and virtue was transferred to the worshippers. Then the goddess may have been separated from that animal which is no longer herself, but which is sacred to her and sacrificed in her rites. And finally, the increasing fear of the sacrilege committed by the slaughter of an animal that is still felt, in some mysterious way, to incarnate the goddess must be reduced by the piacular sacrifice of the priestess. But the priestess is at the same time the goddess, so that the new element is added to, rather than substituted for, the old. This hypothesis, however, gives no account of the divine or human lover of the goddess that we have seen reason to suppose she once possessed. Possibly

---

[1] *Ib.* ii. 439.—In his article ' Sacrifice ' in the 9th edition of the *Encyclopaedia Britannica* Robertson Smith classes the flagellation of the Spartan boys as a piaculum. Possibly the rite is derived from the same source as the bloodletting of the priests at the altar of Rhea-Cybele.
[2] Farnell, *Cults*, ii. 440.   [3] *Ib.* ii. 441.   [4] *Ib.*

he was originally himself the slain animal before it became identified with the goddess.

Although Artemis seems to have had a lover she was originally unmarried. As in the oriental cults, 'orgiastic and lascivious dances and the use of phallic emblems'[1] occurred in her rites. But already in Homer's time, although she remained the goddess of childbirth [2] she had become a virgin [3] proverbial for her chastity.

Aphrodite.—It is probable that Aphrodite was originally an Oriental deity.[4] She was at least identified with Istar as the lover of Adonis. Among the curious features of her cult that may be mentioned a youth at one of her festivals lay down and imitated the cries of a woman in travail.[5] In another the women and the men changed dresses.[6] Aphrodite was best known as the goddess of love—sometimes of profane love. ' In Hierapolis, Armenia, and probably Lydia, she was supposed to demand the sacrifice of virginity before marriage ; and in the legends of Istar and Semiramis the goddess herself was represented as wanton and murderous.'[7] But the distinction between the goddess of free love and the goddess of honourable marriage existed only in later times. She was apparently originally a goddess of fecundity whom the Greeks converted into a goddess of beauty and love.

At Salamis in Cyprus a man was annually sacrificed to Aphrodite, but later an ox was substituted.[8] Her earliest symbol was the conical stone,[9] but later the dove became her most common emblem.[10] She seems to have been yet another form of the great oriental goddess whose lover was ritually slain.

Ge.—Ge seems to have been the great earth goddess,[11] the goddess of that which grows on the land, of agriculture and of the dead. It is a legitimate inference that human victims were once offered to her, and perhaps

---

[1] Farnell, *Cults*, ii. 445.   [2] *Ib.* ii. 448.   [3] *Ib.* ii. 446.
[4] *Ib.* ii. 619.   [5] *Ib.* ii. 634.   [6] *Ib.* ii. 635.   [7] *Ib.* ii. 657.
[8] Frazer, *Golden Bough*, iv. 166, n.   [9] Farnell, *Cults*, ii. 671.
[10] *Ib.* ii. 674.   [11] *Ib.* iii. 19.

their flesh or ashes scattered over the land to make it fertile.[1] In Cyprus in the ritual of Aglauros, who seems to have been another form of Ge, a human victim was made to run thrice round the altar, after which he was speared by the priest.[2] Ge was worshipped 'at Athens, Mykonos, and probably once at Delphi in association with the dead and the ghostly realm'.[3] At Mykonos seven black lambs were offered to Zeus Chthonios and Ge Chthonia. The worshippers seem to have partaken of the sacrificial meal. There is an interesting legend that the Athenian Aglauros cast herself from the Acropolis to save her country in time of peril.[4] Is this a further example of a priestess who was sacrificed for, or to, her goddess?

Demeter and Kore-Persephone.—There is a good deal of similarity between the legend of Demeter and Persephone and that of Astarte or Aphrodite and Adonis. But whereas Adonis is the son of Astarte, Persephone is the daughter of Demeter. And whereas Adonis was killed by Ares in the form of a wild boar, Persephone was carried off to the under world by Pluto to be his bride. Like Attis, Adonis, and Osiris, Persephone was mourned. Like Osiris she ruled in the under world, but as queen not as king. But, since Demeter refused to allow the crops to grow until Persephone had been returned, Zeus ordered that she should spend two-thirds of every year in the upper world with her mother and the gods and only one-third of the year with her husband. This myth, according to Frazer, represents the decay and return of vegetation, which was dramatized and magically controlled. The drama of Demeter and Persephone seems to have formed the chief feature of the Eleusinian mysteries and of the festival of the Thesmophoria. These rites are excessively confusing, and it is impossible to reconstruct them accurately. We hear of living pigs thrown into underground sanctuaries,[5] of serpents that are

[1] See *ib.* iii. 19-20.   [2] *Ib.* iii. 19.   [3] *Ib.* iii. 23.
[4] *Ib.* iii. 21.   [5] *Ib.* iii. 89.

in the vault,[1] of an earth goddess whose local form was a snake,[2] of the sacrifice of a priestess, of a combat after the sacrifice,[3] of prisoners who were released,[4] of the absence of men during one night of the festival, of sexual abstinence mingled with intentional obscenity, and of some kind of flagellation,[5] of a passion play,[6] of representations of the abduction and rape of Kore, the double and daughter of Demeter,[7] and perhaps of the birth of a sacred child.[8]

Rhea-Cybele.—Rhea-Cybele was probably of Cretan or Phrygian extraction, and some opposition was given to her introduction into Greece.[9] Her worship was associated with that of her sacred son. She was a goddess of fertility and of death. She was the Great Mother, the Mother of the Gods. Snakes and lions, trees and pillars, were among her emblems. Her priests were eunuchs who mutilated themselves in religious frenzy. She may have been thought of as a virgin mother. But her cult is obscure and difficult to reconstruct with certainty.[10]

The ritual of the goddess seems to have commemorated the death and resurrection of Attis, her lover and perhaps her son.[11] Frazer describes the spring festival of Cybele and Attis in Rome as follows: 'On the twenty-second day of March, a pine-tree was cut in the woods and brought into the sanctuary of Cybele, where it was treated as a great divinity. . . . The trunk was swathed like the corpse with woollen bands and decked with wreaths . . . and the effigy of a young man, doubtless Attis himself, was tied to the middle of the stem. On the second day of the festival, the twenty-third of March, the chief ceremony seems to have been a blowing of trumpets. The third day, the twenty-fourth of March, was known as the Day of Blood: the Archigallus or high-priest drew blood from his arms and presented it as an offering. Nor was he

---

[1] Farnell, *Cults*, iii. 89. [2] *Ib.* iii. 52-3. [3] *Ib.* iii. 93-4. [4] *Ib.* iii. 97.
[5] *Ib.* iii. 103-4. [6] *Ib.* iii. 173. [7] *Ib.* iii. 134, 176, 181.
[8] *Ib.* iii. 177. [9] *Ib.* iii. 303. [10] See *ib.* iii. ch. vi.
[11] Frazer, *Golden Bough*, v. 264.

alone in making this bloody sacrifice. Stirred by the wild barbaric music of clashing cymbals, rumbling drums, droning horns and screaming flutes, the inferior clergy whirled about in the dance with waggling heads and streaming hair, until, rapt into a frenzy of excitement and insensible to pain, they gashed their bodies with potsherds or slashed them with knives in order to bespatter the altar with their flowing blood. . . . Further, we may conjecture, though we are not expressly told, that it was on the same Day of Blood . . . that the novices sacrificed their virility. Wrought up to the highest pitch of religious excitement they dashed the severed portions of themselves against the image of the cruel goddess. These broken instruments of fertility were afterwards reverently wrapt up and buried in the earth or in subterranean chambers sacred to Cybele, where, like the offering of blood, they may have been deemed instrumental in recalling Attis to life and hastening the general resurrection of nature, which was then bursting into leaf and blossom in the vernal sunshine. Some confirmation of this conjecture is furnished by the savage story that the mother of Attis conceived by putting in her bosom a pomegranate sprung from the severed genitals of a man-monster named Agdestis, a sort of double of Attis.'[1]

There were also secret or mystic ceremonies. ' In the baptism the devotee, crowned with gold and wreathed with fillets, descended into a pit, the mouth of which was covered with a wooden grating. A bull, adorned with garlands of flowers, its forehead glittering with gold leaf, was driven on to the grating and there stabbed to death with a consecrated spear. It's hot reeking blood poured in torrents through the apertures, and was received with devout eagerness by the worshipper on every part of his person and garments, till he emerged from the pit, drenched, dripping, and scarlet from head to foot, to receive the homage, nay, the adoration of his fellows as one who had been born

[1] *Ib.* v. 267-9.

again to eternal life and had washed away his sins in the blood of the bull.'[1]

Poseidon.—Among the sacrifices to Poseidon may be mentioned the offering of the first fruits of the season at Troezen,[2] of a white ram to Poseidon *Temenites* and a white lamb to Poseidon *Pukios* at Mykonos,[3] of a horse by throwing it into the sea,[4] of bulls, of the legendary sacrifice of a maiden,[5] and of a thanksgiving offering to Poseidon Soter after the storm that scattered the Persian fleet.[6] In historic times Poseidon was a sea god, but he was also the god of fertilizing streams and so of vegetation, and was regarded as the cause of earthquakes.[7] He was further considered to be in some sense an ancestor,[8] and his cult seems to have been fused with that of Erechtheus, a hero who was buried but who was believed to continue to live underground, and who in the *Iliad* was honoured with sacrifice.[9] It is not unlikely that this deity was originally a horse, and that a human representation of him was thrown into the sea in sacrifice.[10]

Apollo.—Apollo was perhaps originally a wolf god,[11] the supposed ancestor of certain Ionic gentes who made their way into the Athenian state,[12] but other animals, and especially the goat, seem to have been sacred to him.[13] He was also a pastoral god,[14] a god of trees and vegetation,[15] and of agriculture.[16]

According to a scholiast ' a man who killed a wolf in Attica used "to make a collection" for its burial, that is to say, buried it with costly and propitiatory offerings ',[17] and this custom suggests the originally divine or totemic nature of the wolf, which may once have been eaten sacramentally. There is further some evidence of the sacramental eating of the god in the form of a goat.[18]

Human sacrifices seem to have been offered to

---

[1] Frazer, *Golden Bough*, v. 274-5. [2] Farnell, *Cults*, iv. 6.
[3] *Ib*. iv. 7.   [4] *Ib*. iv. 15.   [5] *Ib*. iv. 26.   [6] *Ib*. iv. 13.
[7] *Ib*. iv. 5-7.   [8] *Ib*. iv. 36-7.   [9] *Ib*. iv. 47-51.   [10] *Ib*. iv. 15-26.
[11] *Ib*. iv. 113.   [12] *Ib*. iv. 160.   [13] *Ib*. iv. 254-5.   [14] *Ib*. iv. 123-4.
[15] *Ib*. iv. 124.   [16] *Ib*. iv. 130.   [17] *Ib*. iv. 115-16.   [18] *Ib*. iv. 258.

Apollo, and the god himself may have been slain in the person of his priest.[1] Of a festival, probably the Thargelia, a festival of Apollo, Tzetzes says : ' In time of plague, famine, or other disaster, the ugliest man in the city was led to sacrifice, as a purification and an expiation of the city ; bringing him to a suitable place they put cheese into his hand, and cakes, and figs, and having smitten him seven times on his genital organs with squills, wild figs, and other wild growths, they at last burnt him with wood of wild (fruit) trees and scattered his ashes to the winds into the sea '.[2] Originally the victim may have been treated with great honour and identified with the god so that he might communicate his virtue to the crops.[3] At Leukos human sacrifice was mitigated first by choosing criminals who were destined to die anyhow, and later by fastening parachutes of feathers to those who were thrown from the high place so that they were not killed but rescued and banished.[4] In the Thargelia the victim still seems to have retained some of the attributes of the god, to be in fact a sort of mock god. But the ugliest instead of the most beautiful human representative was chosen ; either because he is less valuable, or because his very ugliness, an attribute which is often characteristic of phallic symbols, made the victim peculiarly appropriate in a rite designed to stimulate the fertility of the crops.

According to a Megarian story cited by Farnell, the king ' Alkathous was sacrificing at the altar of Apollo, when his own son rushed up and with innocent intent threw the burning wood off the altar, whereupon the father instantly slew him with the sacred faggots. The legend', continues Farnell, ' gives us strong testimony that at Megara, in ancient times, human victims were offered to Apollo, and that the victim might even be the king's own son.'[5]

But there is little certain evidence of a sacramental

---

[1] *Ib.* iv. 263.　　[2] *Ib.* iv. 271.　　[3] See *ib.* iv. 279-81.
[4] *Ib.* iv. 274-5.　　[5] *Ib.* iv. 274.

eating of the god. There are 'only two examples of a nightly and mystic service, namely, the special purification of the Argive priestess and the Kharian prophet; and here the officiating individuals enter into communication with the deity through sacrament. Otherwise the sacrifices are mainly of the usual Hellenic form, being occasionally bloodless oblations, but far more frequently animal-offerings, among which we must reckon with the survival of human sacrifice.'[1]

Apollo was also intimately associated with divination. The diviner was always a woman. She seems to have been originally a virgin, but later the only obligation was that she should dress as one. She chewed laurel to establish communication with the deity, a practice which may have been equivalent to the sacramental eating of the god. Then, possessed with the spirit of the god, she prophesied in his name.

In the earliest monuments Apollo seems to have been represented by a conical pillar, and later the bow is his most constant attribute. Both these emblems are common phallic symbols, and it seems probable that at least the pillar was consciously intended to be such.

Dionysus.—The myth of Dionysus is described by Frazer as follows: 'Zeus in the form of a serpent visited Persephone, and she bore him Zagreus, that is, Dionysus, a horned infant. Scarcely was he born, when the babe mounted the throne of his father Zeus and mimicked the great god by brandishing the lightning in his tiny hand. But he did not occupy the throne long, for the treacherous Titans, their faces whitened with chalk, attacked him with knives while he was looking at himself in a mirror. For a time he evaded their assaults by turning himself into various shapes, assuming the likeness successively of Zeus and Cronus, of a young man, of a lion, a horse, and a serpent. Finally, in the form of a bull, he was cut to pieces by

[1] Farnell, *Cults*, iv. 253.

the murderous knives of his enemies.'[1] In the Cretan version his destruction is brought about by Juno, the wife of Jupiter.[2] After his death he rose again and his limbs were pieced together, either at the command of his father or through the efforts of his mother, or because his father Zeus swallowed his heart and begat him again by Semele.[3]

The ritual of Dionysus appears to have been a sort of mystery play, in which his life, death, and resurrection were acted; but it is probable that here as elsewhere the myth was invented to explain the cult. The main act in the drama seems to have been the tearing to pieces of Dionysus in the form of an animal by the Maenads, or wild women, who devoured his raw flesh in frantic haste, and who presumably imagined that they thus absorbed his divine virtue.[4] The festival was by night, in the forest and on the mountain and often in the depth of winter.[5] 'The tragedy of Euripides is eloquent concerning the joy " of the banquet of raw flesh ", and the Christian fathers and the scholiasts attest the long survival of this practice in the orgiastic ritual.[6] . . . The wild excitement going with the fear lest the spirit should escape, allowed no time for the formal mode of sacrifice and the slower processes of cookery.'[7] And, according to Firmicus Maternus, ' even in the latter days of paganism, the Cretans solemnize a divine funeral festival, and organize a sacred year with trieteric rites, performing everything that the boy god did or suffered. They rend a living bull with their teeth, and they simulate madness of soul as they shriek through the secret places of the forest with discordant clamours.'[8]

Dionysus was usually consumed in the form of a bull, but the goat and fawn were also his embodiments.[9] and snakes, too, were dismembered in his ritual.[10] Human victims seem to have been not uncommon. A

---

[1] Frazer, *Golden Bough*, vii. 12-13.   [2] *Ib.* vii. 13.   [3] *Ib.* vii. 14.
[4] Farnell, *Cults*, v. 164-6.   [5] *Ib.* v. 153.   [6] *Ib.* v. 164.
[7] *Ib.* v. 166.   [8] *Ib.* v. 157.   [9] *Ib.* v. 97.   [10] *Ib.* v. 165-6.

child who personated Dionysus seems to have been dismembered and eaten by Minyan and Argive women,[1] and Pentheus, the priest who incarnated the god, was led through the city in female attire, which the deity himself occasionally affected, hung on a tree and pelted at ; ' then follows the dismemberment, and then —we may suspect—either in reality or simulation, " the sacrificial banquet of men's flesh " '.[2]

Not only the deity and his human representatives, but also his female votaries seem to have come in for rough usage. In the festival of the *Agrionia* these women ' were pursued by the priest of Dionysus with a drawn sword, and anyone that he could catch was slain ; ... And we have a right to suspect that the Maenad was originally slain sacramentally '.[3]

The Maenads seem to have been not only sometimes killed but often scourged, as is suggested by the legend of Lykurgos, who, armed with an ox-goad, drove the ox-god into the sea and pursued the Maenads. ' It is well known ', writes Farnell, ' that whipping is a commonly used practice in vegetation rites, whether to increase the fructifying power of the patients, in cases where the rods were cut from a tree or plant of a specially quickening potency, or more usually perhaps to drive out from the body impure influences or spirits, so that it may become the purer vehicle of divine force. Therefore Lykurgos pursued and struck the Maenads with ox-thongs ; the women of Alea in Arcadia were scourged in the festival of Dionysus ; and there is reason to think that the modern Bacchanalian mummers at Bizyi were at one time accustomed to be whipped in the course of the miracle-play.'[4]

Among other characteristics of the rites of Dionysus may be mentioned a general intoxication, for Dionysus was also a god of wine and with wine his divine essence could be sacramentally absorbed,[5] a mock marriage with the queen-archon,[6] and the use of a model

---

[1] Farnell, *Cults*, v. 167. [2] *Ib.* v. 168. [3] *Ib.* v. 169-70.
[4] *Ib.* v. 163. [5] *Ib.* v. 122. [6] *Ib.* v. 159-60.

phallus which seems to have been paraded at the festivals.[1]

From such legends and survivals it is a little difficult to discover whether Dionysus was originally sacrificed in the form of an animal or of a king or of a prince ; whether he was sacrificed by his priests or by his Maenads ; or whether his priests or his Maenads were sacrificed to him. Or even whether he was male or female himself. The accepted purpose of his rites seems to have been to stimulate fertility.

Reviewing these examples of Greek sacrifice we find in the rites of Cronus, Zeus, and Apollo cases of the sacrifice *of* a god, either in the form of an animal or of a king-priest, followed at a later stage by the sacrifice of a victim *to* the god ; and in the rites of Artemis the sacrifice *of* a theriomorphic goddess, of her priestess, and of animals who may have represented the goddess herself and have been at the same time substitutes for her priestess. That is, we find examples of sacrifices both *of* and *to* both gods and goddesses. We find that chastity was an article of value that could be sacrificed to Aphrodite, and that virility was offered as a sacrifice to Rhea-Cybele, and that blood was given to Attis to renew his life. Finally, we find that Dionysus was torn in pieces and devoured by women. It is possible that the purpose here was not only to become the god as in the usual sacramental meal, but to become his mother.[2] Attis was reborn by his mother who consumed the pomegranate that sprang from the severed genitals of his double Agdestis, and the eating of the severed members of Dionysus, the mock marriage, the use of the phallic emblems, and the whipping of the women with ox-thongs cut from the sacred ox may have been intended to produce a similar effect. The crops may have been renewed by reincarnating the new god of vegetation in the wombs of the women who ate the old.

There is no clear trace of an original connection of

---

[1] *Ib.* v. 107-8, 125.   [2] Roheim, *Australian Totemism*, 391.

burial rites with sacrifice as in Egypt, where the rites for the dead seem to have been derived from the sacrifice of Osiris. It is, however, likely that the great games that formed so striking a feature of Greek civilization were once funeral rites. But as in the cult of Osiris many elements in the funeral may have originally preceded the death. Frazer suggests that the divine king was perhaps the victor in the race, and that his vanquished predecessor may have been ritually slain. Each king, he supposes, may have reigned for eight, or four years, the interval between the races, and have been required at the end of this period to risk his crown and life to the hazard of a new contest.[1] Perhaps he lengthened his reign by requiring his sons to compete on his behalf. Such a development might account for the myths of the substitution of sons for fathers as sacrificial victims. But we cannot yet be sure whether sons were substituted for fathers or fathers for sons, or whether both kinds of substitution occurred.

8. *Sacrifice in Rome*

The Romans ' were more interested in the cult of their deities, that is, in the ritual and routine by which they could be rightly and successfully propitiated, than in the character and personality of the deities themselves '.[2] For this reason it is easier to describe the festivals than to trace the history of the gods.

The Roman month contained three fixed points, the Kalends, the Nones, and the Ides, which originally corresponded to the phases of the moon, and intervening dates were described in terms of the number of days

---

[1] Frazer, *Golden Bough*, iv. 104. It is possible that the races may have been originally combats. Rose in his paper ' Suggested Explanation of Ritual Combat' (*Folk-lore*, xxxvi.) suggests that ritual combats purified by stimulating excitement and mana. This seems rather vague, but if games started as ritual combats at tombs they may have been related to the blood feud. All the members of a bereaved family are sometimes expected to fight together after the funeral. And by this means, especially if one of them is killed, they are purified of their guilt.

[2] Fowler, *Roman Festivals*, 333.

which separated them from the day after the next fixed point. Thus if the Kalends were the day after to-morrow a Roman would describe to-day as the *third* day before the Kalends. Each festival had its fixed day, and it was celebrated with great precision and elaborate detail. Here, as it is not possible to describe them all, I have made an arbitary selection which is based on Fowler's *Roman Festivals*.

In spite of the work of the systematizers the Roman calendar still contains ' in a fossilized condition the remains of three different strata of religious or social development '.[1] There are, first, survivals of ' the most primitive condition of human life in ancient Latium ; that of men dwelling on forest-clad hill-tops, surrounded by a world of spirits, some of which have taken habitation in, or are in some sort represented by, objects such as trees, animals, or stones '.[2] Next there is the remnant of ' a period in which the ordered processes of agriculture, and the settled life of the farm-house, are the distinctive features. We have the beginnings of a calendar in the observation of the quarters of the moon and their connection with the deities of light.'[3] And finally, there is the systematization of the religious life in the city, and even of the Latin federation.[4]

The old Roman year began in March, and on the Ides of this month, or on the day before the Ides, ' a man clad in skins was led in procession through the streets of Rome, beaten with long white rods, and driven out of the city. He was called Mamurius Veturius . . . .'[5] According to a late myth the rite was in commemoration of the expulsion of Mamurius the Smith, because misfortune had fallen on the Romans when they used his shields instead of those that had fallen from heaven. But Frazer holds that the victim represented the Mars of the old year who was driven out at the beginning of the new, and that this god ' was originally not a god of

---

[1] *Ib.* 334.   [2] *Ib.*   [3] *Ib.*   [4] *Ib.* 335.
[5] *Ib.* 48. Quoted from Frazer, *Golden Bough*.

war, but of vegetation '.[1] The rite is interesting, since it seems to suggest the former combination in one act of the sacrifice of a god and the expulsion of a scapegoat.

At the Tubilustrium, on the 23rd of March (x. Kal. Apr.), the day before the meeting of the comita, the tubae were purified by the sacrifice of a lamb. These were long, straight brass tubes with bell mouths, used in military and religious ceremonies.[2] Such purificatory rites are often called cathartic, because by means of them an excessive purity or impurity can be removed from any object, that is, through cathartic sacrifice an object may be consecrated to the service of the gods or deconsecrated for the service of men.

At the Fordicidia on April 15 (xvii. Kal. Mai.), ' one of the oldest sacrificial rites in the Roman religion ', pregnant cows were slaughtered, ' one in the Capitol and one in each of the thirty *curiae*. . . . The cows were offered . . . to Tellus, who . . . may be an indigitation of the same earth power represented by Ceres, Bona Dea, Dea Dia, and other female deities. The unborn calves were torn by attendants of the virgo vestalis maxima from the womb of the mother and burnt, and their ashes were kept by the Vestals for use at the Parilia a few days later. This was the first ceremony in the year in which the Vestals took part, and it was the first of a series of acts, all of which are connected with the fruits of the earth, their growth, ripening, and harvesting. The object of the burning of the unborn calves seems to have been to procure the fertility of the corn now growing in the womb of mother earth, to whom the sacrifice was offered.'[3] It is not clear how much of the rite was magical, how much propitiatory. Perhaps by anticipating the birth of the calves, the birth of vegetation was magically stimulated, and by burning them the earth compensated for what was to be taken from her.

At the Cerialia on April 19 (xiii. Kal. Mai.), burning brands seem to have been fastened to the tails of foxes.

---

[1] Fowler, *Roman Festivals*, 48. Quoted from Frazer, *Golden Bough*.
[2] Fowler, *Roman Festivals*, 63-4.   [3] *Ib.* 71.

This was, according to Ovid, in commemoration of the act of a boy who caught a fox that had done damage to the farm, tied it up in straw and hay and set fire to it, but who allowed it to escape, so that it burnt the crops. Modern research, however, gives the rite a more distant origin. Preller thinks that the ceremony had something to do with the *robigo*, or red fox, a red mildew that attacks cereals, and Gubernatis that the tail of the fox was a phallic symbol, and that the ceremony was a piece of imitative magic to promote the growth of the crops.[1]

At the Parilia on April 21 (xi. Kal. Mai.) 'The sheep-fold was decked with green boughs and a great wreath was hung on the gate. . . . At the earliest glimmer of daybreak the shepherd purified the sheep . . . by sprinkling and sweeping the fold ; then a fire was made of heaps of straw, olive-branches, laurel, to give good omen by the crackling, and through this apparently the shepherds leapt, and the flocks were driven. . . . After this the shepherd brought offerings to Pales, of whom there may perhaps have been in the farmyard a rude image made of wood ; among these were baskets of millet and cakes of the same, pails of milk, and other food of appropriate kinds. The meal which followed the shepherd himself appears to have shared with Pales. Then he prays to the deity to avert all evil from himself and his flocks ; whether he or they have unwittingly trespassed on sacred ground and caused the nymphs or fauni to fly from human eyes ; or have disturbed the sacred fountains, and used branches of a sacred tree for secular ends '.[2] Lastly, a bowl was brought out of which milk and heated wine were drunk until the shepherd was sufficiently inspired to leap over the burning heaps.[3] It is interesting to note that the ancients were themselves uncertain whether Pales was a male or female deity.[4]

At the Robigalia on April 25 (vii. Kal. Mai.) reddish

[1] *Ib.* 77-8.   [2] *Ib.* 80-1.   [3] *Ib.* 82.
[4] Frazer, *Golden Bough*, ii. 326.

suckling whelps seem to have been sacrificed to Robigus, the spirit who works in the mildew. He was probably invoked to avert the evil that he caused.[1] The reddish whelps may have been originally the incarnations of Robigus himself. If so, such a ritual slaughter of the demon of the mildew seems more rational than those sacrifices in which a beneficent god is the victim. We begin to wonder whether those slain gods, of which we have found so many examples, were really not demons at some stage of their existence, or in some strata of the minds of those who killed them.

The Feriae Latinae, the great festival that united in a common kinship all the Latin race, was not fixed in the calendar. It took place in April, and its precise date was determined by the consuls on their entrance upon office on the Ides of March. After the magistrates (or their deputies) from all the Latin cities had collected in the temple, ' the Roman consul offered a libation of milk, while the deputies from the other cities brought sheep, cheeses, or other such offerings '.[2] The consul sacrificed a pure white heifer, the flesh of which was afterwards consumed by the deputies. This rite is typical of ceremonies to make or renew contracts. The participants cement their fellowship in a common meal.

May 1 (Kal. Mai.) was the traditional day of the dedication of a temple to the Bona Dea. This goddess seems to have been an Earth-Mother ; neither men nor wine nor myrtle were allowed in her temple. The latter two restrictions were due, according to a legend, to the fact that the goddess had been beaten by her father with a myrtle rod ' because she would not yield to his incestuous love or drink the wine he pressed on her '.[3]

Fowler thinks that the myth may have grown out of a cult in which a victim or the image of a deity was beaten—a cult which would have many parallels, and which may have been intended to drive away evil and promote fertility.[4] A pig seems to have been sacri-

---

[1] Fowler, *Roman Festivals*, 88-91. [2] *Ib.* 96. [3] *Ib.* 103.
[4] *Ib.* 104.

ficed to this deity. Perhaps she was herself originally a pig.

May 9, 10, and 13 seem to have been devoted to the expulsion or pacification of the hostile dead, that is, those who had died by violence and who had not received orderly burial. The father of the family rises at midnight, and with ' bare feet and washed hands, making a peculiar sign with his fingers and thumbs to keep off the ghosts, he walks through the house. He has black beans in his mouth, and these he spits out as he walks, looking the other way and saying, " With these I redeem me and mine " '.[1] From the fact that those who have not received due burial are believed to be hostile and active we may infer that funeral rites originally included rites to lay the ghost as well as to propitiate him.

On May 15 (Id. Mai.) a number of bundles of rushes, which seem to have resembled men bound hand and foot, ' were taken down to the *pons sublicius* by the Pontifices and magistrates, and cast into the river by the Vestal Virgins. The Flaminica Dialis, the priestess of Jupiter, was present at the ceremony in mourning '.[2] This looks like the survival of yet another example of a mourning goddess and her slain sons.

On May 29 (iv. Kal. Iun.), at the Ambarvalia, there was ' a procession of victims—bull, sheep, and pig—all round the fields, driven by a garlanded crowd, carrying olive branches and chanting '.[3]

At the Poplifugia on July 5 (iii. Non. Quinct.), a festival of which little is known, it seems probable that after the sacrifice the priest and the people fled from the spot. This may have been either to escape the blood-guilt as in the Athenian Bouphonia, or, as Fowler suggests with less probability, to avoid a scapegoat who had become infected with the excessive purity or impurity that had been imparted to it.[4] A late myth states that the festival was in commemoration of the

[1] *Ib.* 109. [2] *Ib.* 112. [3] *Ib.* 126.
[4] *Ib.* 176.

flight of the people after the disappearance of Romulus in the darkness of an eclipse or sudden tempest.[1] It seems likely that this myth contains a germ of truth. The flight is reminiscent of the panic that follows the death of a leader. This leader may have been at once a god and a victim. If he was slain in sacrifice by his own worshippers their flight would be justified at once as an escape from blood-guilt and as the result of the panic that automatically followed his death. Perhaps there is an element of guilt in every panic after the death of a leader. Analysts tell us that leaders are father substitutes and that the attitude towards them is ambivalent. If so, their death may be unconsciously attributed to unconscious hostile wishes, and the vengeance of their ghosts feared.

At the Volcanalia on August 24 (x. Kal. Sept.) small fishes were thrown into the fire by the heads of Roman families.[2]

On the Ides of October (15 Oct.) there was a two-horse chariot race in the Campus Martius. The near horse of the winning pair seems to have been sacrificed to Mars, and killed with the spear that is sacred to this deity. 'The tail of the horse was cut off and carried with all speed to Regiá so that the warm blood might drip upon the focus or sacred hearth there. The head was also cut off and decked with cakes; and at one time there was a fight for its possession between the men of the two neighbouring quarters of the Via Sacra and the Surburba.'[3] Mannhardt believed that the head was 'an object possessed of power to procure fertility'.[4]

The Faunalia rustica on December 15 (Non. Dec.) is described by Fowler after Horace as follows: 'There is an ancient altar—not a temple—to a supernatural being who is not yet fully a god, who can play pranks like the "Brownies" and do harm, but who is capable of doing good if duly propitiated. On the Nones of December, possibly of other months too, he is coaxed

---
[1] Fowler, *Roman Festivals*, 175. [2] *Ib.* 209. [3] *Ib.* 242.
[4] *Ib.* 244.

with tender kid, libations of wine, and incense; the little rural community of farmers (pagus), with their labourers, take part in the rite, and bring their cattle into the common pasture, plough-oxen and all. Then after the sacrifice, they dance in triple measure, like the Salii in March.'[1]

The Saturnalia began on December 17 (xvi. Kal. Ian.) and lasted seven days. The festival began with sacrifice at the temple of Saturn, followed by a public feast. The Senators and Equites wore the toga during the sacrifice, but laid it aside for the convivium. During the festival the slaves were waited on by them.[2]

But the Saturnalia seems originally to have been a grimmer ceremony than the festival of later times. Frazer has collected strong evidence that at one time a representative of the god Saturn was elected as king of the festivals, that during them he was allowed every licence, and that he was sacrificed at their termination. And this custom seems to have survived in the provinces into the third century of our era. Frazer further argues that the human representative of the god was probably married to a divine consort and that their union was supposed to be of great assistance to agriculture. There is some evidence that the old Latin kingships were inherited through the female line, and it seems not improbable that the Saturn of the year was originally mated with the queen. If so, in the Saturnalia, which still survives in the Carnival, may linger traces of a festival in which the new king was conceived and the old king required to die.[3]

From February 13 (Id. Feb.) to February 22 were the *dies parentales*, in which the family ghosts, or manes, were propitiated and cared for. During this festival, or on the anniversary of the death of some relation, the members of the family 'would go in procession to the grave, not only to see that all was well with him who abode there, but to present him with offerings of water,

---

[1] *Ib.* 257.   [2] *Ib.* 268-73.
[3] Frazer, *Golden Bough*, ii. 310 *sq.*, ix. 306 *sq.*

wine, milk, honey, oil, and the blood of black victims: to deck the tomb with flowers, to utter once more the solemn greeting and farewell (Salve, sancte parens), to partake of a meal with the dead, and to petition them for good fortune and all things needful'.[1] This festival seems to have been a kind of 'love feast of the family'. The Lares shared in the sacred meal.

At the Lupercalia on February 15 (xv. Kal. Mart.) goats and a dog were sacrificed at a cave called the Lupercal. 'Next, two youths of high rank . . . had their foreheads smeared with the knife bloody from the slaughter of the victims, and then wiped with wool dipped in milk. As soon as this was done they were obliged to laugh. Then they girt themselves with the skins of the slaughtered goats, and feasted luxuriously; after which they ran round the base of the Palatine Hill, or at least a large part of this circuit, apparently in two companies, one led by each of the two youths. As they ran they struck at all the women who came near them or offered themselves to their blows, with strips of skin cut from the hides of the same victims. . . .'[2] The whipping of the women, as usual in such rites, was intended to produce fertility.[3] The skins were donned presumably to establish an identity between the youths and the divine victims,[4] and the blood may have been wiped off to purify them from the blood-guilt.[5] Thus the youths seem to have represented both the sacrificer and the victim which was itself both god and offering.

The Terminalia on February 23 (vii. Kal. Mart.) seems to have been a rite designed to guarantee the boundaries between neighbouring estates. 'The two landowners garlanded each his side of the boundary-stone, and all offerings were double. An altar is made; and fire is carried from the hearth by the farmer's wife, while the old man cuts up sticks and builds them in a framework of stout stacks. Then with dry bark the fire is kindled; from the basket, held ready by a boy,

[1] Fowler, *Roman Festivals*, 308.   [2] *Ib.* 311.   [3] *Ib.* 320.
[4] *Ib.* 318.   [5] *Ib.* 315.

the little daughter of the family thrice shakes the fruits of the earth into the fire, and offers cakes of honey. Others stand by with wine ; and the neighbours (or dependents) look on in silence and clothed in white. A lamb is slain, and a suckling pig, and the boundary-stone sprinkled with their blood; and the ceremony ends with a feast and songs in praise of holy Terminus.'[1] The original ceremony by which the boundary was first fixed is 'described by the gromatic writer Siculus Flaccus. Fruits of the earth, and the bones, ashes and blood of a victim which had been offered were put into a hole by the two (or three) owners whose land converged at the point, and the stone was rammed down on the top and carefully fixed.'[2]

The Regifugium on February 24 (vi. Kal. Mart.) may have been the flight of the crowd as from the guilt of murder after a sacrifice of a divine victim. Ovid, however, believed that it was in commemoration of the expulsion of Tarquin,[3] and Frazer that it may have been a survival of a race in which the king had to gain and retain his crown.[4]

Reviewing these examples we see that Roman festivals seem to include all varieties of sacrifice. There are elements of communal sacrifice, in which the god is consumed, especially in the Ferae Latinae, of deificatory sacrifice, in which a tutelary deity is supposed to be created, in the Terminalia, and of at least one form of mortuary sacrifice in the Parentalia. An example of the piaculum is perhaps to be found in the ceremony of pacification of the hostile dead and in the Robigalia. The Tubilustrium is clearly cathartic, that is, designed to remove impurity, and certain elements in the Parentalia must have been wholly honorific.

9. *Sacrifice among the Slavs*

As typical of ancient Slav sacrifices may be mentioned their harvest thanksgiving ceremony and their

[1] *Ib.* 325.   [2] *Ib.* 325.   [3] *Ib.* 327-8.   [4] Frazer, *Golden Bough*, ii. 308-9.

burial rites. At the harvest thanksgiving, when the people had gathered together, the priest entered alone into the sanctuary of the god Svantovit. There he examined the tankard that was in the right hand of the idol, which contained the remains of the liquid offering of the year before. Whether the coming harvest would be good or not depended on whether the liquid reached or failed to reach a certain mark on the tankard. After the priest had prophesied the future of the crops, he poured out the old wine as a libation, and twice refilled the tankard, once for himself and once for the god in whose right hand he placed the cup. Meanwhile he prayed for the happiness and prosperity of himself and the people. Next the priest took an offering of honey cake almost as big as a man, and standing behind it asked if he could still be seen. If the people answered yes, the priest said that he hoped that they would not see him at the same festival the next year. Finally, after a warning to honour the gods and the old morals, began the feast. Besides animal sacrifices there were sometimes human victims determined by lot. Especially relished by the god was the blood of Christians. In order to become more sensitive to the gift of prophecy the priest drank of the blood of the victims.[1]

The fact that the offering of the honey cake was supposed to be as large as the priest suggests that it was a substitute for a man, perhaps for the priest himself. And the belief that drinking the blood of the victims inspired the priest to prophesy is evidence that here again the victims were originally divine. Possibly the priest once died in the character of the god.

The Slavonic funeral was as follows : Over the body there were night watchmen to prevent the soul of the departed from interfering with those who were asleep. Then there were complaints and reproaches that the dead had left his own ; but these ended in feasting,

[1] Brückner, *Lehrbuch der Religionsgeschichte*, 4. Aufl. ii. 513-4; Loisy, *Le Sacrifice*, 265.

drinking, and games. The corpse was burned on the funeral pyre; after which the ashes were collected in an urn and buried under a tumulus. A wife of the dead man, his horse and weapons, or models of these, were also burnt. Finally there were games with prizes that were paid for out of the property of the deceased. And in order to propitiate him for this misuse of his goods there was celebrated an Easter feast for the dead after that for the living, even in Christian times.[1]

There is an interesting myth that purports to account for the origin of cremation. Sovij, the God of the Dead, was once a man who hunted a wild boar and took nine pieces of spleen out of it and gave them to his children to cook. But the children ate them themselves. On discovering this the father was very angry and tried to go to the underworld. At eight doors he failed; but at the ninth, with the help of his youngest son, he succeeded. Then were the other brothers angry with the youngest, so that he too, with their permission, went to the underworld, to seek his father. After their evening meal the son made for his father a bed in the earth. But the next morning as the son asked his father how he slept the father complained that he had been disturbed by snakes and worms. The next night the son made the bed in a wooden coffin, but this time the father was disturbed by bees and gnats. On the third night the son made the bed in the fire and here the father slept as sweetly as a babe in a cradle.[2]

We know that primitive people often believe that the spirits of the departed enter into snakes and worms. We have only to invert certain elements of the story to recover its original meaning. It was not the father whose sleep was disturbed, but the sons. They were troubled by the ghost of their father in the form of snakes, worms, bees, or gnats. Belief in ghosts seems to be due to an unconscious refusal to accept the death of loved persons. A great part of the ceremony of

[1] Brückner, *Lehrbuch der Religionsgeschichte*, 4. Aufl. ii. 517-8.   [2] *Ib.* 526-7.

funeral rites is designed to free the participants from the fear of ghosts. This purpose is achieved by bringing conviction of the fact of death right into the unconscious layers of the mind. And cremation, which utterly destroys the body whatever other purpose it may fulfil, does help to bring this conviction.

Behind the other portions of the myth we may perhaps dimly discern a story in which the youngest son kills his father and is in turn killed by his brothers. And, behind this story again, an account of the killing and eating of the totem father by the tribesmen. We shall return to this myth, for, if it is treated analytically, it seems to contain the whole history of sacrifice from the totemic communion, through the later piaculum, to the pious mortuary rites of later times. But I am anticipating the argument of later sections.

There is slight evidence that the Slav kings, like those of many other peoples, may have been once periodically killed and succeeded by their assassins. ' When the captives Gunn and Jarmerik contrived to slay the king and queen of the Slavs and made their escape, they were pursued by the barbarians, who shouted after them that if they would only come back they would reign instead of the murdered monarch, since by a public statute of the ancients the succession to the throne fell to the king's assassin.'[1] Perhaps the assassin was thought to incarnate his victim. If he had been a cannibal as well as a murderer he would have incarnated his victim in the literal sense. To absorb the virtues of others is known to be one of the motives of cannibalism. Possibly the successor to the throne once ate the late monarch, though I know of no direct evidence of such a custom.

We know that gods were eaten and that kings personated gods, so that there is nothing intrinsically improbable in the suggestion that the new king secured his title to the throne by literally incarnating his predecessor. The custom of the slayer eating a portion

[1] Frazer, *Golden Bough*, iv. 52.

of the man he has slain, and of the eating of aged relatives is not unknown.[1] Such rites may have had at least two purposes, to absorb the virtue of the deceased, and to prevent his ghost from doing harm, for it is thought that the ghost will recognize his own flesh in the murderer and will not injure it.

10. *Sacrifice among the Germans*

The dead chiefs of the Germans, like those of the Slavs, were burnt together with their arms and perhaps their horses; afterwards their ashes were buried under a tumulus.[2] There was also a feast for the dead. 'On the third, sixth, ninth and fortieth days after the funeral the old Prussians and Lithuanians used to prepare a meal, to which, standing at the door, they invited the soul of the deceased. At these meals they sat silent round the table and used no knives, and the women who served up the food were also without knives.'[3] There was further a custom for anyone who passed a place where someone had died by violence to add to the pile of sticks or stones that covered the spot.[4] This may have been to prevent the ghost from rising.[5]

To determine the future of an important expedition the Germans procured a man from the people of the enemy, and made him fight with one of their own men. On the issue of this fight would depend the issue of the greater battle that was to come.[6]

There is also evidence of propitiatory sacrifices to nature spirits. 'In some parts of Austria and Germany, when a storm is raging, the people open a window and throw out a handful of meal, saying to the wind, "There, that's for you, stop."'[7] But sometimes they throw knives at a whirlwind.[8]

[1] *Ib.* iii. 174; iv. 14.
[2] Loisy, *Le Sacrifice*, 153.
[3] Frazer, *Golden Bough*, iii. 238.
[4] *Ib.* ix. 15.
[5] Roheim, *Australian Totemism*, 361 *sq.*
[6] Loisy, *Le Sacrifice*, 264.
[7] Frazer, *Golden Bough*, i. 329, n.
[8] *Ib.* i. 329.

Traces of totemism may have survived well into our era. 'At the beginning of the eighth century, Popes Gregory III and Zacharas enjoined Boniface, the apostle of the Germans, to see that his converts abstained from the flesh of horses. To eat the horse is a filthy and execrable crime, adds Gregory. It is evident that the Popes were concerned, not for the hygiene of the Germans, but for their religion. The meats they proscribe are those of sacred animals, which were eaten ritually.'[1]

Descent among the Germans was probably once through the female line, and the maternal uncle, rather than the father, was the ruler of the family.[2] Great reverence was shown for women, and queens were sometimes defied.[3] Perhaps there were once queen-priestess-goddesses and rituals of slain son gods as among so many other peoples.

11. *Sacrifice among the Celts*

After victories the Celts sometimes sacrificed their prisoners, and such sacrifices were cannibalistic, possibly among the Celts of Britain, and almost certainly among those of Ireland.[4] These people also appear to have kept the heads of those they slew and to have used the skulls as cups for libations.[5]

If an important Celt was ill he sacrificed someone else thinking that the gods would accept the substitute.[6] The Celts also divined from the entrails of a victim, or from the way he fell.[7]

Every four or five years several victims were burnt by the Druids in great man-like cages of basket work.[8] Frazer in early editions of the *Golden Bough* adopted a theory from Mannhardt that the men and animals who were burnt in these wicker cages personated the corn-

---

[1] Reinach, *Orpheus*, translated by Florence Simmonds, 134.
[2] Frazer, *Golden Bough*, ii. 285.   [3] *Ib*. i. 391.
[4] Loisy, *Le Sacrifice*, 111.   [5] *Ib*. 111.   [6] *Ib*. 497.
[7] *Ib*. 277-8.   [8] *Ib*. 497 ; Frazer, *Golden Bough*, xi. 32-3.

spirit. But in the third edition he holds that these victims were witches and wizards who might otherwise blight the crops.[1] It is strange that the attitude of primitive peoples to their good and evil spirits was sometimes so similar that it is difficult to determine in a given sacrifice whether the victim was a god or a devil.

Anwyl finds 'some traces in the folklore of such a practice as the dispatch of an aged parent by his able-bodied son' and seems to conclude that the real motive for this, and for human sacrifices that were later offered as an expiation and atonement, ' was probably, in the main, real or supposed economic pressure'.[2] We may suspect that such a motive, if it existed, was a rationalization. We remember that the sons of the Celts were not allowed to go into the presence of their fathers armed, and that generally they were brought up in strange families. This suggests that these fathers had real grounds to fear their sons and took precautions accordingly. The reasons for the fear were probably repressed and it would be simply regarded as unlucky for a son to approach his father armed. The unconscious hatred of the father may have found an ultimate satisfaction in the pious duty of dispatching him when he was too old to be of any further use, if such a custom existed.

12. *Sacrifice in Mexico*

Frazer has collected from Mexican rites many examples of sacrifice in which the victim died in the character of a god. A short account of some of these I have taken from his *Golden Bough*.

A general description of such rites he quotes from a sixteenth-century Spanish authority. 'They took a captive', says the Jesuit Acosta, ' such as they thought good ; and afore they did sacrifice him unto their idols, they gave him the name of the idol, to whom he should

---

[1] Frazer, *Golden Bough*, xi. 43-4.
[2] Anwyl, *Encyclopedia of Religion and Ethics*, xi. 11.

be sacrificed, and apparelled him with the same ornaments like their idol, saying, that he did represent the same idol. And during the time that this representation lasted, which was for a year in some feasts, in others six months, and in others less, they reverenced and worshipped him in the same manner as the proper idol; and in the meantime he did eat, drink, and was merry. When he went through the streets, the people came forth to worship him, and every one brought him an alms, with children and sick folks, that he might cure them, and bless them, suffering him to do all things at his pleasure, only he was accompanied with ten or twelve men lest he should fly. And he (to the end he might be reverenced as he passed) sometimes sounded upon a small flute, that the people might prepare to worship him. The feast being come, and he grown fat, they killed him, opened him, and ate him, making a solemn sacrifice of him.'[1]

Such a victim was a man or a woman according to whether he, or she, died in the character of a god or a goddess. The method of execution was nearly always the same—the victim was held on his back on the sacrificial stone while the priest cut open his chest and tore out his heart. Sometimes after his execution his head was cut off and stuck on a pike, and sometimes he was flayed and his skin worn by one of the priests. We read also that parts of the victim were eaten,[2] and that communicants partook of paste idols[3] that were no doubt believed to contain by a miracle the physical presence of the god.

In this manner young men were annually sacrificed in the character of Tezcatlipoca, 'the god of gods'[4] of Vitzilopochtli or Huitzilopochtli,[5] and of Quetzalcoatl.[6] Frazer describes the end of the human representative of Tezcatlipoca as follows: 'Twenty days before he was to die, his costume was changed, and four

[1] Frazer, *Golden Bough*, ix. 275-6.
[2] Westermarck, *Origin of Moral Ideas*, ii. 563.
[3] Andrew Lang, *Ency. Brit.*, 9th ed., xvii. 150.
[4] Frazer, *Golden Bough*, ix. 276-9.   [5] *Ib.* ix. 280.   [6] *Ib.* ix. 281-3.

damsels, delicately nurtured and bearing the names of four goddesses—the Goddess of Flowers, the Goddess of Young Maize, the Goddess " Our Mother among the Water ", and the Goddess Salt—were given him to be his brides, and with these he consorted. During the last five days divine honours were showered on the destined victim. The king remained in his palace while the whole court went after the human god. Solemn banquets and dances followed each other in regular succession and at appointed places. On the last day the young man, attended by his wives and pages, embarked in a canoe covered with a royal canopy and ferried across the lake to a spot where a little hill rose from the edge of the water. It was called the Mountain of Parting, because here his wives bade him a last farewell. Then, accompanied only by his pages, he repaired to a small and lonely temple by the wayside. Like the Mexican temples in general, it was built in the form of a pyramid ; and as the young man ascended the stairs he broke at every step one of the flutes on which he had played in the days of his glory. On reaching the summit he was seized and held down by the priests on his back upon a block of stone, while one of them cut open his breast, thrust his hand into the wound, and wrenching out his heart held it up in sacrifice to the sun. The body of the dead god was not, like the bodies of common victims, sent rolling down the steps of the temple, but was carried down to the foot, where the head was cut off and spitted on a pike. Such was the regular end of the man who personated the greatest god of the Mexican pantheon.'[1]

Similarly women were sacrificed in the characters of the goddesses of Salt and of the Young Maize, of the goddess ' Our Mother ' and of the Mother of the Gods.[2]

Sometimes the victim was flayed after being killed, and the skin used in certain rites. Thus in the sacrifices of the human embodiment of the Mother of the Gods, ' The body, still warm, was skinned, and a tall, robust

[1] *Ib.* ix. 278-9. [2] *Ib.* ix. 283-8.

young man clothed himself in the bleeding skin, and so became in turn a living image of the goddess. One of the woman's thighs was flayed separately, and the skin carried to another temple, where a young man put it over his face as a mask and so personated the maize-goddess Cinteotl, daughter of the Mother of the Gods. Meantime the other, clad in the rest of the woman's skin, hurried down the steps of the temple. The nobles and warriors fled before him, carrying blood-stained besoms of couchgrass, but turned to look back at him from time to time and smote upon their shields as if to bid him come on. He followed hard after them, and all who saw that flight and pursuit quaked with fear. On arriving at the foot of the temple of Huitzilopochtli, the man who wore the skin of the dead woman and personated the Mother of the Gods, lifted up his arms and stood like a cross before the image of the god; this action he repeated four times. Then he joined the man who personated the maize-goddess Cinteotl, and together they went slowly to the temple of the Mother of the Gods, where the woman had been sacrificed. All this time it was night. Next morning at break of day the man who personated the Mother of the Gods took up his post on the highest point of the temple; there they decked him in all the gorgeous trappings of the goddess and set a splendid crown on his head. Then the captives were set in a row before him, and arrayed in all his finery, he slaughtered four of them with his own hand; the rest he left to be butchered by the priests. A variety of ceremonies and dances followed. Amongst others, the blood of the human victims was collected in a bowl and set before the man who personated the Mother of the Gods. He dipped his finger into the blood and then sucked his bloody finger; and when he had sucked it he bowed his head and uttered a dolorous groan, whereat the Indians believed the earth itself shook and trembled, as did all who heard it. Finally the skin of the slain woman and the skin of her thigh were carried away and deposited separately at two towers, one of which stood on the border of the enemy's country.'[1]

The human incarnation of the Maize Goddess, a young slave girl of twelve or thirteen years, was also flayed. At the end of a long ceremony the priests ' threw her on her back on the heap of corn and seeds (collected in the temple), cut off her head, caught the gushing blood on the wooden image of the goddess, the walls of the chamber, and offerings of corn, peppers, pumpkins, seeds, and vegetables which cumbered the floor. After that they flayed the headless trunk, and one of the priests made shift to squeeze himself into the bloody skin. Having done so, they clad him in all the robes which the girl had worn ; they put the mitre on his head, the necklace of golden maize-cobs about his neck, the maize-cobs of feathers and gold in his hands ; and thus arrayed they led him forth in public, all of them dancing to the tuck of drum, while he acted as fugelman, skipping and posturing at the head of the procession as briskly as he could be expected to do, incommoded as he was by the tight and clammy skin of the girl and by her clothes, which must have been much too small for a grown man.'[2]

This sacrifice of the Maize Goddess ' was preceded by a fast of seven days, during which old and young, sick and whole, ate nothing but broken victuals and dry bread and drank nothing but water, and did penance by drawing blood from their ears '.[3] On the eve of the sacrifice the people brought this blood that they had taken from their ears, in saucers, and one by one they came before the girl who personated the goddess and cast it before her.[4] This looks like an offering to appease the goddess for her approaching sacrifice.

Victims to the fire-god were also regarded as the incarnations of the deity, at whose festival they died. But in this ceremony there were many divine victims, of both sexes, and their deaths were more elaborate than usual. 'In the eighteenth and last month of their

[1] *Ib.* ix. 290-1.   [2] *Ib.* ix. 294-5.   [3] *Ib.* ix. 291-2.   [4] *Ib.* ix. 294.

year, which fell in January, the Mexicans held a festival in honour of the god of fire. Every fourth year the festival was celebrated on a grand scale by the sacrifice of a great many men and women, husbands and wives, who were dressed in the trappings of the fire-god and regarded as his living images. Bound hand and foot, they were thrown alive into a great furnace, and after roasting in it for a little were raked out of the fire before they were dead in order to allow the priest to cut the hearts out of their scorched, blistered, and still writhing bodies in the usual way.'[1] The intention of this sacrifice was, according to Frazer, probably ' to maintain the Fire-god in full vigour, lest he should grow decrepit or even die of old age, and mankind should be deprived of his valuable services. This important object was attained by feeding the fire with live men and women, who thus as it were poured a fresh stock of vital energy into the veins of the Fire-god and perhaps of his wife also. But they had to be raked out of the flames before they were dead; for clearly it would never do to let them die in the fire, else the Fire-god whom they personated would die also. For the same reason their hearts had to be torn from their bodies while they were still palpitating; what use could the Fire-god make of human hearts that were burnt to cinders?'[2]

By these and similar rites the Mexicans slaughtered many thousands of victims every year. Probably those who were selected, in so far as they were not enemy captives, were buoyed up with pride in their divinity and in the sense of high service that they rendered to their fellow-men; and that they would no more have thought of escape than would a soldier seek to avoid a post of honour or the decoration that it brought him.

13. *Sacrifice among Primitive Peoples*

So far we have classified sacrifices by the races that have practised them rather than by any characteristics

---
[1] Frazer, *Golden Bough*, ix. 300-1.   [2] *Ib.* ix. 301.

of the rites themselves ; that is, we have classified geographically not anthropologically, by contiguity not by similarity. Such a method helps to prevent the neglect of rites that do not fit into theories, but it is hardly appropriate to the present section. Primitive peoples do not form a bounded area either in geography or history. To divide them up and to describe the rites of each tribe in turn would take too much space in anything but an encyclopaedia of the subject. There is, therefore, no alternative but to introduce some classification according to inherent similarities between the rites themselves.

In most sacrificial rites there is a god, a spirit, or a ghost, in short, a supernatural being who is either the victim, the recipient, or the beneficiary of some offering. Thus we may commence by classifying sacrifices according to the rôle of this being. There are, however, other rites in which a revered being appears to play no rôle. Such practices should perhaps strictly be classed not as sacrifices, but under the wider head of rites of destruction for magical purposes. But, lest I should be guilty of trimming my definitions to suit my theories, I will include examples of these rites in the discussion. I shall, therefore, arrange sacrifices among primitive peoples under the four heads of sacrifices *of, to*, and *for* supernatural beings, and miscellaneous rites of destruction.

1. *Sacrifices of Supernatural Beings.*—Supernatural beings have been widely destroyed in sacrificial rites in the form of animals, plants, or men, or in the form of substitutes for any of these.

The custom of sacrificing a divine or at least a revered animal is common. Usually the flesh is consumed as a sacrament. Frazer distinguishes two types of such sacrifice. In one, the Aino type, the species from which the victim is drawn is not specially protected. In the other, the Egyptian type, it is taboo for profane purposes.[1] It is uncertain whether these

[1] *Ib.* viii. 310 *sqq.*

practices have developed independently, or, if not, which is derived from which. In remote times the Australian tribes, who now only destroy their totems for sacred purposes, killed them apparently for food.[1] But we do not know whether they passed through an intermediate stage in which they killed their totems for both profane and sacred purposes; or whether, with the development of that contempt of the divine that is so often a correlate of advancing civilization, this is a state to which they will some day attain. In other words we do not know, in general, whether the idea of the sacredness of an individual victim succeeded or preceded the idea of the sacredness of the species, nor even whether the two ideas are historically related.

Perhaps the most primitive sacrament, if indeed the rite deserves this name, occurs in the Australian *intichiuma*. The general purpose of these rites is, according to Frazer, the multiplication of the totem for food.[2] But since the totem is usually taboo to its people this purpose would seem to require a more altruistic regard for the appetites of other groups than might be expected from such primitive savages. The rites are complex and are perhaps performed without a clear conscious purpose. They include, for instance in the witchery grub totem, a pantomime representation of the fully developed insect emerging from the chrysalis, or, in the emu totem, the pouring of the blood from the arms of the totemists upon the ground until it forms a hard surface on which to paint the design of an emu. But there is also often a definite sacrament. For instance, the men of the kangaroo totem not only eat a little kangaroo but also anoint their bodies with kangaroo fat.[3]

A famous example of an animal sacrament which has been assumed by Robertson Smith, and after him by Freud, to have been typical of a form of sacrifice from which most other types have been evolved, is the sacrifice of a camel by the desert Beduins witnessed

[1] Frazer, *Golden Bough*, i. 107.   [2] *Ib.* i. 85 *sqq.*   [3] *Ib.* viii. 165.

and described by Nilus in the fourth century. The camel, a member of the sacred and protected species, was fastened on a rough altar, hacked to pieces, and totally consumed in frantic haste by the clan. Many similar rites have been recorded, but the assumption that all peoples have practised them is an inference which has not remained unquestioned.

Sometimes the sacred animal is destroyed only in effigy. Thus in Australia the men of the Wollunqua totem make an image out of sand of the mythical water-snake Wollunqua, and after various ceremonies they attack it with their weapons and hack it to pieces. After this the ceremony of subincision is practised on the youths.[1] But I know of no evidence that a mimic sacrament is also performed.

Perhaps a relic of the transition from hunting to agriculture is to be found in the common practice of killing the corn-spirit in animal form of which Frazer has collected many examples. 'These customs', he writes, 'bring out clearly the sacramental character of the harvest-supper. The corn-spirit is conceived as embodied in an animal; this divine animal is slain, and its flesh and blood are partaken of by the harvesters. Thus, the cock, the goose, the hare, the cat, the goat, and the ox are eaten sacramentally by the ploughmen in spring. Again, as a substitute for the real flesh of the divine being, bread or dumplings are made in his image and eaten sacramentally; thus pig-shaped dumplings are eaten by the harvesters, and loaves made in boar-shape (the Yule Boar) are eaten in spring by the ploughman and his cattle.'[2] Frazer thinks that the finding of such animals in the corn when it is cut is a sufficient explanation for their identification with its spirit. But, while it is not absolutely necessary to assume that these animals were once totems, it seems likely that a people passing into the

---

[1] Frazer, *Belief in Immortality*, i. 110-11. Wollunqua is a single animal and not a species like other Australian totems.
[2] Frazer, *Golden Bough*, vii. 303.

agricultural stage might well have selected as the embodiments of the spirits of their crops those beasts which, in their hunting stage, they had already learned to revere and to sacrifice.

Not only animals but also vegetables have been revered and eaten sacramentally. At a Fijian initiation ceremony, after a drama of death and resurrection, there was a sacramental meal of yams. 'Four old men of the highest order of initiates now entered the Holy of Holies. The first bore a cooked yam carefully wrapt up in leaves so that no part of it should touch the hands of the bearer; the second carried a piece of baked pork similarly enveloped; the third held a drinking-cup full of water and wrapt round with native cloth; and the fourth bore a napkin of the same stuff. The first elder passed along the row of novices putting the end of the yam into each of their mouths, and as he did so each of them nibbled a morsel of the sacred food; the second elder did the same with the hallowed pork; the third elder followed with the holy water, with which each novice merely wetted his lips; and the fourth elder wiped all their mouths with his napkin. Then the high priest or one of the elders addressed the young men, warning them solemnly against the sacrilege of betraying to the profane vulgar any of the high mysteries which they had witnessed, and threatening all such traitors with the vengeance of the gods. The general intention of the initiatory rites seems to have been to introduce the young men to the worshipful spirits of the dead at their temple, and to cement the bond between them by a sacramental meal.'[1] I do not know whether the yam and pork was supposed to be eaten in common by ghosts and men, or whether these commodities were once believed to incarnate the ancestral spirits.

The latter conclusion is supported by the avowed intention of the ceremonies that accompany the eating of the firstfruits among many peoples. Certain

[1] Frazer, *Golden Bough*, xi. 245-6.

North-West American Indian tribes, for instance, believe that the plant they are about to eat 'is animated by a conscious and more or less powerful spirit, who must be propitiated before the people can safely partake of the fruits or roots which are supposed to be part of his body. If', continues Frazer, 'this is true of wild fruits and roots, we may infer with some probability that it is also true of cultivated fruits and roots, such as yams, and in particular that it holds good of the cereals, such as wheat, barley, oats, rice, and maize. In all cases it seems reasonable to infer that the scruples which savages manifest at eating the firstfruits of any crop, and the ceremonies which they observe before they overcome their scruples, are due at least in large measure to a notion that the plant or tree is animated by a spirit or even a deity, whose leave must be obtained or whose favour must be sought before it is possible to partake with safety of the new crop. This indeed is plainly affirmed of the Aino: they call the millet "the divine cereal", "the cereal deity", and they pray to and worship him before they will eat of the cakes made from the new millet. And even where the indwelling divinity of the firstfruits is not expressly affirmed, it appears to be implied both by the solemn preparations made for eating them and by the danger supposed to be incurred by persons who venture to partake of them without observing the prescribed ritual. In all such cases, accordingly, we may not improperly describe the eating of the new fruits as a sacrament or communion with a deity, or at all events with a powerful spirit.'[1]

If, then, the firstfruits that are eaten sacramentally incarnate a deity it is not unlikely that the yams which are consumed sacramentally in the Fijian initiation rites may also incarnate a supernatural being, such as an ancestral ghost. If so, this sacrament, like the sacrament of firstfruits, may be compared to what Frazer calls the Aino type of animal sacrament. For, only a

[1] *Ib.* viii. 82-3.

sample of the yams, or of the cereal, is eaten sacramentally; the rest is used for profane purposes.

The idea that the firstfruit is shared with the deity, instead of being an incarnation of him, is probably later than the true sacrament. But it may be present in savage as well as in developed religions. Thus a house-father among the Ewe negroes of West Africa 'takes a raw yam and goes with it under the house-door and prays: "O my guardian-spirit (*aklama*) and all ye gods who pay heed to this house, come and eat yams! When I also eat of them, may I remain healthy and nowhere feel pain! May my housemates also remain healthy!"'[1] Here the dominant idea is that the fruits are shared with a diety, but the old belief that the yam itself incarnates a spirit seems to lurk behind the householder's obvious uneasiness lest through eating he should fall ill.[2]

Sometimes, especially among peoples of a higher culture, the sacred cereal is fashioned in the form of a god before it is eaten. Thus the Mexicans prepared an image of their god Huitzilopochtli out of seeds of various sorts, kneaded into a dough with the blood of children; and this image they pretended to kill and then ate.[3] Here the seeds, which were probably once supposed to be in themselves endowed with consciousness and power, seem later to have acquired an independent soul, or spirit, in human form.

Live men, too, have been killed, and sometimes eaten, in the character of a god. The kings of the Shilluk tribe, who were supposed to incarnate the founder of their dynasty Niakang, had to defend their lives and thrones against any of their sons who chose to challenge them. But the king, even if he survived these duels, was put to death as soon as he began to fail to satisfy the sexual passions of his numerous wives. When this symptom of incompetence appeared the king was walled

---

[1] Frazer, *Golden Bough*, viii. 60.
[2] At a still later stage the idea that the firstfruit is given to the god rather than shared with him would probably emerge.
[3] Frazer, *Golden Bough*, viii. 90-1.

up in a hut with his head resting on the lap of a nubile virgin until both died of thirst and hunger. But in more recent times a speedier death was substituted for this prolonged suffering. When the king was dead and buried a shrine was built over his grave where services and sacrifices were offered. Frazer argues that the processes of all nature were supposed to depend on the king's virility and that for this reason it was desirable to transfer his sacred spirit, the spirit of Niakang, to a healthy successor at the first sign of advancing impotence.[1] The peculiar mode of his death may have symbolized a return to the womb as a preliminary to his rebirth or reincarnation.

In like manner the pontiffs of the people of Congo were not allowed to die a natural death. When they fell ill and seemed about to die their successors-elect entered their houses and strangled or clubbed them to death.[2] And again : ' The Ethiopian kings of Meroe were worshipped as gods ; but whenever the priests chose, they sent a messenger to the king, ordering him to die and alleging an oracle of the gods as their authority for the command. This command the king always obeyed down to the reign of Ergamenes, a contemporary of Ptolemy II., king of Egypt. Having received a Greek education which emancipated him from the superstitions of his countrymen, Ergamenes ventured to disregard the command of the priests, and, entering the Golden Temple with a body of soldiers, put the priests to the sword.'[3]

In these examples a divine or semi-divine king was slain, but not eaten. There are, however, other examples of gods in human form who were eaten as well as killed. The young man who died in the character of the Mexican Tezcatlipoca was chopped up small and distributed among the priests and nobles as a blessed food.[4] And, although there are not many records of such rites, stories like that of Lycurgus, who was rent in pieces by those notorious cannibals the Bacchanals,

[1] *Ib.* iv. 17-26.   [2] *Ib.* iv. 14.   [3] *Ib.* iv. 15.   [4] *Ib.* viii. 92.

and the general analogy of eating the god in animal or vegetable form, suggest that a sacramental meal off the the body of a human embodiment of a god may once have been common.

2. *Sacrifices to Supernatural Beings.*—By sacrifices offered to supernatural beings I understand gifts made in order to induce the favour or avert the anger of the recipient. Thus I do not include offerings made only to benefit him who receives them, since such offering may be classed as sacrifices *for* a supernatural being.

The recipient of sacrificial gifts may be a ghost, a spirit, or a god; the gifts may be either to induce his favour or to avert his anger, and they may be either bloody or bloodless. Thus there are at least twelve types of sacrifices to supernatural beings as follows: bloody sacrifices to induce the favour of a ghost, bloodless offerings for the same purpose, bloody and bloodless sacrifices to avert the anger of a ghost, as well as four similar types offered to spirits and to gods. Numerous examples of each of these kinds of offering are to be found in the practices of primitive peoples all over the world. But, since it is not always easy to distinguish between a ghost, a spirit, and a god, or between an offering made to induce favour from an offering to avert anger, and because I do not regard these distinctions as of major importance, I shall give only a few examples of bloody and bloodless sacrifices, without regard to the theological status of the recipient or the conscious motives of the giver.

Blood Sacrifices.—The Yabim of New Guinea have a curious initiation ceremony in which the lads are supposed to be swallowed by a monster, whose name 'Balum' is also applied to the bull-roarer which imitates his voice and to any ancestral ghost. But if the monster is given pigs he is supposed to allow the youths to return from his stomach to the light of day, with no further injury than that of circumcision. Thus it seems that both the circumcision and the pigs are accepted as vicarious sacrifices instead of the youths.[1] The cere-

[1] Frazer, *Belief in Immortality*, i. 250 *sqq.*

mony has also been interpreted as a drama of death and rebirth. But perhaps the two interpretations are not incompatible, for, here as in Christian symbolism, the idea of rebirth seems to be associated with the idea of escape by means of a vicarious offering from an otherwise inevitable doom. Reminiscent of this New Guinea initiation rite is the Maori myth that life would have been immortal if their national hero Maui had only succeeded in climbing in and out of the mouth of his ancestress Hine-nui-te-po, the Great Woman of Night, the Goddess of Death. Unfortunately, however, Maui did not get off so easily as the Yabim initiates, for he was bitten in half by the monster.[1] Perhaps the underlying idea in both the myth and the rite is that the problem of immortality is the same as the problem of birth and that neither can be solved without sacrifice. In the Yabim rite the sacrifice includes circumcision. Perhaps the emasculation of the priests of Cybele, whose severed genitals were deposited in underground vaults, was a variant of the same motive.

Circumcision has not only been practised to redeem the self but also to save the lives of others. In certain districts of Viti Levu, the largest of the Fijian Islands, sacrifices and prayers were offered to the ancestral spirits in a sort of open-air temple. Here the firstfruits of the yams were presented. But ' of these offerings perhaps the most curious was that of the foreskins of young men, who were circumcised as a sort of vicarious sacrifice or atonement for the recovery of a sick relative, it might be either their father or one of their father's brothers. The bloody foreskins, stuck in the cleft of a split reed, were presented to the ancestral gods in the temple by the chief priest, who prayed for the sick man's recovery.'[2]

The commonest bloody sacrifices to win favour or avert anger are animal offerings. And these may be made to gods, spirits, or ghosts. They were, for instance, offered to trees, or tree-spirits, to propitiate them for

---

[1] *Ib.* ii. 16-19.   [2] Frazer, *Golden Bough*, xi. 243-4.

being felled. Thus among the Tradjas of Central Celobes, when a tree was felled, a goat, a pig, or a buffalo was killed and the wood smeared with the blood.[1]

But human victims were also often offered in sacrifice, and there is perhaps no people whose history is free from such rites. Thus the Mairs, a Hindoo tribe, used to sacrifice a first-born son to the smallpox goddess Mata, and the sacrifice of first-born children to the Ganges was common till the beginning of the nineteenth century.[2] Young girls, too, have been drowned in rivers as brides to the crocodile spirit. 'It is said that once, when the inhabitants of Cayeli in Buru (an East Indian Island) were threatened with destruction by a swarm of crocodiles, they ascribed the misfortune to a passion which the prince of the crocodiles had conceived for a certain girl. Accordingly, they compelled the damsel's father to dress her in bridal array and deliver her over to the clutches of her crocodile lover.'[3]

Perhaps the desire to propitiate an angry ghost was also the motive of the mourners who mutilated themselves at funerals. In central Australia certain male relations of the deceased will sometimes cut right through the muscles of their thighs, while the women cut open their scalps with yam-sticks and sear the scalp wounds with red-hot fire-sticks. Similarly, at the death of the Tongan kings, the mourners cut and wound their heads and bodies with clubs, stones, knives, or sharp shells. Their behaviour at the death of King Finow has been graphically described by Mariner, who is quoted by Frazer. 'As one ran out into the middle of the ground he would cry, "Finow! I know well your mind; you have departed to Bolotoo (the land of the dead), and left your people under suspicion that I, or some of those about you, were unfaithful; but where is the proof of infidelity? where is a single instance of disrespect?" Then, inflicting violent blows and deep cuts on his head with a club, stone, or knife, he would again

---

[1] Frazer, *Golden Bough*, ii. 39.   [2] *Ib*. iv. 180-1.   [3] *Ib*. ii. 152.

exclaim at intervals, "Is this not a proof of my fidelity? does this not evince loyalty and attachment to the memory of the departed warrior?"[1] Such exaggerated manifestations of sorrow are probably dictated by the belief that the ghost of the dead might take vengeance on the living if they did not thus show their genuine sorrow at their loss and thereby prove that they had no complicity in his unnatural death. For primitive people generally hold that death is due to sorcery. Perhaps also the piacular idea, that guilt is expiated in suffering, or at least the idea that a self-inflicted injury will be accepted in lieu of a deserved punishment, is present in such rites. For however innocent of evil actions the mourners may be, their consciences are not clear; indeed, if a medicine man accuses one of them he is sometimes ready to admit his crime, even against the evidence of his own senses.

But, though the mutilations of mourners were probably in part vicarious offerings, the blood that was sometimes allowed to drip upon the corpse may have had the purely altruistic purpose of strengthening the dead.[2]

Besides rites which are more or less consciously designed to propitiate ghosts, spirits, or gods, offerings to win the favour of the recipient are very common. There is a general tendency for gods, like men, to become more kindly as they grow older, so that rites which were once intended to avert the anger of a jealous demon are later employed to win the favour of a paternal god. And, finally, when the god has outgrown his bribability, the offering is supposed merely to honour him. But in the Unconscious the motives may have remained the same.

Bloodless Sacrifices.—Bloodless sacrifices to avert anger or to win favour seem to be derived from many sources, among which are bloody sacrifices of propitiation, vegetable sacraments, and offerings to benefit, or revivify, the dead.

[1] Frazer, *Belief in Immortality*, ii. 135.   [2] *Ib.* i. 156-9.

'In Tibet, when a man is very ill and all other remedies have failed, his friends will somtimes, as a last resort, offer an image of him with some clothes to the Lord of Death, beseeching that august personage to accept the image and spare the man.'[1] Perhaps, originally, a real man or child was offered in exchange for a sick chief. With the softening of manners and the spread of aristocratic customs to classes that could not afford them the live substitute may well have given place to the dummy.

Offerings of firstfruits are very common. Thus the Ovambo of South-West Africa assemble at the end of harvest. The head of the family takes some porridge made of the corn, ' dips it in melted fat, and throws it to the east, saying, "Take it, ye spirits of the East!" Then he does the same towards the west, saying, "Take it, ye spirits of the West!" This', continues Frazer, ' is regarded as a thank-offering presented to the spirits of the dead for not visiting the people with sickness while they were cultivating the fields, and especially for sending rain.'[2] But these people no doubt believe that, if the ceremony were omitted, famine and drought would result, so that the sacrifice is propitiatory as well as honorific. At an earlier stage it may also have been expiatory; for the corn was probably once regarded as the special possession of a spirit who was injured when it was cut. And still earlier, when the corn was itself thought to be animate, the rite may have been a sacrament in which the body of the new corn-spirit was consumed in common by the people, so that they might imbibe its virtue, and perhaps so that they should all share the guilt of cutting it.

Food has often been offered to the dead, and here the purpose may have been disinterested love as well as fear. But ghosts have been feared all over the world, and one purpose of mortuary offerings was certainly propitiatory, and even expiatory. The primitive savage does not recognize natural death, which he attributes

[1] Frazer, *Golden Bough*, viii. 103.   [2] *Ib.* viii. 110.

to the sorcery of a wizard or an evil spirit. And, however clear his conscience ought to be, he always seems to believe that the dead may accuse him of complicity in the crime. For this reason he displays exaggerated grief,[1] and we may suppose that this is also one reason for the offerings that he brings.

That the mourner is in some way believed to be guilty of the death for which he mourns is further suggested by the rites of purification which he, like the manslayer, is often required to undergo before he is readmitted to the society of his fellows. These rites have all been attributed solely to the taboo of the infection of death. But the infection of death itself requires an explanation. Perhaps it is nothing but the ghost which pursues anyone who has been guilty of complicity either in his death, or in what to the savage is perhaps the same thing, in the disposal of his remains.

Often the property of the dead is destroyed at the funeral, and one purpose of such rites is certainly to transfer the spirits of this furniture to the other world for the use of the deceased. But a forgotten, or unconscious, purpose may also have been the taboo of the dead man's property to which his ghost might be expected to cling. Perhaps even the destruction of his weapons, which may have been the earliest mortuary sacrifice, was once intended to prevent him using them to wreak his vengeance upon those to whom he attributed, however erroneously, his death. Where, however, the dead man's property is not destroyed, but laid with him in the grave, we may suppose that the conscious purpose, at least, is to transfer them to his use.

In the Boulia district of Queensland the things that belonged to the dead man are sometimes burnt, sometimes buried with him, and sometimes distributed among his tribal brothers.[2] The Dieri place food on the grave for many days, and light a fire when it is cold.[3] Such customs are world-wide, and the multiplication of examples would be profitless.

---
[1] Frazer, *Belief in Immortality*, 134 *sqq*.   [2] *Ib.* i. 147.   [3] *Ib.* i. 144.

3. *Sacrifices for Supernatural Beings.*—Many of the customs which are intended to propitiate a supernatural being, or to expiate a sin, are also intended to benefit the recipient. There are, however, sacrifices which seem solely to serve this latter purpose. But even where these are not intended to win the favour or avert the anger of a supernatural being, but solely to benefit him, their purpose is not always directly altruistic. Thus sacrifices of horses were made to the sun, not to win his favour, but to enable him better to perform his daily task of riding or driving across the sky. They were made to benefit him not in his own interest but in that of his worshippers. Though this purpose may not have been the original, or the unconscious, intention of the rite.

Again, men of the Dieri tribe wound themselves and pour their blood on a sand hill in which a mythical ancestor is supposed to be buried. And this rite is believed to multiply carpet-snakes and iguanas, which are important articles of diet. It seems to be magical, not religious, for it operates automatically, not through divine intervention.

Sometimes, however, altruism seems to be the sole motive for sacrifice. Among the tribes of the River Darling after a death 'several men used to stand by the open grave and cut each other's heads with a boomerang, and then hold their bleeding heads over the grave so that the blood dripped on the corpse at the bottom. . . . Further, it is a common practice with the Central Australians to give human blood to the sick and aged for the purpose of strengthening them ; and in order that the blood may have this effect it need not always be drunk by the infirm person, it is enough to sprinkle it on his body. For example, a young man will often open a vein in his arm and let the blood trickle over the body of an older man in order to strengthen his aged friend ; and sometimes the old man will drink a little of the blood.'[1] It may be unusual, but it is not unique,

[1] Frazer, *Golden Bough*, i. 90.

to care for others more than for oneself, and there is no doubt that sacrifices have been made solely, as far as conscious motives are concerned, to benefit the ghost, or spirit, or god, who receives them.

4. *Miscellaneous Rites of Destruction.*—Some rites of destruction, which are regularly classed as sacrificial, do not fall into any of the above categories. In them a supernatural being is not slain, nor is anything given to him or destroyed for his benefit. There are also other rites which, though not usually described as sacrificial, resemble sacrifices. In this section examples of a few such rites will be recorded under the title of miscellaneous rites of destruction.

Circumcision, subincision, the extraction of teeth, and other mutilations are commonly practised at primitive initiation ceremonies, and we have seen examples in which such mutilations seem to be regarded as vicarious sacrifices of a part for the whole, or of a vital part of one man for the life of another. But sometimes the purpose is less clear. Often the severed foreskin, or the extracted tooth, is hidden in the tree or rock which harbours the external soul of the initiate. And in such cases the rite, as Frazer suggests, may have been 'originally intended to ensure the rebirth at some future time of the circumcised man by disposing of the severed portions of his body in such a way as to provide him with a stock of energy on which his disembodied spirit could draw when the critical moment of reincarnation came round. This conjecture is confirmed', continues Frazer, 'by the observation that among the Akinkuyu of British East Africa the ceremony of circumcision used to be regularly combined with a graphic pretence of rebirth enacted by the novice.'[1] We may perhaps anticipate the argument of a later section by pointing out that, for the psycho-analyst, death commonly symbolizes castration, and that circumcision or the extraction of teeth is a substitute for castration. Hence circumcision might well help to

[1] *Ib.* i. 96-7.

relieve the neurotic fear of death. And, if this interpretation is correct, such mutilations, even when they are consciously intended to remove the fear of death and thereby to secure the hope of rebirth, are vicarious sacrifices. They are accepted by the super-ego in place of the self-castration that it would otherwise demand. Further, since a relation of identity often seems to subsist between the external soul and the soul of the ancestor, the foreskin that is hidden in the tree may, from one point of view, be regarded as made over to the ancestral spirit, which is itself nothing more than the projection of the super-ego. Such a sacrifice might well be combined with a pantomime of rebirth, or with what is perhaps more important, a pantomime return to the womb.

Akin to rites of expiation on the one hand and to ceremonies of rebirth on the other are rites of purification. 'Among the Bechuanas a man who has killed another, whether in war or in single combat, is not allowed to enter the village until he has been purified. The ceremony takes place in the evening. An ox is slaughtered, and a hole having been made through the middle of the carcase with a spear, the manslayer has to force himself through the animal, while two men hold its stomach open. Sometimes instead of being obliged to squeeze through the carcase of an ox the manslayer is merely smeared with the contents of its stomach.'[1] Sometimes, also, the manslayer is obliged to eat a piece of the ox or even a piece of the skin of the murdered man. Again, he may be required to allow the medicine-man to make a gash in his thigh for every man he has killed.[2] Until these, or similar, rites have been performed the manslayer is more or less taboo and secluded. Some of these rites are probably intended to appease the ghost of the slain. But others must also be intended to control or to avert it. If part of the slain man, or something representing him, is eaten he is perhaps converted from a dangerous enemy

---

[1] Frazer, *Golden Bough*, iii. 172-3.   [2] *Ib.* iii. 174.

into a powerful part of the self, and this is certainly one motive of cannibalism. On the other hand, the ablutions, that so often form a part of purificatory rites, may have been intended to produce the opposite effect, namely, to wash off the ghost that clings like a leech to his murderer. Thus the spirit of the slain may either be propitiated, absorbed as a valuable part of the personality, or removed.

The idea that the ghost of the slain adheres, like a leech, to the slayer is perhaps akin to the idea of a sin that sticks to the sinner, but which may be transferred to a scapegoat and driven away. If the same goat, or another, is slain, a magical rite to transfer sin is combined with a vicarious sacrifice. Ultimately the sin, like the ghost of the slain, is perhaps the spirit of the man, or god, who has been sinned against. If so, sin is another name for conscience. It is an anthropomorphic demon that haunts the sinner and which he will seek to propitiate or to transfer to someone else.

But purificatory rites, like initiation ceremonies, often seem to symbolize a rebirth. The crawling through the body of the slain ox, for instance, would seem to have this meaning.

It was once a common practice to bury men below the foundations of new buildings, or beneath the gate posts. And it was believed that the ghosts of these victims would become guardian angels.[1] The inconsistency of this belief with the dread that primitive man usually feels for the souls of those he has slain has led Westermarck to argue that such rites were originally intended to propitiate a deity rather than to obtain a new guardian. In many cases this view is probably a sufficient explanation of the foundation sacrifice, but the many examples of the killing by primitive and ancient peoples of the beings that they worship should warn us that the idea of manufacturing a god by killing a man is not unthinkable.

As among the Semites many peoples have had the

[1] *Ib.* iii. 90 *sq.*

custom of sacrificing their children, generally the first-born. But the victim does not always appear to have been offered to a supernatural being. 'In some tribes of New South Wales the first-born child of every woman was eaten by the tribe as part of a religious ceremony.'[1] Again, in Uganda, 'if the first-born child of a chief or any important person is a son, the midwife strangles it and reports that the infant was still-born. "This is done to ensure the life of the father; if he has a son first he will soon die, and the child inherit all he has (Roscoe)."'[2] Here the child does not appear to be sacrificed to any supernatural being, but to be killed because he might usurp his father's place. But this motive seems to be repressed and rationalized by the theory that the first-born son incarnates his father, that, in fact, he has stolen his father's soul.

Sometimes, however, the son is killed because he incarnates his grandfather. 'At Whydah, on the slave coast of West Africa, where the doctrine of reincarnation is firmly held, it has happened that a child has been put to death because the fetish doctors declared it to be the king's father come to life again. The king naturally could not submit to be pushed from the throne by his predecessor in this fashion; so he compelled his supposed parent to return to the world of the dead from which he had very inopportunely effected his escape.'[3]

[1] Frazer, *Golden Bough*, iv. 179-80.   [2] *Ib.* iv. 182.   [3] *Ib.* iv. 188.

CHAPTER II

THE THEORIES OF SACRIFICE

IN the last chapter examples were given of rites which are usually described as sacrificial, among some of the main peoples of the world. In this we will consider some of the theories that have been put forward to explain them.

1. *Tylor's Theory*

Tylor's theory of sacrifice is, in the main, the consequence of his theory of animism. He showed that primitive people not only thought of men, animals, and things as possessed of souls, or living principles within them, but also that they generalized this concept and came to personify all causes as spirits, even when these possessed no material abode. Thus, in Tylor's terminology, a spirit is to an immaterial cause what a soul is to a material object.[1]

In funeral sacrifice Tylor finds an example of the consequences of the belief in souls, and at the same time of the general theory of sacrifice that he develops later. ' When a man of rank dies and his soul departs to its own place, wherever and whatever that place may be, it is a rational inference of early philosophy that the souls of attendants, slaves, and wives, put to death at his funeral, will make the same journey and continue their services in the next life, and the argument is frequently stretched further, to include the souls of new victims sacrificed in order that they may enter upon the same ghostly servitude. It will appear from the ethnography of this rite that it is not strongly marked in the very lowest levels of culture, but that, arising in the lowest barbaric stage, it develops itself

[1] Tylor, *Primitive Culture*, 3rd ed., i. 417 *sq.*; ii. 108-10.

in the higher, and thenceforth continues or dwindles in survival.'[1]

Further, 'the sacrifice of property for the dead is one of the greatest religious rites of the world'[2] and this Tylor derives from the belief in souls of objects; though he admits that such beliefs may not always have been explicit.[3] Similarly, I suppose that he would derive offerings to nature deities from the belief in personified causes or spirits.

But Tylor is always careful not to exclude the possibility that other motives may be operative. 'Efficient motives' for mortuary sacrifice 'may be affectionate fancy or symbolism, a horror of the association of death leading the survivors to get rid of anything that suggests the dreadful thought,' or 'desire to abandon the dead man's property'—motives that do not necessarily presuppose a belief either in the soul of the dead or in the soul of the objects destroyed at his funeral. Or 'the hovering ghost may take pleasure in or make use of the gifts left him' even if, as Tylor must have meant, these objects had no souls.[4]

Once the false beliefs that have determined sacrificial rites have been disclosed it is easy for Tylor to discover rational motives for these rites. 'Sacrifice has its apparent origin in the same early period of culture and its place in the same animistic scheme as prayer, with which through so long a range of history it has been carried on in the closest connection. A prayer is a request made to a deity as if he were a man, so sacrifice is a gift made to a deity as if he were a man. The suppliant who bows before his chief, laying a gift at his feet and making his humble petition, displays the anthropomorphic model and origin at once of sacrifice and prayer. But', continues Tylor, 'sacrifice, though in its early stages as intelligible as prayer is in early and late stages alike, has passed in the course of religious history into transformed conditions, not

---

[1] Tylor, *Primitive Culture*, 3rd ed., i. 458.   [2] *Ib.* i. 483.
[3] *Ib.* i. 484-5.   [4] *Ib.* i. 483-4.

only of the rite itself but of the intention with which the worshipper performs it.'[1] Thus the 'ruder conception that the deity takes and values the offering for itself gives place, on the one hand, to the idea of mere homage expressed by a gift, and, on the other, to the negative view that the virtue lies in the worshipper depriving himself of something prized. These ideas may be broadly distinguished as the gift theory, the homage theory, and the abnegation theory.'[2]

This development from gift to homage and from homage to abnegation Tylor describes in detail. The 'idea of the practical acceptableness of the food or valuables presented to the deity begins early to shade into the sentiment of divine gratification or propitiation by a reverent offering, though in itself of not much account to so mighty a personage'.[3] And besides this development from gift to homage, 'there arises also a doctrine that the gist of sacrifice is rather in the worshipper giving something precious to himself, than in the deity receiving benefit. This may be called the abnegation theory....'[4]

This account, I think, sums up Tylor's main views on sacrifice. They are illustrated with great detail in his *Primitive Culture*. His theories seem indubitably correct as far as they go; they give an adequate account of the conscious motives in certain kinds of rite. But there are kinds of sacrifice, apparently the most primitive kinds from which many of the others seems to have been derived, of which Tylor gives no account and no explanation. How, for instance, can we explain, on Tylor's theory, the motive of the communicant who eats his god? Yet this form of sacrifice is found in every cult from the Australian Intichiuma to the Christian Eucharist.

Nevertheless Tylor's method is instructive. In discussing, for instance, the cause of the development of the abnegation theory of sacrifice he says, 'Taking our own feelings again as a guide, we know how it

[1] *Ib.* ii. 375. [2] *Ib.* ii. 375-6. [3] *Ib.* ii. 394. [4] *Ib.* ii. 396.

satisfies us to have done our part in giving, even if the gift be ineffectual'.[1] Tylor always takes his own feelings as a guide. When, therefore, he comes across a strange custom he asks himself, What should I have to believe in order to do that? And in this way he reconstructs many of the false beliefs of primitive peoples. But he cannot imagine desires very different from those he consciously possesses. And for this reason he is prevented from discovering the most fundamental motives in primitive customs. Later anthropologists, finding that the thought of primitive peoples is not as theirs, have not hesitated to impute to them any motive, however strange, that seemed to account for their rites. But to do this is to discard psychology as useless in folk-lore. The best method would seem to be that of Tylor supplemented by the greater knowledge of oneself that psycho-analysis can give.

2. Robertson Smith's Theory

For Tylor sacrifice was originally a gift; for Robertson Smith it was a communion, a method of establishing or re-establishing the solidarity between the group and its god. Yet the two theories complete rather than contradict each other. Tylor gives an account of the evolution of honorific and abnegatory sacrifice from the gift sacrifice; while Robertson Smith reconstructs some of the earliest motives of sacrifice before such rites had been rationalized as gifts.

Robertson Smith starts from the totemic communion in which the clan ritually kill and eat an animal belonging to a species which they believe to be akin to themselves. This animal is not thought of so much as an individual but as the 'Platonic Idea' of the class composed of its species and the tribe, together with the ancestors of both. It is at once their father, their brother, and their god.

[1] Tylor, *Primitive Culture*, 3rd ed., ii. 396.

The community ' is conceived as a circle of brethren, united with one another and with their god by participation in one life or life-blood. The same blood is supposed to flow also in the veins of the victim, so that its death is at once a shedding of the tribal blood and a violation of the sanctity of the divine life that is transfused through every member, human or irrational, of the sacred circle. Nevertheless the slaughter of such a victim is permitted or required on solemn occasions, and all the tribesmen partake of its flesh, that they may thereby cement and seal their mystic unity with one another and with their god.' [1]

The idea of the piaculum Robertson Smith finds already in the primitive communion from which he believed it to be evolved. ' If the physical oneness of the deity and his community is impaired or attenuated, the help of the god can no longer be confidently looked for. And conversely, when famine, plague, or other disaster shows that the god is no longer active on behalf of his own, it is natural to infer that the bond of kinship with him has been broken or relaxed, and that it is necessary to retie it by a solemn ceremony, in which the sacred life is again distributed to every member of the community. From this point of view the sacramental rite is also an atoning rite, which brings the community again into harmony with its alienated god, and the idea of sacrificial communion includes within it the rudimentary conception of a piacular ceremony. In all the older forms of Semitic ritual the notions of communion and atonement are bound up together, atonement being simply an act of communion designed to wipe out all memory of previous estrangement.' [2]

From the same primitive rite Robertson Smith also derives the idea of purification. ' In the most primitive form of the sacrificial idea the blood of the sacrifice is not employed to wash away an impurity, but to convey to the worshipper a particle of holy life. The con-

[1] Robertson Smith, *Religion of the Semites*, 1889, 294-5.
[2] *Ib.* 302.

ception of piacular media as purificatory, however, involves the notion that the holy medium not only adds something to the worshipper's life, and refreshes its sanctity, but expels from him something that is impure. The two views are obviously not inconsistent, if we conceive impurity as the wrong kind of life, which is dispossessed by inoculation with the right kind.'[1]

We may doubt if the conception of vicarious atonement can be so easily disposed of. But to Robertson Smith the idea that guilt may be wiped out in suffering, especially in the suffering of others, necessarily seems so irrational that he has to explain it away. Thus he writes: 'The one point that comes out clear and strong is that the fundamental idea of ancient sacrifice is sacramental communion, and that all atoning rites are ultimately to be regarded as owing their efficacy to a communication of divine life to the worshippers, and to the establishment or confirmation of a living bond between them and their god.'[2]

Robertson Smith not only derives the piaculum and the purificatory sacrifice from the primitive communion; he also derives the gift-offering from this source. 'Originally all sacrifices were eaten up by the worshippers. By and by certain portions of ordinary sacrifices, and the whole flesh of extraordinary sacrifices, ceased to be eaten. What was not eaten was burned, and in process of time it came to be burned on the altar and regarded as made over to the god. Exactly the same change took place with the sacrificial blood, except that here there is no use of fire. In the oldest sacrifice the blood was drunk by the worshippers, and after it ceased to be drunk it was all poured out at the altar. The tendency evidently was to convey directly to the godhead every portion of the sacrifice that was not consumed by the worshipper; but how did this tendency arise? . . . A holy thing is taboo, *i.e.* man's contact with it and use of it are subject to certain restrictions,

[1] Robertson Smith, *Religion of the Semites*, 1889, 406-7.
[2] *Ib.* 418.

but this idea does not in early society rest on the belief that it is the property of the gods. . . . In later heathenism the conception of holy kinds and the old ideas of taboo generally had become obsolete and the ritual observances founded upon them were no longer understood. And, on the other hand, the comparatively modern idea of property had taken shape, and began to play a leading part both in religion and in social life. The victim was no longer a naturally sacred thing, over which man had very limited rights, and which he was required to treat as a useful friend rather than a chattel, but was drawn from the absolute property of the worshipper, of which he had a right to dispose as he pleased. Before its presentation the victim was a common thing, and it was only by being selected for sacrifice that it became holy. If, therefore, by presenting his sheep or ox at the altar, the owner lost the right to eat or sell its flesh, the explanation could no longer be sought in any other way than by the assumption that he had surrendered his right of property to another party, viz. the god. Consecration was interpreted to mean a gift of man's property to the god, and everything that was withdrawn by consecration from the free use of man was conceived to have changed its owner.'[1]

In this way Robertson Smith evolves the gift-theory and the piacular-theory of sacrifice from the original mystic communal meal that united the tribe with its god incarnate in the victim. His work is one of the foundations of modern anthropology. But his explanation of sacrifice seems incomplete; for it does not take into consideration the magical purposes of such rites that have been pointed out especially by Frazer, nor fully recognize or explain the guilt that has always characterized man's relation to his god. The motive of expiation through direct or vicarious suffering, which he has so ingeniously explained away, is probably fundamental and can be detected alike in the primitive

[1] *Ib.* 370-2.

communion and in the gift. The religious satisfaction which is derived from direct or vicarious suffering is surely, in part, masochistic or sadistic; and, since such impulses were probably operative at the origin of sacrifice, those rites which satisfy them cannot be dismissed as due solely to the conservative observance of purer customs which have lost their original significance.

3. *Frazer's Theory*

It is difficult to give a precise account of Frazer's theory of sacrifice. His works abound with illustrations of sacrificial rites; but his interpretations of their ends and his explanations of their means is almost as varied. Nevertheless I will try to give his main conclusions, and as far as possible in his own words.

The fundamental idea of Frazer's work seems to be his theory of magic. For him religion in general and sacrifice in particular is a development of magic. ' Led astray by his ignorance of the true causes of things, primitive man believed that in order to produce the great phenomena of nature on which his life depended he had only to imitate them, and that immediately by a secret sympathy or mystic influence the little drama which he acted in forest glade or mountain dell, on desert plain or wind-swept shore, would be taken up and repeated by mightier actors on a vaster stage.'[1] In short man imitates nature and believes that nature will be magically compelled to follow his example. Thus, for instance, the primitive farmer will stimulate the growth of his crops by copulating in his fields.

Frazer adopts the conception of the slain god, which is due to Robertson Smith, but generalizes it and explains it differently.[2] For Robertson Smith the main purpose of sacrifice is to cement the kinship between a totemic god and his people through a sacramental meal off the flesh of the slain animal divinity. For Frazer

---

[1] Frazer, *Golden Bough*, iv. 266-7.   [2] *Ib.* i. Preface to first edition.

the slain god may be a man or an animal who incarnates a nature spirit. And this nature spirit is, I suppose, what Tylor would call a personified cause. It is killed ritually, and its death is believed to have a good effect on agriculture. Frazer has collected, and drawn attention to, innumerable examples of such rites, and has shown that they existed almost universally.

It is difficult to see how primitive man could have ever come to the idea that the killing of the spirit of the crops could stimulate their growth. To explain this belief Frazer writes: 'The motive for slaying a man-god is a fear lest with the enfeeblement of his body in sickness or old age his sacred spirit should suffer a corresponding decay, which might imperil the general course of nature and with it the existence of his worshippers, who believe the cosmic energies to be mysteriously knit with those of their divinity'.[1] Thus Frazer believes that one motive for killing a god is to preserve him from senility, and therefore to preserve the crops from imitating his old age. But he also points out that the slaying of the god is combined with the rebirth, or reincarnation, of his spirit in the person of his successor. 'For the killing of the tree-spirit in spring is associated always (we must suppose) implicitly, and sometimes explicitly also, with a revival or resurrection of him in a more youthful and vigorous form.'[2]

We may agree that the idea of rebirth is fundamentally associated with the idea of sacrifice. But the view that the motive of deicide was the belief that killing the god was the necessary condition for his rebirth or rejuvenation seems hardly adequate to explain these rites. Possibly the ceremony of rebirth and rejuvenation was the conscious reaction to the unconsciously motivated deicidal act. If an unconscious hatred of a consciously loved god found an expression in his murder, it is natural that his worshippers should both rationalize and seek to undo their act. Such an explanation would be immediately intelligible if a motive for unconscious hate

[1] *Ib.* iv. Preface.   [2] *Ib.* iv. 212.

could be discovered. It would account at once for the murder, the inadequate reasons given for the murder, and for the attempts to revive the victim.

Though we cannot accept Frazer's view that the desire to rejuvenate a god is an adequate reason for killing him, we may agree that the sacrifice of victims *for* a god may have had this purpose. The ancient Mexicans called the sun Ipalnemohuani, ' He by whom men live '. ' But ', writes Frazer, ' if he bestowed life on the world he needed also to receive life from it. And as the heart is the seat and symbol of life, bleeding hearts of men and animals were presented to the sun to maintain him in vigour and enable him to run his course across the sky. Thus the Mexican sacrifice to the sun was magical rather than religious, being designed not so much to please and propitiate him, as physically to renew his energies of heat, light, and motion.'[1] Such a rite is a rejuvenating sacrifice; but it is *for* rather than *of* a god. In it, as in the communal sacrifice, the spiritual virtue of a victim is absorbed; but by the god rather than the worshipper.

It is, however, difficult to separate sacrifices of a victim *for* a god, to rejuvenate him, from sacrifices *to* a god, to propitiate him, and still more difficult to separate either of these types of offering from the sacrifice *of* a god. In Mexico the victim was identified with the god, and although the sacrifice may have been intended both to benefit and to propitiate him, it also destroyed him.

The deity can be assisted indirectly as well as directly. His devotees can attack his rival. Primitive man not only fancied ' that by masquerading in leaves and flowers he helped the bare earth to clothe herself with verdure ', but also ' that by playing the death and burial of winter he drove that gloomy season away, and made smooth the path for the footsteps of returning spring '.[2]

Thus Frazer recognizes at least three ways of assisting through sacrifice the gods on whom depend the lives

[1] Frazer, *Golden Bough*, i. 314-15. [2] *Ib.* iv. 267.

of men. By killing them in order that they may escape death and decay; by feeding them on victims in order that they may acquire fresh life; and by destroying their enemies so that they may be unimpeded in their resurrection.

But Frazer admits that the rejuvenation of the god is not the only aim of sacrifice, and his works are rich in examples of sacramental, piacular, and cathartic rites. 'We have seen', he says, 'that the spirit of the corn, or of other cultivated plants, is commonly represented either in human or in animal form, and that in some places a custom has prevailed of killing annually either the human or the animal representative of the god. . . . We may suppose that the intention was to guard him or her (for the corn-spirit is often feminine) from the enfeeblement of old age by transferring the spirit, while still hale and hearty, to the person of a youthful and vigorous successor. Apart from the desirability of renewing his divine energies, the death of the corn-spirit may have been deemed inevitable under the sickle or the knives of the reapers, and his worshippers may have felt bound to acquiesce in the sad necessity. But, further, we have found a widespread custom of eating the god sacramentally, either in the shape of the man or animal who represents the god, or in the shape of bread made in human or animal form. The reasons for thus partaking of the body of the god are, from the primitive standpoint, simple enough. The savage commonly believes that by eating the flesh of an animal or man he acquires not only the physical, but even the moral and intellectual, qualities which were characteristic of that animal or man; so when the creature is deemed divine, our simple savage naturally expects to absorb a portion of its divinity along with its material substance.'[1] Here, then, is a clear recognition of the communal sacrifice. May we not assume further that one of the purposes of this procedure was, through absorbing, to master the corn-spirit and thus

[1] *Ib.* viii. 138-9.

to guard against retaliation ? The corn, like the animal, possessed an immortal soul that might be more dangerous in death than in life. How could this soul be dealt with better than by absorbing it as the cannibal absorbs the virtues of his slain foes ? And, further, is not the pretence that the corn-spirit is killed for its own good analogous to the pretence in many sacrifices that the sacrificer has no evil intentions against his victim ? May not the motive be the same—namely, to add a precaution, in case the attempt to master the soul of the dead fails, and to lessen the likelihood of revenge ?[1]

As the confidence of man to dominate his gods still further fails we should expect such pretences to be more pronounced and to be supplemented by piacular rites. Frazer admits the propitiatory element in sacrifice and has collected innumerable examples to illustrate it in all its forms. 'The same motive, which leads the primitive husbandman to adore the corn or the roots, induces the primitive hunter, fowler, fisher, or herdsman to adore the beasts, birds, or fishes which furnish him with the means of subsistence. . . . For the most part he assumes as a matter of course that the souls of dead animals survive their decease ; hence much of the thought of the savage hunter is devoted to the problem of how he can best appease the naturally incensed ghosts of his victims so as to prevent them from doing him a mischief.'[2]

Thus, piacular sacrifice is offered to vegetation spirits and to sacred animals. 'Among the Ewe-speaking peoples of the Slave Coast the indwelling god of this giant of the forest (silk-cotton tree) goes by the name of Huntin. Trees in which he specially dwells— for it is not every silk-cotton tree that he thus honours —are surrounded by a girdle of palm-leaves ; and sacrifices of fowls, and occasionally of human beings, are fastened to the trunk or laid against the foot of the tree. A tree distinguished by a girdle of palm-leaves

---

[1] See Westermarck, *Origin of Moral Ideas*, ii. 559.
[2] Frazer, *Golden Bough*, vii. Preface, vi.

may not be cut down or injured in any way ; and even silk-cotton trees which are not supposed to be animated by Huntin may not be felled unless the woodman first offers a sacrifice of fowls and palm oil to purge himself of the proposed sacrilege. To omit the sacrifice is an offence which may be punished with death.'[1]

Frazer further distinguishes two types of animal sacrament, the second of which involves a piaculum. 'On the one hand, when the revered animal is habitually spared, it is nevertheless killed—and sometimes eaten —on rare occasions. . . . On the other hand, when the revered animal is habitually killed, the slaughter of any one of the species involves the killing of the god, and is atoned for on the spot by apologies and sacrifices, especially when the animal is a powerful and dangerous one ; and, in addition to this ordinary and everyday atonement, there is a special annual atonement, at which a select individual of the species is slain with extraordinary marks of respect and devotion.'[2]

Sacrifice, according to Frazer, as to Tylor and to Robertson Smith, can sometimes be a mere homage free from ulterior motives. He seems to derive this form of sacrifice, like Robertson Smith, from the communal form, but interposes one of his three rejuvenating sacrifices, that in which the god is benefited by nourishment. Primitive peoples, he says, ' often partake of the new corn and the new fruits sacramentally, because they suppose them to be instinct with a divine spirit or life. At a later age, when the fruits of the earth are conceived as created rather than as animated by a divinity, the new fruits are no longer partaken of sacramentally as the body and blood of a god ; but a portion of them is offered to the divine beings who are believed to have produced them. Originally, perhaps, offerings of first-fruits were supposed to be necessary for the subsistence of the divinities, who without them must have died of hunger ; but in after times they came to be looked on rather in the light of a tribute or mark of homage

[1] *Ib.* ii. 15.   [2] *Ib.* viii. 312.

rendered by man to the gods for the good gifts they have bestowed on him.'[1]

Finally Frazer devotes a volume to the scapegoat which seems to form yet another separate category of sacrifice. Speaking of the scapegoat he says : ' If I am right, the idea resolves itself into a simple confusion between the material and the immaterial, between the real possibility of transferring a physical load to other shoulders and the supposed possibility of transferring our bodily and mental ailments to another who will bear them for us '.[2] Thus for Frazer the destruction of a scapegoat is not primarily an offering to propitiate an outraged deity, but a piece of magic to transfer an evil from one thing or person to another. It may therefore justly be described as cathartic sacrifice.

To sum up this account of Frazer's views we may say that he distinguishes at least three types of rejuvenating sacrifice, the killing of a god to save him from decay and facilitate his rebirth, the killing of a victim to feed and strengthen him, and the killing of his rival. He also distinguishes a communal sacrament, a piaculum, a homage, and a cathartic rite. All these are illustrated many times within his pages. His main contribution to the theory of sacrifice is, however, his view that gods were destroyed to save them from decay. But he is modest about his theories and is of the opinion that his ' contribution to the history of the human mind consists of little more than a rough and purely provisional classification of facts gathered almost entirely from printed sources '.[3] Even if his work consisted of nothing more than this its value would still remain immense.

4. *Hubert and Mauss' Theory*

For Hubert and Mauss a sacrifice is ' a religious act which, by the consecration of a victim, modifies the moral state of the sacrificer or of certain objects in

[1] Frazer, *Golden Bough*, viii. 109.   [2] *Ib.* ix. Preface.
[3] *Ib.* x. Preface, vi.

which he is interested '.[1] This definition, as the authors remark, not only limits the object of their research, but it assumes the genetic unity of sacrifice.[2] But this unity they find more in a unity of method (*procédé*) than in a unity of origin. Thus they criticize Robertson Smith's view that all sacrifices are derived from the totemic communion. But they believe that every sacrificial rite is 'a procedure to establish a communication between the world sacred and the world profane through the intermediary of a victim, that is to say, of a thing destroyed in the course of the ceremony '.[3]

The main idea underlying this theory, as far as I understand it, is that primitive man, on the one hand, desires to establish communication with the supernatural world (*monde sacré*), and, on the other hand, hesitates to do so directly for fear of getting something analogous to an electric shock. He therefore requires an intermediary who is there to succumb to these dangerous influences.[4] Thus while Tylor starts out from the idea of a gift, Robertson Smith from that of the totemic communion, and Frazer from magic, Hubert and Mauss find in mana, or something like it, the primitive concept from which everything can be explained. 'If', they write, 'religious forces are the very principle of vital forces, if they are in fact these vital forces, they are of such a nature that contact with them is dangerous to the vulgar. Especially when they reach a certain degree of intensity they cannot be concentrated in a profane object without destroying it. Hence the sacrificer, however much he may need them, cannot absorb them without the greatest prudence. For this reason he inserts intermediaries between him and them ; and of these the principal is the victim. If he penetrated to the end into the rite he would find death instead of life. The victim replaces him. It alone penetrates into the dangerous sphere of the sacrifice, it succumbs to it, and it is there to succumb to it.'[5]

---

[1] Hubert and Mauss, ' Essay sur le sacrifice ', *L'Année Sociologique*, ii. 41.
[2] *Ib.* 41.   [3] *Ib.* 132-3.   [4] *Ib.* 134.   [5] *Ib.* 134.

Now there is no doubt that to the primitive mind certain things are invested with dangerous and mysterious properties so that they cannot be approached without extreme caution, and often only through intermediaries. But there seems very little evidence that the victim of a sacrifice is such an intermediary. On the contrary it seems that the victim is itself the holy thing that cannot be lightly touched, and which often can be approached only by an intermediary or priest. In sacrifices where the victim is itself the god it is difficult to see what else more holy there can be which the victim relates to man.

5. *Westermarck's Theory*

Most writers on sacrifice, as we have seen, refuse to accept the idea of vicarious atonement as ultimate. They seek to explain it away as a degenerate form of a more primitive rite such as the communion or the gift. For Westermarck, however, the main element in sacrifice is expiation. He does not deny the existence of other types, but he considers that expiation is often the original purpose of sacrifices that have later developed a second meaning, such as the transference of sin or the rejuvenation of a dying corn god. He admits that sin may be transferred to a scapegoat who is driven away and not sacrificed, but points out that such transference of evil may be combined with the vicarious sacrifice of the scapegoat.[1] Expiation, however, he takes to be the original purpose of the sacrifices to secure the future of the crops. Thus, he writes:
'For people subsisting on agriculture failure of crops means starvation and death, and is, consequently, attributed to the murderous designs of a superhuman being, such as the earth-spirit, the morning star, the sun, or the rain-god. By sacrificing to that being, a man, they hope to appease its thirst for human blood; and

---

[1] Westermarck, *Origin and Development of Moral Ideas*, i. 61-2.

whilst some resort to such a sacrifice only in case of actual famine, others try to prevent famine by making the offering in advance. This I take to be the true explanation of the custom of securing good crops by means of human sacrifice, of which many instances have been produced by Dr. Frazer. . . . So far as I can see, Dr. Frazer has adduced no satisfactory evidence in support of his hypothesis; whereas a detailed examination of the various cases mentioned by him indicates that they are closely related to human sacrifices offered on other occasions, and explicable from the same principle, that of substitution.'[1] But the second type of rejuvenating sacrifice recognized by Frazer, namely, that in which the recipient is fed and strengthened by a victim, is accepted by Westermarck, at least in the case of funeral rites, when he alludes to sacrifices to dead men ' to vivify their spirits '.[2]

Westermarck believes that foundation sacrifices may also have been originally piacular. These sacrifices are often supposed to be designed to provide a guardian deity for a building. 'But,' writes Westermarck, 'whatever be the present notions of certain peoples concerning the object of building sacrifice, I do not believe that its primary object could have been to procure a spirit-guardian. According to early ideas, the ghost of a murdered man is not a friendly being and least of all is he kindly disposed towards those who killed him.'[3]

Finally, of special interest is Westermarck's comparison between sacrifice and the blood-feud. ' The duty of blood-revenge is, in the first place, regarded as a duty to the dead, not merely because he has been deprived of his highest good, his life, but because his spirit is believed to find no rest after death until the injury has been avenged. The disembodied soul carries into its new existence an eager longing for revenge ; and, till the crime has been duly expiated, hovers about the earth, molesting the manslayer or trying to compel its

[1] *Ib.* i. 443-4.   [2] *Ib.* i. 472.   [3] *Ib.* i. 464.

own relatives to take vengeance on him. . . . From one point of view, blood-revenge is thus a form of human sacrifice.'[1]

Westermarck has stressed the elements of vicarious suffering, guilt, and expiation, which have been neglected by other writers. But, as far as I know, he has given no explanation of the killing of a god.

6. *Loisy's Theory*

Loisy prefaces his own theory of sacrifice with a survey of those of his predecessors. He admits that the gift, the communion, and the agricultural rite all play their part, but denies that all sacrifices are derived solely from any of these forms.[2] And this is a conclusion which Frazer, at least, would readily accept; for he has written that he is 'unwilling to leave' his readers 'under the impression, natural but erroneous, that man has created most of his gods out of his belly'.[3]

But with the theories of Hubert and Mauss, Loisy is more severe. He denies that sacrifice is a process for establishing communication between the world sacred and the world profane. 'One would say, after this definition, that the two worlds are radically distinct and even separate, almost in opposition with each other, whereas in reality the two are in perpetual contact, and man employs the "process" of sacrifice often to disengage himself from the influences of what is called the "world sacred". Sacrifice, in this case, is not used to "establish a communication" positive and direct, but much more to sever a communication which is grievous in its results.'[4]

Sacrifice, for Loisy, is not derived from a single source, but from two, the magical act and the ritual gift; and neither of these, he thinks, in its earliest

---

[1] Westermarck, *Origin and Development of Moral Ideas*, i. 481-2.
[2] Loisy, *Essay historique sur le sacrifice*, 6-7.
[3] Frazer, *Golden Bough*, vii. Preface, vii. Loisy, *Le Sacrifice*, 7-8.

form, constitutes a sacrifice.[1] Thus his main explanatory principles combine Frazer's views on sympathetic and homeopathic magic and Tylor's theory of the gift. He applies them systematically to the explanation of a number of distinct rites. I will try to summarize his account.

Funeral Rites.—In the cult of the dead Loisy finds the purest example of the gift of nourishment.[2] Such offerings, like those offered to the gods, were designed not only to assuage their anger but to utilize their power.[3]

Seasonal Rites.—At the root of all ancient religions there are rites to control and regulate the processes of nature, the growth of vegetation, and the course of the seasons. And such rites are not the mere symbolic accompaniment of the phenomena they represent, but their magical cause. By them the corn is made to die or to revive.[4] But since such necessities are believed to be semi-personal powers, they are not merely magically controlled but also propitiated 'to induce these beings to accept, and even to assist, their exploitation by man for his profit.'[5]

Divinatory Rites.—'It was inevitable that men should search for signs of the future or of secret things in the same beings that were supposed to contain a mystic virtue useful for the government of the affairs of the world. Thus were born the sacrifices of divination, which, in themselves, were not concerned in the cult of any god.'[6]

Contractual Rites.—A victim is often killed by the parties to a contract. Loisy thinks that they believe that this rite will ensure that the same fate will overtake him who breaks his word. If so it is an example of a magical act (*action sacrée, figuration rituelle*) 'which is in itself neither an offering, nor a communion, nor an homage to any god, but a rite effective in itself, conditionally effective, for it operates solely against the perjurer, if there is a perjurer'.[7]

[1] *Ib.* 10-11.   [2] *Ib.* 11-12.   [3] *Ib.* 162-3.   [4] *Ib.* 12-13.
[5] *Ib.* 202.   [6] *Ib.* 13.   [7] *Ib.* 14.

Purificatory and Expiatory Rites.—'Primitive man has, one may say, a physical conception of sin and a moral conception of illness; or rather he does not know how to distinguish clearly between a physical and a moral evil, and he uses the same process to eliminate both. . . . The sacrifices said to be for purification or expiation tend essentially to rid men from the evil influences under which they have fallen. . . . The fundamental idea has been to transfer the evil from man to another being, through the destruction of which the evil is supposed to be itself destroyed or driven away. Then the gods were supposed to have prescribed this remedy for these evils which men finally attributed to the gods themselves as a punishment for their sins. And thus developed the idea, absurd in itself, that sin could be expiated with blood, an idea that has found its highest expression in the Christian myth of the redemption of the world by the death of Christ.'[1] Thus Loisy, like Tylor and Robertson Smith, is unable to accept the idea of expiation through suffering as primitive. But whereas for Tylor the idea of abnegatory sacrifice is derived from the gift and for Robertson Smith the piaculum is a retieing of the blood bond, for Loisy, as for Frazer, the expiatory rite has its origin in the magical transferrence of evil.

Consecratory Rites.—Loisy thinks that rites of consecration of things, or of initiation of persons, are the converse of rites of expiation. In them a virtue is conveyed from the victim to the thing or person consecrated. He believes that the foundation sacrifices, which are often supposed to procure a guardian spirit, are examples of this kind of consecration.[2]

Sacrifice in the Religion of Personal Gods.—In the formed religions or the religions of personal gods Loisy finds the idea of sacrifice fully developed for the first time. In it he distinguishes two elements, the magical or mystic act and the ritual gift. The magical act he again subdivides into the positive act of pro-

[1] Loisy, *Le Sacrifice*, 14-15.   [2] *Ib.* 15-16.

duction and the negative act of destruction, that is, I suppose, into the act which transfers a virtue from the victim to the worshipper and the act that transfers an evil from the worshipper to the victim. ' The combination of the ritual gift, or its idea, with the magical rite of positive effect makes the communal sacrifice in the divine service ; the combination of the ritual gift, or its idea, with the magical rite of negative effect forms the so-called expiatory sacrifice, which from the time that it included an offering, also enters, to some extent, into the service of the gods. But neither the magical rite of destruction nor the ritual gift are in themselves sacrifices, if by sacrifice one understands a method of communicating with invisible beings, and not simply acting on them.' [1]

Loisy's account of sacrifice is thus both systematic and comprehensive ; everything seems to be explained and to find its place in a tidy structure on two neat foundations. But, like the authors that precede him, he does not seem to have given a convincing explanation of the custom of killing a divine being, nor of the guilt which seems to be so intimately involved in sacrifice.

7. *Freud's Theory*

In Freud's theory of sacrifice entirely new factors are introduced. Before him anthropology ignored the unconscious and considered conscious impulses alone, so that it missed some of the most vital forces that conditioned the seemingly irrational behaviour it studied. But Freud's researches into the minds of his patients had convinced him that they were influenced by unconscious motives, so that when he found parallels between their beliefs and actions and those of primitive peoples he naturally supposed that the unconscious motives for these beliefs and actions were present also in the unconscious of the primitive peoples who behaved

[1] *Ib.* 521.

so like them. Unfortunately his interpretations cannot be adequately judged by those who have not mastered the psycho-analytic technique that he invented to obtain them. And this technique is difficult to learn.

Briefly, Freud's view is that sacrifice was originally one of the results of the Oedipus complex of primitive man. Darwin, long ago, supposed that our first ancestors lived in small families dominated by one old man, the father, who killed or drove out his adolescent sons as soon as they threatened his sole enjoyment of his wives.[1] This condition is now nowhere to be observed. The most primitive society still found consists of bands of men who are gerontocratic and exogamous, and who call themselves after some species of animal (their totem) which they hold sacred, but sacrifice periodically with every expression of apology and regret.

Freud adopts Darwin's view of the life of primeval man and sets himself the problem of reconstructing the development from this state to the totemic system. His investigation of neurotics had revealed a common but unconscious wish on the part of men to possess those women with whom they first were brought in contact, namely, their mothers, and consequently to eliminate their fathers : and further, that the unconscious fear of the father which results from such unconscious wishes frequently expresses itself symbolically as a phobia of and respect for certain animals. Freud next assumed that the same impulses existed in the unconscious of primitive peoples, and suggested that their exogamy is perhaps nothing but an exaggerated reaction against the incest wish, and that their reverence for that sacred animal, from which they believe themselves descended, is a reaction to a parricide which may actually have taken place and which is symbolically repeated at the sacrifice of the animal. His theory may perhaps best be summarized by a single quotation from his *Totem und Tabu*. ' One day the exiled brothers (who had been driven out of the horde by its jealous

---

[1] Darwin, *Descent of Man*, ii. 395.

leader) came together and killed and ate their father, and so made an end to the Father-horde. . . . The totem meal, perhaps the first festival of man, was the repetition and the commemoration of this memorable and criminal act, with which so much began, social organization, moral limitations, and religion.'[1]

This description has been called ' a just-so story ' ; but Freud has himself anticipated his critics in a note. ' The vagueness, the temporal compression, and the compression of the content, of the above account may be regarded, in view of the nature of the object of the investigation, as a desirable restraint. It would be as senseless, in this subject, to seek exactitude, as it would be useless to require certainty.'[2] In spite of this warning the temptation to attempt a stage further along the road that Freud has opened is too strong to be resisted.

[1] Freud, *Totem und Tabu*, 2. Aufl. 190.   [2] *Ib.* 191.

CHAPTER III

THE ESSENCE OF SACRIFICE

ANYONE who is convinced of at least the approximate correctness of the findings of the psycho-analytic school will feel no doubt that certain sacrificial rites are, in some sense, the 'repetition and commemoration' of a parricide. That parricide was the usual termination of most primeval hordes is a natural consequence of Darwin's view and was assumed by Atkinson[1] long before the days of psycho-analysis. And anyone who has detected the unconscious detestation of fathers in the deeper strata of the minds of even the most dutiful sons can hardly doubt that such feelings must once have found a more direct expression. It is therefore no great flight of fancy to see in the sacrifice of a god more than a mere parallel to the slaughter of a father.

We may agree that the primeval parricide took place, and that the inability of the sons severally to enjoy the fruits of their collective crime, together with their ambivalence towards their father, led them to desire to undo their act.[2] But there is a big gap between the killing of and the mourning for a father and the killing of and the mourning for a totem. This gap Roheim has done something to fill. He writes: 'If we picture to ourselves the psychical situation of the victorious brother clan assembled round the cairn, which they had piled up in triumph (over the body of their slain sire) yet trembling from what might follow after their victory, we may very well understand the exact moment in which the projection of the Father-Imago into an animal took place.

'The conscience-stricken murderer sees the image of

[1] Atkinson, *Primal Law*, 228.
[2] Freud, *Totem und Tabu*, 2. Aufl. 191-2.

the man he has killed in every tree of the forest, he hears his voice in the rustling boughs and, at last, so popular belief will have it, he is compelled by irresistible force within him always to return to the scene of his crime. These parricides at the dawn of human evolution must have been subject to these emotions in an enhanced measure, for was not their victim their beloved father, the very source of their being? Their attitude towards him was ambivalent, a compound of hatred and love; after hate had obtained free play in the bloody deed it was natural that love should get the upper hand in the mourning period. They now felt a lively desire to resuscitate their powerful leader as a help in the struggle for life against other species, although this desire was not unmingled with a very natural dread of what he would do to his murderers if he came back again. At any rate, they were expecting his return, and so it was very natural that they should identify the wild beasts of the jungle or desert with his now thrice sacred person.'[1]

Thus we may picture to ourselves, without intellectual discomfort, a set of primeval parricides bitterly repenting their deed and worshipping an animal which they believed to be the reincarnation of their victim.

We next find these parricides, or their descendants, treating their totem as they treated their sire, killing him, eating him, and mourning him; and Freud describes their action as the 'repetition and commemoration' of their crime. But the causal relation between deicide and parricide does not seem to be adequately expressed by these words.

Freud now regards a blind impulse to repeat the past as more ultimate than the hedonic principle. Are we then to suppose that the totem sacrifice is due to a compulsion to repeat (*Wiederholungszwang*),[2] that, like the curse that compels earth-bound spirits to repeat their crimes, has pursued humanity throughout the

---
[1] Roheim, *Australian Totemism*, 384.
[2] Freud, *Jenseits des Lustprinzips*, ch. iii.

ages ? Or is there some simpler explanation ? The compulsion to repeat may be the ultimate principle of psychology, but it does not seem to explain why some things should be repeated more than others, and reference to it should be supplemented by the designation of a specific motive. And even if this principle were a sufficient explanation for individual fixations, it would have to be extended from individuals to races before it could be used to explain the continuance of sacrifice. This extension is often made implicitly or explicitly by analysts. Reik, for example, writes : ' The mental constitution, which the individual brings with him into the world, is perhaps nothing more than the precipitate of the experiences of his ancestors—that which life gave them '.[1] It is universally admitted that our dispositions are inherited from the innate dispositions of our ancestors ; but that we are affected by their actions and experiences otherwise than through tradition is still a dangerous assumption. There is an axiom of science that hypotheses be not multiplied without necessity ; and, if the inheritance of acquired characters, and in particular the racial compulsion to repeat, can be dispensed with by biology, it seems likely that these assumptions are mere burdens to psychology.

Hence the word 'repetition', to describe the causal relation between the totem communion and the primeval parricide, if it is not inadequate, seems likely to be false. It is inadequate if it merely records a parallel between deicide and parricide without giving the cause of the connection. It is probably false if by repetition we understand the product of a non-existent racial compulsion to repeat.

Again, the word ' commemoration ' is perhaps misleading and certainly inadequate. It is misleading if it suggests too much the activities of a committee appointed to revive the memory of some great calamity and the lessons that it taught. We may picture our

[1] Reik, *Probleme der Religionspsychologie*, Einleitung, xx.—Ferenczi also finds himself more in sympathy with Lamarck than with Darwin (*Versuch einer Genitaltheorie*, 69, 91).

ape-like ancestors, having destroyed their father, quarrelling over his wives, and then, to prevent a repetition of this misfortune, subjecting themselves to exogamy and instituting a solemn and symbolic commemoration of their crime to remind them of the first occasion on which they vowed to respect each other's wives.

The word ' commemoration ' is, further, inadequate, for the same reason that the word ' repetition ' is inadequate ; because it does not suggest a motive. It leaves the unjustified impression that Freud has discarded psychology for history. After using psychology to reconstruct the primeval parricide he appears to neglect it in his subsequent derivation of the totem feast from this act. Hence his theory assumes the same one-sidedness as is apparent in the views of the diffusionists. It becomes, in fact, a sort of diffusionism. The possibility of spontaneous invention of sacrifice, for no other reason than because it was satisfying to the individual, seems to be ignored. Instead it is derived, by a sort of ancestral diffusion, from the primeval forebears of the race. But in the last pages of *Totem und Tabu* Freud has himself drawn attention to these difficulties.

It is true that sacrifices were often described by those who practised them as commemorations of the death of some god ; and even in the early records of Christian communion, the faithful are instructed to eat the body and drink the blood of Christ in ' remembrance ' of Him. But it is probable that this word was selected to conceal from the devout their deeper motives which had survived only in the Unconscious from the oldest totemic communion, and which would have been regarded as the worst abomination. That there were operative motives more fundamental than the desire to revive the memory of an ancient tragedy is shown by the tendency, which in the Roman Church is largely successful, to regard the sacrament as a medicine to secure immortality, as a sort of prophylactic against the second death. Even this motive is probably not sufficient to explain the survival of the rite. But the words 'repetition and commemoration' give no motive at all.

When we do the same thing again we do it usually, not merely because we have done it before, but also because the same motives are operative. And where we seem to act as we did before without a motive, it is probably because the motive has become unconscious. The fact that we have reacted adequately, on a past occasion, to a certain stimulus in a certain way may determine that we react in the same way on a recurrence of the stimulus. But without the repetition of the stimulus the reaction would not be repeated. Similarly, we may suppose that when one generation perpetuates the customs of the last they do so both because they have the same needs and because the customs of their fathers provide them with an example of one method of satisfying these needs; not merely because their fathers have so acted. Thus it would seem that tradition and motive are both necessary, and neither sufficient, to produce a custom. Without motive the tradition would die out. Without tradition the motive might find some other outlet.

If this argument is correct, the assertion that deicide is a repetition and commemoration of parricide is only half an explanation of the facts. Parricide may provide the example for deicide; but unless the same motives are operative the example would not be followed.

I believe that the other half of the explanation is already implicit in Freud's writings; but it seems important that it should be made explicit. He says that the inheritance of psychical dispositions is in part responsible for the psychical continuity of successive generations.[1] This I take to mean that all men inherit an innate, not an acquired, disposition to incest, which under the conditions of almost every type of family organization will bring them inevitably into conflict with their fathers. In primeval days this conflict was probably expressed by an act of parricide. Later it

[1] Freud, *Totem und Tabu*, 2. Aufl. 212.

was repressed and found only a distorted outlet in such rites as the totemic sacrifice.

We have seen in an earlier section that the son is not easily freed from the influence of his father by the mere fact of his death, that a new Imago arises to take the place of the old, and that the same conflicts recur again. We have seen that an Imago, either imaginary or real, is likely to oust the original father even before his death, as the distance between the superman he appeared to the child of two and the man he is recognized to be by his growing son widens into a gulf. And, lastly, we have seen that this transference is additionally determined by the necessity of finding a new recipient for affects which are no longer permitted to reach their first object. Both the character of the Imago and the emotions that he excites preclude his continued identification with the person from whom he was derived. Sometimes he is split in two and reappears as two individuals, as god and devil, as loving friend and remorseless foe. To primitive man, as to children, one of his commonest manifestations is theriomorphic ; he appears as the totem of the clan and provokes the same conflicts among his people as did their fathers when they were little, or the fathers of their ancestors in primeval days. He, like them, is loved consciously and unconsciously detested. And the repetition of this ambivalence explains his murder. His sacrifice is the repetition of a parricide, not necessarily because there is a blind impulse to repeat the past, not necessarily because it is desired to commemorate the past, but because he excites the same ambivalent affects as the rival and protector that each child learnt to hate, love, and fear.[1]

It is not even essential to the Freudian theory of sacrifice to assert that the primeval parricide actually and habitually took place. And this Freud himself admits.[2] If the unconscious hatred of fathers that

---

[1] Roheim, *Australian Totemism*, 384.
[2] Freud, *Totem und Tabu*, 2. Aufl. 213-16.

psycho-analysis detects to-day was present at all times, it must have been responsible for the killing of father-symbols. If the present conscious repudiation of this hatred was also present, it must have concealed from the sacrificer the true motive of his act. No analyst would doubt that the hatred once found a still more direct expression in the act of parricide. But this inference is not an essential premise in the deduction that the sacrifice of gods was a result of the Oedipus complex.

Thus we may amend the wording of Freud's theory of the origin of the totem feast. The feast was a symbolic parricide. Its motive was a displaced and unconscious hate. It may also have been the repetition and commemoration of such a crime, indeed it seems certain that it was; but we need make no burden of this additional assumption.

Guilt and fear, we have seen, are largely the manifestations of the paralysis of a combined love and hate. And these affects characterize the attitude of the sacrificer to his victim. With the discovery of his unconscious hatred they are at once explained. That love and fear helped to determine the behaviours of men to the beings on whom they believed themselves dependent is obvious and recognized by all. That hate and envy were also present is less evident because these feelings are not admitted. Without the work of Freud they might still have been overlooked, in spite of the obviously hostile nature of the act of sacrifice, which cannot be explained away.

Motives for the Sacrifice of Gods

Love, hate, and fear seem, then, to have all played their part as motives in the earliest sacrificial rites. We will consider these affects in detail.

Hate and Destruction.—Hate is a destructive impulse. ' The ego hates, abhors, and pursues· with intent to destroy all objects which cause it pain (*Unlustempfindungen*), whether this pain is due to a sexual deprivation or to the loss of something necessary to self-preservation.'[1] This description of hate can be accepted without equating the destructive impulse with the organic death impulse that has recently acquired prominence in psycho-analytic literature. It may be that the ultimate urge of organic matter is due to a sort of elasticity that tends to resume forms of equilibrium that have been disturbed, and that the final aim of life is death. But, although hate may lead to murder, or when inverted to suicide, it does not seem to be a direct manifestation of the organic death impulse. This death impulse seems to have no positive aim like hate that pursues an object. It does not kill, but it allows to perish when it is not counteracted by a positive desire. In melancholia death seems sometimes to occur for no other reason than because life has lost all value. In the same disease hate is inverted against the self and may lead to suicide, but such deliberate self-destruction seems distinct from cases in which life is given up without effort. Perhaps the Buddha, who conquered all desire, may have died in this manner. Similarly, it may be that we do not lose interest in life because we grow old, but that we grow old because the life impulses exhaust or satisfy themselves. Unlike this death instinct, hate is an active desire; it actively pursues an aim, whether this aim be the destruction of the self or of another.

Hate has also been confused with the impulse of repulsion. But whereas this impulse avoids its object, hate follows it. And in this, hate is akin to love. But unlike love, hate pursues its object only to destroy it.

We know from analysis that the father is regularly an object of unconscious hatred. We have inferred that the totem is a father substitute, and that its slaughter is the expression of this unconscious hate. That it is in fact hated can be inferred from two moments: from the taboo that protects its life, and

[1] Freud, 'Triebe und Triebeschicksale', *Sammlung kleiner Schriften*, 2. Aufl. Folge 4, 275.

from the act that destroys it. As Freud has shown, the taboo exists only where there is a desire to repress; and since one of the oldest taboos is that which protects the totem, one of the strongest desires must have threatened to destroy it.[1] Further, this taboo was occasionally and ceremoniously broken, and the aim of the repressed realized in action.

We have seen in an earlier section how the Oedipus situation recurs throughout life between an individual and the various persons that come to stand to him in the same relation as did his father. The same ambivalence, the same love and hate returns, and the victim of this complex finds himself again in the same intolerable situation which he has experienced before, but which he has forgotten. We have seen that there are two developments to this untenable position: the direct and the inverted solution, the destruction of, or the capitulation to, the new Imago. The one is masculine and aggressive, the other feminine and masochistic. Primitive man finds himself in the Oedipus relation to his totem; the distribution of psychic forces is unstable; one of the conflicting impulses must be diverted. In the sacrifice of the totem-god it is the love, an impulse that strives to retain its object, that must change its aim, and the impulse to destroy that is first satisfied.

We have seen further that it is only with difficulty that a son frees himself from the ghost of his Imago, and that it is hard for him to realize that such a one is really dead. Unless he sees the body rot away or disintegrate before his eyes he is haunted by the spirit of the slain even more than he was haunted by him in life. The totem feast in which the god was torn in pieces and eaten provided just such a proof of his annihilation as is required to free the tribesmen, if only for a moment, from his influence.

That the desire to be free from the very ghost of the dead is in fact a motive for the destruction of the totem-

[1] Freud, *Totem und Tabu*, 2. Aufl. 42-3.

god is suggested by numerous analogies. Of cannibalism Westermarck remarks: 'The idea that a person is annihilated or loses his individuality by being eaten has led to cannibalism not only in revenge but as an act of protection, as a method of making a dangerous individual harmless after death. Among the Botocidos warriors devoured the bodies of their fallen enemies in the belief that they would thus be safe from the revengeful hatred of the dead.'[1]

Funeral rites, of mutilation or destruction, often served a similar purpose, as has been pointed out by Rhode[2] and by Levy-Bruhl.[3] The Greeks burned their dead in order that they might be banished to Hades, and there live a life of as complete annihilation as the mind of man can conceive; and many primitive peoples have mutilated or dismembered their dead to prevent them from influencing the living. In a Slavonic myth, that has already been quoted, the man Sovij hunted a boar and took nine pieces of spleen and gave them to his children to cook for him. But they ate them themselves. On discovering this the father was very angry and tried to go to the underworld. With the help of his youngest son he succeeded. If this myth is analysed as a dream its latent content is not far to seek. The father was killed and eaten by the sons; his youngest son was perhaps the ringleader. This is the fantasy, and perhaps also the fact, that underlies the myth. In the manifest content the killing of the father by the sons is replaced by the killing of the boar by the father; the eating of the father by the eating of the boar; and the death of the father by his voluntary descent to the underworld. Thus the mechanism of distortion imputes actions and motives to the father which belonged to his sons, but which they could not consciously accept. It produces as manifest content a myth that is hardly coherent; for why should the father wish to die because he was angry with his sons? In the second part of the

---

[1] Westermarck, *Moral Ideas*, ii. 559. [2] Rhode, *Psyche*, 8. Aufl. i. 325-6.
[3] Levy-Bruhl, *L'Âme primitive*, 328.

myth the youngest son visits his father in the underworld, and, after their common meal, makes a bed for his father, first in the earth, then in a wooden coffin, and lastly in the fire. Here only can the father sleep untroubled as sweetly as a babe in a cradle. Here again the method of distortion is the same; motives are imputed to the father that belong to the sons. They had killed their father whom they loved and they were troubled by his ghost; and, like many primitive peoples, they saw it in the snakes and the worms that frequented his grave. Then they buried him in a wooden coffin, but again they could not destroy his memory, and they saw him in the bees and the gnats that infested the coffin. Lastly, they burned his body and saw it melt in the fire before their eyes. So they were convinced that he was gone beyond recall and would trouble their sleep no more.

If there is a similarity between the destruction of a totem in sacrifice and the destruction of the body of the dead in a funeral rite, there is also an analogy between these funeral customs and certain acts of sympathetic magic. It is commonly believed among primitive peoples that a person may be injured by destroying a model of him, or some of his appurtenances, or something that has been in contact with him. 'Thus the North American Indians, we are told, believe that by drawing the figure of a person in sand, ashes, or clay, or by considering any object as his body and then pricking it with a sharp stick or doing it any other injury, they inflict a corresponding injury on the person represented.'[1]

Here an injury to the model is supposed to injure the original. In funeral rites, in which the corpse is mutilated, dismembered, or burnt, the soul or spirit may be supposed to be similarly affected, even where this purpose is not admitted. In the sacrifice of the totem the clansmen free themselves, for the moment at least, from his influence; but here this aim is wholly

[1] Frazer, *Golden Bough*, i. 55.

unconscious. Thus the repression of the motive increases with the sanctity of the victim. The motive is apparent in the rite designed to injure an enemy; less so in the funeral ceremony that banishes a fellow-tribesman from the society of his neighbours; and invisible in the sacrifice that destroys a god.

A type of behaviour that seems to belong to the same category as the magical injury of an enemy is illustrated by children who destroy their toys. Analyses have shown that such a practice is an alternative to the destruction of the child's rivals,[1] though the child, unlike the sorcerer, is neither aware of the origin of his temper nor deluded as to the effectiveness of its outlet. Even the cultivated adult is not always free from similar futilities, such, for instance, as that of a man who was so enraged by someone that he was discussing, but who was beyond his reach, that he hurled a decanter of his best port into the fire.

How are we to explain such irrational behaviour? As a means of abreacting, or working off pent-up feelings? Such practices do provide an outlet for repressed or suppressed impulses, but relief, in the case of sympathetic magic, is accompanied by a delusion. It is possible that this delusion is present, to some extent, in all vicarious outlets for indignation. If the injured object is in the true sense a symbol, it may be that some part of the mind is satisfied that the injury to the symbol has reached the real object, and that the peculiar relief that the destruction of the port decanter gave the gentleman in the story was due to the unconscious conviction that the broken bottle really was the object of his irritation. Freud believes that the earliest satisfaction that we receive was hallucinatory, and that only painful experience taught us the difference between milk that was imaginary and worthless as a permanent diet and milk that was real and filling. It may be that our unconscious is as easily

---

[1] Freud, ' Eine Kindheitserinnerung aus " Dichtung und Wahrheit " ', *Sammlung kleiner Schriften*, 4. Folge.

pleased to-day, and that the man or child believes unconsciously that he has removed his father when he has eaten a bear, stuck pins into a doll, broken his toys or his decanter.

But the inability to distinguish between image and sensation can overlook a real satisfaction as easily as it can accept a false one. The ghost, that is, the image of the dead, survives his death, and may have to be laid by a further destruction of his body on the funeral pyre. Such may be one purpose of the funeral, as of the sacrificial rite. If so, it owes its success and its failure to the same cause: to an inability to distinguish sensations from ideas and to realize that sensations, unlike ideas, are only indirectly controlled by desire. In the unconscious all images may be as vivid as sensations. There may be no internal difference between them.

That the destruction of the totem-god does, at least for a time, free the worshippers from his influence may be inferred from their reaction to his death. After the sacrifice there follow often the orgy, in which all taboos, including the incest taboo, may be systematically broken.[1] In this orgy the sacrificer may be compared to the manic depressive in the manic stage, who is without conflict or restraint; for the Imago that is responsible for repression has vanished. We may compare such orgies with the great games and festivals of antiquity which are held to have been instituted as part of a funeral rite. Frazer suggests that the Olympic games were originally contests in which the king competed and staked both his crown and his life.[2] Such funeral games, if they celebrated the ritual death of the king or of his opponent, may have been a variant of the sacrificial orgy.

Love and Introjection.—If the hate of the father is satisfied by his destruction in effigy, what outlet is left for the love that also existed and which strives to

---

[1] Freud, *Totem und Tabu*, 2. Aufl. 188.
[2] Frazer, *Golden Bough*, iv. 104.

retain its object ? We know that even after a loved object has been destroyed, that is, when it is no longer a possible sensation, the Id[1] refuses to give it up. It is recognized in its symbols, that is, an unconscious image or hallucination of the object is evoked by them.[2] We have seen that such a symbol may be either a new external object or the subject's own ego. The original object may be either reprojected or introjected.

This process of introjection is obscure, but we may suppose that the ego becomes a symbol of the object to the unconscious like any external Imago ; and that the unconscious recognizes the lost object in the ego and suffers no deprivation. It is the victim of an agreeable hallucination—an hallucination which is responsible for the firm character and confidence of the individual who has introjected his Imago.

Thus when a loved object is lost and introjected, the Id is satisfied because the ego has become the symbol of this object. And this is what seems to happen to the slaughtered totem. It is eaten, its skin is worn, and its adorers believe that they themselves have become the object that they have destroyed. Its introjection is not only psychical but physical. And the belief is strengthened by the act. In the same way the cannibal believes that he absorbs, with the flesh and blood of his victim, the moral virtues as well.

But the eating of the totem-god is not only an exquisite expression of the destruction and introjection of an object of ambivalent feelings and the most perfect resolution of this ambivalence ; in its very act it satisfies both apparently incompatible desires. It is at once an expression of love and hate.

There is an old saying that all love starts as cupboard love, and in an earlier section reasons were given for supposing that oral love preceded, and colours, the later forms. The little boy, I have often quoted, at the age of four and a half, once said to his father : ' I wish, Daddy, you were made of chocolate, I would eat you

---

[1] *I.e.* the infantile unconscious.   [2] Part I, Chapter i.

all up'. And on another occasion: 'I would eat fingers made of blood and cake'. 'Whose blood?' 'Nobody's blood.' 'It must be somebody's blood.' 'Your blood, Daddy.' His brother of two and a half similarly remarked on several occasions to his mother: 'Mummie, I would cut you up, take your clothes off, run over you with a steam roller, and eat you up for lunch, I would, I would'. To these children a cannibalistic fantasy was an expression of love; and it seems likely that this oral sadistic form of love was one of the motives of the totem feast.

The favourite game of these same children was bear-hunting. Their father had to be the bear which they pretended to hunt, kill, and eat. They were thus true totemists in play. But soon the older child said that such games gave him nightmares. He dreamed that he was himself being eaten by bears. An analyst would say that indulgence in the game had stimulated his unconscious desire to kill and eat his father, and that, in consequence, he had had to project his cannibalistic desires to prevent them from becoming conscious. If, however, this child had been reared in a primitive society, with the examples of totemic sacrament around him, it is likely that he would have readily adopted their rites. His conscious motive might have been a pious conservatism that perpetuated the customs of his clan. But his unconscious motive would have included hate of his father, which, surviving from infancy, vented itself in the destruction of a father-symbol, and an almost equally unconscious love which was satisfied both in the oral sadistic act and in the resulting introjection.

Fear and Propitiation.—The father Imago is not only hated and loved; it is also feared, and the fear is largely the result of ambivalence. The hate which is constant in the lower strata of the mind is unowned in the upper strata, projected, turned against the self, and consequently feared. Thus fear of the victim before the sacrifice shows that the worshippers are not wholehearted in their act and fear after the sacrifice shows that the resolution of ambivalence has not been complete.

Before the sacrifice the worshippers treat the divine animal with great respect and do everything to persuade it that they who are about to kill it have no really ill intent. They beseech it not to be angry with them ; they offer it libations. Sometimes they make a rule that no blood be shed, and in consequence stone, burn, or drown the victim, and believe that they thereby reduce their guilt. And these things they do because they are afraid of their own hate which is repressed and projected.

But even the destruction of the object of love and hate does not permanently relieve the worshippers of fear. Their introjection of the Imago is incomplete and short lived. The ghost of the slain animal lives on in their imagination, the object of a love they cannot escape, and the carrier of an unconscious and projected hate, which is the stronger because it has failed to destroy its object, and because there is now no longer a concrete object to destroy. The Imago can no longer be pierced by arrows or crushed by stones, and the hate of it, bereft of the possibility of external expression, tends to turn inwards and threatens the self. It is this inversion of the destructive impulse that causes the self-injuries, or the injuries to the sacrificer's own group, that are supposed to expiate the crime, as well as the defences against this reaction.

The first defence against the inverted hate is perhaps the covenant to share the guilt. Robertson Smith believed that the earliest form of sacrifice was the covenant in which the members of the tribe consumed an animal which was at the same time their god, and thereby renewed their kinship with him and with each other. Freud's theory accepts and elaborates this view. For him the animal represents the primeval father and is eaten in commemoration of his murder. The sons at the same time make a covenant together to respect the laws of exogamy and to refrain from the free expression of the lusts which once before threatened the unity of the clan. But as Zulliger[1] has pointed out, this covenant is also the covenant to share the guilt. Everyone must participate in the crime, and admit his guilt in the fullest sense by eating the flesh of the victim. Each revolutionary is terrified at what he is about to do and wavers in his resolve. His greatest fear is that others may waver too and leave him to face the blame alone. He is suspicious of his brothers and sees to it that their hands are as red as his. Once he has forced them to join him in the act, they are committed, and shut off from all hope of returning to the side of the father. This seems to be the deepest motive for forcing all the clan to partake of the flesh of the slain.

Sometimes it is consciously admitted that the command that all shall eat is a protection ; for the victim will recognize his own flesh in his devourers and will be unable to harm them. But the deeper motive seems to be less an anxious solicitude, lest others should be unprotected against revenge, than the wish that they should not escape the guilt. Thus the motive that inspires each individual to make others eat of the flesh of the victim is probably different from the motive that inspires him to eat the victim himself. The individual eats because he wants to introject the victim, and he may believe that in this way he also secures his immunity from revenge.[2] But he compels others to eat that they may share his guilt. If they are united they will the better resist vengeance.

Not only is the guilt shared, but it is disowned ; the axe that did the deed is sentenced and destroyed. And not only is the guilt disowned ; its very existence is denied. The ox is stuffed with straw and yoked to the plough ; the murderers undo the past and declare it null and void.

Fear after the sacrifice, fear of vengeance, is, we have argued, the fear of a projected hate which lacks

---

[1] Zulliger, ' Totemmahl eines fünfeinhalbjährigen Knaben ', *Imago,* xiii.
[2] Westermarck, *Moral Ideas,* ii. 565-6.

a concrete object. By forcing others to join in the crime, or by pretending that the crime had not occurred, this fear is temporarily relieved. But its source remains. The projected hate remains ; and is turned against the self, or against something that can be identified with the self. And it is this projected hate that commits those repetitions of the crime that are known as acts of direct or vicarious atonement.

Direct expiation is vengeance against the self. The self executes the sentence which it fears. The self succumbs to a hate which it imagines to be external, but which is in reality its own. The self is inverted and masochistic. Vicarious expiation, on the other hand, is vengeance against the self by proxy. Thus it is psychologically similar, though practically different, from the direct variety. It is masochistic by proxy, that is, it is sadistic.

We can now understand what is meant by the sense of guilt and the desire for punishment. The desire for punishment is nothing more than the destructive impulse of an inverted hate, and the sense of guilt is simply the fear of this hate. The voice of the avenger within the self is ventriloquized and heard as the voice of God. And this voice is persistent and allows no rest until in despair its hearer turns and rends himself, or finds someone else to injure in his place.[1]

But there are compensations for succumbing to an inverted hate. Even pain can be made to give sexual satisfaction. We may suppose that the religious flagellants of old beat themselves as much for their own pleasure as do the perverts of to-day, though they may have been more reluctant to admit it. For those whose normal passions are inhibited such practices may be the only erotic outlet that they possess. And these are the more ready to listen to the voice of conscience when it bids them expiate their crimes.

There is, however, another and a grimmer way by

[1] See Flügel's review of Freud's ' The Ego and the Id ', *Int. Journal of Psycho-Analysis*, viii. 411.

which the nemesis of guilt can be accepted. Masochism converts the torments which it seeks into the female erotic pleasures which biology or a morbid disposition has denied. But there is no feeling and no sensation which cannot be experienced by proxy. The masochist enjoys the feminine rôle in his own person and the active rôle in the person of his partner, and the acts which excite this pleasure are not the acts of adult sexual life, but are aggressive and such as inflict injury and pain. But it is possible to acquire a secondary inversion, to readopt the aggressive rôle, and to enjoy the pains of masochism through empathy with greater security and convenience.[1] The sadist, like the masochist, suffers from a projected hate that threatens to turn against himself. Like the masochist he is inhibited and unable to enjoy the normal outlet of his sexual needs. But, unlike the masochist, he protects himself, and succeeds in shunting the destructive impulses from himself to another, and yet enjoys the masochistic compensations by proxy. In Vienna I once witnessed a play, ' Die Peitsche und . . . ', the name of the author of which I have unfortunately forgotten. The sadistic hero explained to the masochistic heroine, after the climax was over, that his erotic pleasure was derived solely from the excitement which he obtained from his acute imagination of all the details of the torture he inflicted. He was more than usually conscious of the source of his pleasure because he could describe it in words. It seems to me that the mechanism of vicarious expiation must be the same, though those who practise it would be less honest in the understanding of their motives.

The facts of conscience and the desire for direct or vicarious self-punishment have often been quoted in disproof of the hedonic principle. On analysis they seem strikingly to confirm it. For, to submit to punishment is, to the inhibited personality, the line of least resistance. In it he derives erotic satisfaction. With-

---

[1] Freud, ' Triebe und Triebschicksale ', *Sammlung kleiner Schriften*, 2. Aufl. 4. Folge, 265.—Havelock Ellis, *Studies in the Psychology of Sex*, 2nd ed. iii. 160.

out succumbing to it he would remain utterly inhibited and tormented with fear of an inverted hate which was unfulfilled. Sometimes, however, the inverted hate is not eroticized. This can happen in melancholia. Then there is no compensation; the sufferer is of no value as an object to his erotic impulses, he gives himself up and dies. But even here, if hedonism is the flight from pain rather than the pursuit of pleasure, suicide is hedonic, for life has become intolerable.

If this analysis is correct the piacular element is inevitable in sacrifice; for sacrifice is a crime that turns against those who commit it. But the expiation may either follow, or be merged in, the crime. The priest who did the deed may be stoned, or required to fly. The people may beat themselves or beat each other. Or a sacrifice may be made to expiate a sacrifice as in the legend of the African Ngurangurane, who offered human victims to his father, the Giant Crocodile, whom he had killed.[1] But more often the crime and its expiation are merged in one act. The sacrificial victim is both god and man, a symbol at once of the father and of his rebellious son. Thus in the dispute whether the offering represents, or is offered to, the god, both views are right. The totem is both the ancestor and the brother of the clan; its slaughter satisfies both the direct and the inverted hatred, though the latter is satisfied by proxy. In this way the demand for punishment is fulfilled and fear and guilt avoided. As Roheim puts it : ' The symbolic repetition is also a reduced, a neurotically inhibited repetition, for the rebellion against the father is reacted under the guise of a self-punishment for the very deed '.[2]

The Meaning of Sacrifice to Women

Starting from the Oedipus complex of the little boy, we have argued that sacrifice is a symbolic parricide.

[1] Roheim, *Australian Totemism*, 131-2, from Trilles, *Le Totemisme chez les Fan*, 184-202.   [2] *Ib.* 233.

But since women, as well as men, take part in sacrificial rites, some wish corresponding to the essential purpose of sacrifice for men must be present in women also. What, if any, are the special sacrificial derivatives of the female Oedipus complex?

Analysts have in the past given more attention to sons than to daughters, but have supposed that the Oedipus complex in a woman is the mirror image of the same complex in a man. Whereas, it was argued, the main wish of the boy child is to kill his father and marry his mother, that of the little girl must be to kill her mother and marry her father. There is a good deal of evidence that this is so, but certain theoretical considerations seem to show that this desire cannot be primary. The first love of the girl as well as of the boy must be the mother who supplies all the earliest wants. Hence the normal Oedipus complex in the girl, in which she identifies herself with her mother and loves her father, must be inverted. She achieves this inverted position more firmly and more easily than the inverted boy. But if she inverts again and becomes homosexual she is returning, unlike the homosexual boy, to a former psychical position.

If, therefore, I am right, the development of the normal woman starts like that of the normal man, and is throughout its whole course similar to, but more satisfactory than, that of his inverted brother. Like the boy she goes through a stage in which she desires to monopolize her mother and resents the disturbing presence of her father. Unlike the boy, however, she fails to find in her own genital a substitute for the nipple, or the thumb, which she loses after she has been weaned from oral habits. This she can only find in a male partner, so that, unlike the boy, she has to change the sex of the first object of her love. But though the object of the impulse is changed the impulse itself seems to alter less in the girl than in the boy. The act of absorbing the penis into the vagina is believed to be, at least in part, a direct derivative of the act of sucking the nipple.[1] But the act of allowing the penis to be absorbed would seem to be an inverted derivative from the act of sucking. Thus while the girl retains the original form of the impulse and has to find a new object, the boy retains the first object and inverts the impulse. If this analysis of the development of the female Oedipus complex is correct, the eating of gods by women has at its basis the same parricidal tendencies as in men. But, since for women the father is only an obstacle to the possession of another object at the oral stage, the intensity of the destructive impulse must be due to other factors as well.

At the genital stage a woman's father is himself the unconscious object of her sexual impulse. But a loved object is hated if it thwarts the impulse that is directed to it. In fact, this kind of hate is probably the earliest kind there is; for it occurs at the second oral phase, where its purpose seems to be to master a refractory loved object rather than to destroy an impediment. Similarly, a woman may hate her father, less because he stands in the way of some separate loved object than because he is himself a refractory loved object. And this motive is presumably at the basis of the penis envy that is so regularly discovered in her unconscious, for she desires to take what she is not given. Thus, where women destroy their gods as in the Dionysian orgies, the unconscious hate must be due more to rebuffs by the father than to rivalry with him. As with men, the hate is due to thwarted love. But the impediment and the loved object are, to a large extent, the same.

Again the motive for eating the god is not quite the same in women as in men. In both a motive is doubtless to be, or to introject, the Imago. But in women the eating seems also to be a forerunner of coitus. It is supposed, on good evidence, that the desire to suck the

[1] See, for example, Ernest Jones's paper 'The Early Development of Female Sexuality', *International Journal of Psycho-Analysis*, viii., especially pages 465-6.

penis mediates between the desire to suck the nipple and the desire to receive the penis into the vagina.[1] And this intermediary desire seems to be often symbolized in the sacrifice of gods by women. The mother of Attis consumed the pomegranate that sprang from the severed genitals of his double, Agdestis. And there are many examples of fertility rites in which women are supposed to become pregnant by the sacramental eating of a phallic symbol. Even where what is eaten is not obviously a phallic symbol the avowed purpose of the eating is to facilitate conception. Thus, we may believe with Roheim, that 'there was a time in the prehistoric evolution of the Central Australian tribes when the women were supposed to conceive, not from eating the totem, but from eating human flesh. They probably partook of the festival meal and ate the flesh of the murdered father. From the point of view of the Unconscious this was equivalent to having intercourse with him, as eating is a transposition upwards of the sexual act.'[2] More precisely we might say that the eating was a reversion to an antecedent of coitus.

Lastly, I do not think that the motives for direct or vicarious expiation are identical in women and in men. We have seen that self-destruction is determined partly by the turning inwards of a hate that is externally inhibited, and partly by the extent of the masochistic compensation that can be combined with this. But women seem to be less subject to the sense of guilt than men; and this is perhaps because their unconscious hate is less, so that they have less to turn against themselves. When, therefore, women were sacrificed voluntarily to their gods, directly or by proxy, we must suppose that they suffered more from pleasure than from a stern duty that they could not escape. In women there is thus less inverted hate and more masochistic compensation. It is more natural for them to play the passive rôle, and easier for them to learn to enjoy it even when it is painful.

[1] See Note, p. 209.   [2] Roheim, *Australian Totemism*, 391.

Thus, if I am right, deicide symbolizes, within limits, the same things to women as to men. They, like men, act in deicide a symbolic parricide. But their unconscious motives are not quite the same. Hate and love are both present, but these affects are differently conditioned and differently satisfied. Fear of projected aggressive impulses is also present, but these impulses would seem to be more erotic than in men, and less purely destructive.

CHAPTER IV

THE MODES OF SACRIFICE

THE sacrificial prototype that was considered in the last chapter contained two parts—the killing of the god, and the masochistic, or sadistic, expiation. Sometimes these two rites were fused in one act, so that the victim was at once a symbol of the father and of his rebellious son. But, ultimately, even the pure act of self-destructive expiation is symbolic parricide; for, while consciously the object of the destructive impulse is the self, unconsciously it remains the father. Thus, the sacrificial prototype is a symbolic parricide repeated twice: once directly in the killing of the god, once inverted in the masochistic or sadistic expiation. And these two may be either fused in one act or separate.

It is obvious that the motive in the second of these two forms of sacrifice undergoes more distortion in its passage from unconscious to conscious than the motive in the first form. In one the father as the object of destructive impulses is replaced by the god, in the other the father is first replaced by the son as object of an inverted hate, and then, at least in the sadistic form of expiation, the son is replaced by a scapegoat. Thus, although the ultimate meaning of both rites is parricide, the sacrifice of a scapegoat has an intermediary meaning that is absent in the sacrifice of a god.

In other types of sacrifice there may be other intermediary meanings, and, if so, it seems worth while to investigate them systematically, and to classify certain varieties of sacrifice by the intermediary meanings that they may possess. Thus, while in the last chapter we were concerned with a deep stratum of the unconscious, in this we shall attempt to analyse the various meanings of sacrifice at a level intermediate between the deep unconscious and the conscious rationalization.

For clarity it may be convenient to work out the geological and perhaps neurological analogy still further, and to divide the mind into four strata—the pre-Oedipus, the Oedipus, the post-Oedipus, and the conscious. In this chapter, then, we shall be occupied with the post-Oedipus unconscious deposit, and we shall classify sacrifices according to the meanings that they possess at this level. But, as in all analytical classifications, the types will be abstractions separated in artificial purity from their complex setting. The same rite will have different post-Oedipus meanings to the different members of the group, and even many meanings to the same individual. A single meaning will only partially explain a single rite.

Like the conscious representation of the Oedipus fantasy, the representation at the post-Oedipus level is often formed by the displacement of the destructive impulse on to a new object instead of the father, or its projection on to a new subject instead of the son. But at this level, even when there is distortion, the actors in the drama are often confined to the fundamental trio of the family—father, mother, and son. The son, as subject of the destructive impulse, may be replaced by the father or the mother ; and the father, as object of this impulse, may be replaced by the mother or the son. Thus, by a change of subject and object there arise eight important variants of the Oedipus fantasy. And these, together with the prototype, I will tabulate as follows :

1. The Unconscious fantasy of killing the father
2. The Unconscious fantasy of killing the mother } Types in which the object alone is changed.
3. The Unconscious fantasy of killing the self
4. The Unconscious fantasy of the father killing himself } Types in which the subject alone is changed.
5. The Unconscious fantasy of the mother killing the father

6. The Unconscious fantasy of the father killing the mother
7. The Unconscious fantasy of being killed by the father
8. The Unconscious fantasy of the mother killing herself
9. The Unconscious fantasy of being killed by the mother

Types in which both subject and object are changed.

In types 1, 2, and 3 the destructive impulse remains direct; in types 4-9 it is projected; in types 3, 7, and 9 it is inverted, it destroys the self. In types 4 and 5 the object is unchanged, in all the rest it is replaced.

At the conscious level each of these post-Oedipus fantasies may be dramatized symbolically in action. Since it seems likely that there have been sacrificial rites that correspond to each of them, we will proceed to a more detailed examination of each in turn.

1. *The Unconscious Fantasy of killing the Father*

The Oedipus fantasy of killing the father sometimes persists unchanged in form from the Oedipus level of the unconscious to the conscious. There may be some displacement of object and projection of subject, but both object and subject remain of the same type. The father may be replaced by a totem, a brother, a king or a god, and the son as murderer may be replaced by an executioner or a priest. But though there is thus a change in the content of the original fantasy there is no real change in form.

The sacrificial totem feast, where the victim is a direct symbol of the father and the sacrificers are the sons, is largely a dramatization of this fantasy. It was this type of sacrifice that Freud explained as the 'repetition and commemoration' of a primeval parricide. We have seen that his theory seems content to record a parallel and does not give an explicit motive : but that the motive is already implicit in Freud's writings.

Thus, whether or not the projection of the father into an animal, which was revered and slain, occurred first at a level of culture in which parricide was common, or whether it did not develop till much later, is not really fundamental to the psycho-analytic thesis. What is important is to be sure that the totem was, in the psycho-analytic sense, a father symbol. We know that an animal is often such a symbol to our children to-day, and there is a strong presumption that a totem was so to primitive peoples in the past and that it is so to them now. It is often regarded as their ancestor, sometimes as their elder brother, and it is treated with a respect due to a father god. Thus many totems and revered animals or plants have the attributes of father symbols. And this to a psycho-analyst should be a sufficient reason why they should be sometimes killed.

Often, however, the totem appears to be less the symbol of the father than of his important attribute. Where the totem is a tree, an insect, or a plant of peculiar shape, it may well be a phallic symbol. And where to eat it is believed to stimulate fertility this suspicion receives some confirmation. The killing and eating of the totem would here not only symbolize the killing and castrating of the father, a frequent theme of ancient myth, but the acquisition of his potency. And if such a sacrament is practised by women it is presumably further supposed to procure conception.

But it seems that the totem does not always symbolize the father or his attributes directly, although it may still do so indirectly. It may be of female sex; it may be a sort of fetish; or it may be the receptacle of the external soul. And in these cases it is difficult to see how its slaughter can be symbolic parricide. Thus, it is not possible at this stage of the inquiry to assert that every ritual destruction of a totem is a dramatization of an unconscious parricidal fantasy. Our theory of sacrifice, so far, applies with reasonable certainty only to that type of the killing of a sacred beast recorded in Nilus' famous story of the camel.

If there are types of totemic sacrifice that are not obviously parricidal, there are also non-totemic sacrifices which do seem to possess this character. The king is one of the most universal father symbols to-day, and it seems likely that the kings of olden times were even more definitely substitutes for fathers. They were believed to incarnate their ancestors, the gods who made and ruled the universe, and they themselves frequently received divine honours. It seems, therefore, that the custom of sacrificing kings, of which Frazer has collected so many examples, is, like the totemic communion, a symbolic parricide. And we may suppose that the most important motive for such rites was the same unconscious hatred that we have made responsible for the totemic communion.

Consciously, no doubt, the devout murderers believed that their bloody deeds were sacred and magical acts to secure the necessary changes of the seasons and the growth of vegetation. The kings they slew were also nature spirits. The unconscious that at once hates, loves, and fears the father recognizes him in many shapes. Not only the totem and the king, but the great forces of nature, which the primitive man personifies, may thus become his symbols. Like the father they are loved when they are helpful and hated and feared when they menace. Like him they are the object of ambivalent feelings. Like his other symbols they are sometimes propitiated and sometimes slain. Sometimes, as in the Egyptian ceremony to destroy Apepi, these nature spirits are hated openly, but more often the hostility, although manifest in the deicidal act, is not consciously recognized as its motive. Instead, the sacrifice is supposed to be a magical ceremony to effect some other purpose. But the magical purpose and the unconscious purpose are not unrelated. The primitive man interprets the fickleness of nature as the retaliation of nature against his own unconscious hatred of that which nature symbolizes. Natural calamities are punishments inflicted by the malice of the gods, and this malice is ultimately the projection of the malice of the worshippers against their fathers and against all that symbolizes them. Therefore, the primitive man, to free himself from the dread of his own projected hate, will seek to destroy his imagined enemy. If he is successful he is freed, for the moment at least, from fear. The real source of this fear remains unconscious, and it is not removed. Only a symbol is destroyed. Nor is the real cause of a calamity avoided. Only a neurotic fear is temporarily relieved. Therefore, the operation is therapeutic, not agricultural; magical, not scientific.

But because the unconscious will not give up the symbol of a loved object, the whole effect of the magical ceremony is afterwards made null and void. The nature spirit is reincarnated; a new symbol takes the place of the old, and the worshippers declare with joy that their god is risen. For a time they forgive him; but soon he will be required to die again.

A historian would raise the question of priority between the totemic sacrifice and the ritual slaughter of a divine king. If totemism was ever universal it seems likely that kings and gods may have developed out of totems. Perhaps the totem sacrifice came gradually to be the privilege of a special class, and then of the high priest of this caste. If so, since he alone would eat the sacred animal, he alone would inherit its divinity. But he would have to pay for his position with his life. He would be eaten ritualistically by his successor. Out of such a priest, who, like the Egyptian Unis, feasted on gods, might have developed the divine king. And such a being might well have used his powers to delegate the most painful part of his functions. But historical speculations are dangerous. It is safer to stick to the analysis of the motives which must have been necessary, if not sufficient, for the development of various cults.

In an earlier chapter it was argued that the sacrifice of king's sons might have historically preceded the sacrifice of kings. If so, such practices may well have developed not from the totem communion but from the initiation rite. From the point of view of the sons such rites seem to dramatize the unconscious fantasy of being killed by the father. But from the point of view of the fathers the rite is not inverted or masochistic. It is known by analysis that a man's own son is often regarded by his unconscious as the reincarnation of his father. If, then, the son is symbolically killed and castrated, we may suppose that the unconscious purpose is to kill the father. In the typical initiation rite members of the older generation, in the name of a spirit, pretend to kill the youths and at the same time knock out a tooth, remove a testicle,[1] circumcise or subincise them. After this the youths are supposed to be reborn and they are given a new name and admitted into the full citizenship of the tribe. The tooth extraction, the circumcision or subincision, clearly symbolizes castration, and the meaning of the first part of the rite is not hard to guess. The older generation project their own unconscious hatred upon their sons, as they did formerly upon their fathers. They therefore fear them and act accordingly. And such action is effective. It teaches respect for the older generation and is perhaps one of the important bulwarks of primitive society. It performs the same function as did the public school in its more brutal days. There are, however, other features of such rites that concern their effect upon the youths, which will be considered later.

It is impossible to reconstruct the historical origin of puberty rites. They seem to belong psychologically to the same category of practices as the castration of servants and the exposure of infants. They are dictated by that fear which those in authority so often feel for those beneath them. It is a truism that a usurper fears assassination more than a legitimate ruler. He has been himself a rebel; he has never lost his hatred of his own father Imagos. And when he has attained to power

[1] Frazer, *Belief in Immortality*, iii. 146.

he sees the avenging father in all his servants. He is deluded by the conviction that he is pursued. Like Domitian, who built a gallery of glass so that no one could approach him unawares, he will live in constant dread, and his suspicions will as constantly demand fresh victims. So too may well be the lot of the primitive father or chief who has never overcome his ambivalence to his own Imagos. If so, it would be natural that he should desire to castrate his servants and expose his sons. And the act would be sanctioned by custom and tradition, which was itself the cumulative effect of similar subliminal inclinations. There are many stories of kings who killed their sons because they had been warned by a prophet that they would die at their hands. And such myths clearly disclose one motive for exposure. Afterwards such practices may have been exalted into a sacrifice, or rationalized as an economic necessity; but the unconscious motive perhaps remained the same. However, the fact that daughters too were exposed must warn us that other motives may sometimes have been sufficient.

As with the totemic communion and the sacrifice of kings, the puberty rite and the exposure of male children may have been historically direct reactions to primeval parricide. But they may as easily have cropped up spontaneously as reactions to the growing tension of an unconscious ambivalence.

2. *The Unconscious Fantasy of killing the Mother*

Analysis has shown that the roles of father and mother can be reversed in unconscious fantasy. The mother can be hated and the father loved. But such reversal is not primary and an ordinary Oedipus complex is discoverable below. It is therefore a post-Oedipus reaction which, like its predecessor, has become unconscious, but which remains active in its conscious derivatives. The symbolism in the outward expression of this complex will have a double meaning. Female mother symbols will ultimately symbolize the father, and male father symbols the mother. Female Imagos will have male attributes and male Imagos female attributes. Men who are attracted by feminine men and strongly influenced by masculine women must be, to some extent, the victims of this complex.

There are two variants of this situation. In one the ego remains masculine and positive ; in the other it becomes feminine and inverted. Probably the inverted variety is more common. In its typical form a man is capable only of loving masochistically a sadistic woman, who is thought of as equipped with some phallic symbol, such as a whip. Probably this complex is developed as a further reaction to a simple homosexual inversion. If so, the son first inverts and becomes feminine and masochistic towards his father and later replaces his father by his mother, or by a symbol of her, as the object of his now inverted love. In this way he both escapes the Oedipus conflict and retains his mother as the chief object of his affections. His subsequent emotional life may be modelled on these early reactions.

Sometimes, however, he may reacquire the masculine attitude without changing the object of his desires and become sadistic towards masculine women. And I suppose that this complex may develop as a direct reaction to the Oedipus situation without going through these intermediate stages. It is this complex, in which the original hate of the father is eroticised as sadism and turned against the mother that concerns us here. It gives rise to the post-Oedipus fantasy of the killing of the mother by the son. It is realized almost directly by the obsessional wife-murderers, whose activities are periodically curtailed by the police and more symbolically by less dangerous sadists. We may expect that it, like most perversions, has been performed collectively as a religious duty, and that we shall find it dramatized in sacrificial rites.

We have seen that there is some evidence that the

great mother goddess of antiquity may have been killed as well as her son or consort. If so, she was perhaps slain because the unconscious father hatred was turned against her. Where she is most prominent there seems to have been no father god important enough adequately to absorb this hatred. It obtained a semi-masochistic outlet in the sacrifice of son gods, and one reason for the tendency to convert son gods into father gods [1] may have been to find an adequate father symbol to slay. But if the mother goddess was sometimes slain, she would herself have provided the outlet. We have seen that she was often associated with phallic emblems, and even represented by phallic symbols, such as the snake. Sometimes she wore a beard and her true sex has often been a puzzle to archaeologists. Thus, although she symbolized the mother at one level of the unconscious, she probably symbolized the father too.

It is of the utmost importance for a true understanding of the conditions that first enabled men to combine into large societies, that the whole prehistoric chapter of the dread mother be sometime disclosed. At present we can but see her as through a glass darkly, and can only guess at her true shape. It is likely that all the higher civilizations passed at some stage of their development under her influence. And this influence must have been of the greatest importance to the formation of their culture. Without her no culture might have been possible. But the comparison of the history of peoples, like the Jews, who early freed themselves from her sway, with those of her neighbours, suggests that her rule, though stabilizing, was also petrifying. Her cult remains obscure, but she was terrible ; she was unmarried and unchaste, and she destroyed her lovers. Her characteristics are still discernible in the female monster of heroic legend.

In the more usual type of story there is a male monster and a lady in distress. The hero kills the monster and marries the lady. And analysts tell us

[1] Attis sometimes appears as a father god.

that the monster symbolizes the father and the distressed damsel the mother. But in the stories of the type of Perseus and the Gorgon, Theseus and the queen of the Amazons, or Siegfried and Brunhilde, the monster and the damsel are one. The hero slays her ; or he defeats her and forces her to become feminine ; he destroys, as it were, her masculine double.

If we compare the two types of story and at the same time remember the snakes of the Gorgon, the spear of Brunhilde and the bow of the Amazon, we shall suspect that the villainess or heroine is a composite symbol of father and mother, and that the story is a condensed representation of the Oedipus fantasy, in which both rôles are played by one actress. In the story of the Gorgon actor and actress remain inseparable to the end and both are slain. But in that of Brunhilde or the queen of the Amazons only the masculine double is destroyed and the feminine heroine who is left is really a different person from the dread goddess who was defeated.

Thus, the unconscious fantasy of the killing of the masculine mother by the son has been represented in the ancient world in myth and legend. Possibly such legends may record sacrificial rites. More likely they express the attitude of patriarchal peoples to the goddesses of their neighbours. There are, however, definite examples of mother goddesses who have been slain. Such were the European Corn-Mother and the Mexican Mother of the Gods. I do not know how far these goddesses, who died in the persons of their human incarnations, resembled the dread mother of the ancient world. It is tempting to identify the Corn-mother with the Asiatic goddess, so that we could transfer to her the masculine attributes of the older deity. It is important for the psycho-analytic explanation of communal sacrifice that slain goddesses were also father symbols. The similarities between the killing of a god and of a goddess are so great that it seems likely that the two have similar explanations. And if the psycho-analytic explanation of the first is in no way applicable to the second, we shall be forced to suspect its validity even where it seems best to apply. Hence, if the psycho-analytic interpretation of deicide as symbolic parricide is valid, it should be possible to show that it holds for the sacrifice of goddesses as well as for the sacrifice of gods. If the father was the first object of the developed destructive impulse, all that satisfies it may well be ultimately a father symbol. Thus, though we cannot prove that slain goddesses were father as well as mother symbols, there is a strong psycho-analytical presumption that they were. I admit that the argument is not as good as it should be. But negative anthropological evidence cannot prove that it is wrong, and further positive evidence of the masculine attributes of such goddesses might well prove that it is right.

Goddesses may not only be hated because they are father symbols, but also on their own account. Thus the inverted son and the normal daughter hate their mothers as rivals, and such unconscious motives may help to determine their reactions to mother symbols. But in general the destructive impulse is probably more eroticized in the sacrifice of women than in the sacrifice of men. In dreams coitus is sometimes symbolized by murderous onslaughts with a knife or other weapon, and it is likely that the same symbolism may have helped to motivate the sacrifice of mother goddesses.

Rank would doubtless argue that such sacrifice abreacts the shock of birth. And in those Mexican rites in which a priest crawled into the skin of the slain goddess we might find a parallel to the rebirth symbolism which is so common a feature of primitive religion. But Rank would proceed to derive the dread which characterized the attitude of the worshipper to the Great Mother as due to her association with the shock of birth. Freud on the other hand would maintain that the dread was due to her association with castration, that is, with the shock that the boy child experienced when he was first convinced that there were beings devoid of the male organ of procreation. Freud further argues that fetishism results from an attempt to repress this knowledge, and that the fetish ultimately symbolizes the female penis whose non-existence the boy's unconscious refuses to admit. It he is right we can understand a further reason why female deities are so often associated with phallic emblems, and how these attributes make them a fit target for unconscious impulses that were originally directed against the father.

But while the dread of certain female goddesses may well be in part due to their unconscious association with the idea of castration, it seems also due to the fact that behind the mother goddess the unconscious sees the figure of the jealous father. I once saw a small boy of three or four terrified of his mother for no other reason than that she had dressed up as a man with a moustache. I felt sure that the child had seen his mother turn into his father and had thus lost the only protection that he had against that personification of his own projected hate that his unconscious mistakes for his father.

Not only men but also women sacrifice their goddesses. Thus maidens are believed to have impersonated bears at the sacrifice of the bear goddess Artemis. Such a rite looks like the exact equivalent of the ordinary totemic communion. In it a mother symbol is destroyed by daughters instead of a father symbol by sons. Presumably the motives were the same.

3. *The Unconscious Fantasy of killing the Self*

A third type of object that can be chosen by the destructive impulses that were originally directed towards the father is the self. In melancholia the Id treats the ego like a former object of ambivalent affects which was at once loved and hated. So in religious suicide or self-mutilation the aggressive tendencies which are not allowed to find their first object are turned inwards and destroy the self.

We have seen how after the symbolic killing of the father in sacrifice he rises again in some new form, sometimes as an animal, sometimes as a new king, and sometimes as an introjected part of the self. And we have seen how the sacrificial killing of a father-symbol is often followed by some piacular rite in which something belonging to, or representing, the self is in turn sacrificed. The African Fan tribe have a myth that well illustrates this transition from parricide to suicide, from murder to propitiation, as well as the transition from the theriomorphic to the anthropomorphic god. ' In times long gone by the Fans dwelt on the borders of a great river and were subject to the rule of Ombure, the ruler of water and forest, the Giant Crocodile. Every day they had to give him a man and a woman for food, and every month a young girl as wife. As it was difficult to keep up supplies, they had to make war on their neighbours for slaves, and they were victorious, as the powerful Ombure helped them. He spared the life of the chief's daughter, who was also exposed to him, but after nine months she gave birth to a child, who was called Ngurangurane, the Son of the Crocodile. He grew up to be a Chief of the Fans and a powerful wizard. Aided by his mother, he made a beverage and intoxicated Ombure, whom, having secured with strong ropes, he compelled the lightning, hitherto subject to his father, to come and kill. When he had killed his father (which he only managed to do through the magic help accorded to him by his mother), the Son of the Crocodile cut the corpse into pieces; he ate the brains and the heart, gave the best parts to the old men, the entrails to the women and children, but he took care that everybody should get a morsel so that they should not be afraid of the ghost of the murdered father. Ngurangurane, as he was not only the avenger of his race (that is of his mother's people) but also the son of the Crocodile, now ordered a great funeral to be celebrated. For thirty times thirty days the women cried after Ombure and sang songs

P

in his praise for the same period. For thirty months the angry ghost of Ombure ran all along the village thirsting for vengeance, but as he found his own flesh everywhere (as everybody had taken part in the sacramental meal), he was compelled to desist. Ngurangurane then fashioned an enormous image of Ombure out of clay, and in the head of the image he put his father's bones. They recommenced the dances around the image, and killed two men and two women as sacrifices, so that the blood dripped over the statue. The flesh was placed near the statue, the heads to the head, the feet to the feet and so on. Everybody took his portion of the flesh and then they went home, and the Son of the Crocodile said: "This is what we shall do year by year, this is how we shall honour Ombure". And for this reason Ombure, under the mystic name of Ngan, is the Mwamayon (totem) of the sons of Ngurangurane.'[1]

Roheim points out that the men and women who are sacrificed to ' honour ' Ombure are also symbols of him. They too are eaten. They are the sons and daughters who did the deed, or who at least shared the guilt by partaking of the flesh of the murdered father symbol: but they are also reincarnations of him who are forced by their fellows to share his fate. The elder brother and ringleader Ngurangurane forced every member of the clan to partake of the sacrificial meal in order that he, rather than they, might not fear the ghost of Ombure. He feared to bear the guilt alone and forced them to share it. In the subsequent sacrifice he repeated as well as expiated his crime. The father was reincarnated in the sons and forced to die again.

If the totem father were not loved he would not return in the person of a new symbol. If he were not also hated his reincarnation would not be dangerous to this symbol. If this new symbol is some other animal

[1] Roheim, *Australian Totemism*, 131-2, from Trilles, *Le Totemisme chez les Fan*, 184-202.

or a royal or divine successor to the last victim, it will be treated similarly and will go the way of all gods—to destruction. If it is the self, if, that is, the attempted introjection comes about, the ego will be in turn in danger. No sooner had Oedipus killed his father and possessed his mother than Nemesis began to overtake him ; he ended by tearing out his eyes. Such an impulse to self-destruction is called the need for punishment (*Strafbedurfniss*). It is the turning inwards of impulses that are outwardly inhibited, or which have no longer an outside object. In the story of Oedipus it is satisfied masochistically on the self ; in that of Ngurangurane it is satisfied sadistically in a vicarious sacrifice.

Often the heroic story in which the hero carries all before him, in the end to perish as dramatically as he has lived, is compressed. Only the last act occurs in reality ; the first is fantasied consciously or unconsciously and repressed. Similarly there are rites in which the king, or the god, no longer dies by the hands of his worshippers, to be followed to the grave by some of those who slew him. Instead someone is found to take his place, to die for him before rather than after he has been slain. In India the custom that required kings to take their lives at the end of twelve years, itself perhaps derived from rites in which they were sacrificed by their people, seems to have given place to a custom of faithful retainers cutting their heads off in place of their lord. At tombs the practice of suicide has been common in many countries, and even in recent times the general Nogi committed suicide on the day of the funeral of his Mikado Meigi.[1]

To the conscious in former times, as to the unconscious to-day, death was never regarded as an accident. Probably those who commit suicide at the tombs of their masters unconsciously feel guilty of their death and offer themselves in sacrifice. The same motive perhaps accounts for the mortuary sacri-

[1] De la Saussaye, *Lehrbuch der Religionsgeschichte*, 4. Aufl. i. 331.

fice of servants and wives. Those who feel guilty cause some of their members to die. Those who perish are representatives of those who feel the guilt, that is, the need for self-punishment. The destructive impulse is inverted, but finds a vicarious outlet on something that symbolizes the self. Later such sacrifices would be rationalized as rites to secure an adequate retinue for the deceased. But unconsciously they probably remained rites of suicide by proxy.

The Buddhist monks of China sometimes sought their salvation by voluntarily burning themselves; or, rather, they voluntarily entered wooden chests placed in furnaces, which they were prevented from leaving by those who were anxious to compel them to be saved.[1] Similarly, in the Middle Ages, when the approaching end of the world was confidently expected, many thousands of Russians committed suicide, either by starvation, in buildings without doors or windows especially constructed for the purpose, or in the flames.[2] Here the avowed motive was not to save their lord by perishing in his stead, but to secure their own salvation. But whatever the rationalization of such conduct may be, the results of analysis justify the belief that it is always due to the turning inwards of aggressive impulses that were originally directed outwards. Those who were overpowered by the conviction of their sin against God owed this certainty to the fact that they hated him unconsciously. Yet they also desired, no less ardently, to be loved by him. Their hate, unable to find an external outlet, turned upon themselves, and at the same time satisfied masochistically, at least in anticipation, an erotic need.

To be burnt, or to be killed in any way, as to be beaten, symbolizes to be loved to the morbid mind. Thus such deaths satisfy not only the hostile impulse which can find no external outlet, but the erotic impulse that is also inhibited and inverted.

To Rank the situations which are ultimately objects

---

[1] Frazer, *Golden Bough*, iv. 42-3.   [2] *Ib.* iv. 44-5.

of every desire and of every fear are respectively the prenatal state and the event that terminates it. For him, therefore, such religious suicide, especially when the candidate is burnt in a chest or starved in a building without doors or windows, is desired because it symbolizes a return to the place from which the embryo so reluctantly emerged. It is fairly generally accepted that at least most forms of death do in fact symbolize a return to the womb, and burial practices have often consciously sought to assimilate the dead to an unborn babe. It is therefore possible that these Buddhist and Christian suicides did attempt heroically to break through the trauma of birth and return from whence they came. Such an interpretation does not invalidate the one that has been already given. Motives are always overdetermined. The same event may symbolize various events at various levels of the mind. It may have a whole hierarchy of distinct meanings. Those that are more conscious than the one that we happen to be considering are called rationalizations; those that are less conscious are called overdeterminations.

A whole group of sacrifices are classified by anthropologists as divinatory; their purpose is to foretell the future, to prophesy good luck. They were therefore in all probability originally intended to ward off ill luck. The fear of ill luck is the fear of guilt. It results from ambivalence, and can be seen most clearly before undertakings that symbolize the parricide that is at once desired and repudiated. War, which is not merely self-preservative, is, if the conclusions of Part I are correct, one of the first substitutes for parricide. Hence, before military expeditions, where the enemy is a father symbol, the old ambivalence recurs and is manifest as fear, as the foreboding of ill luck. At such times especially some offering to appease the Fates is urgently desired, and found in a vicarious sacrifice. And sacrifices of divination are probably derived, at least in part, from such rites.

But other motives may be also present. As Rank has pointed out, the desire to foretell the future is the conscious counterpart of the desire to probe the past, to satisfy the first sexual curiosity of the child who seeks to find out whence he came. It is therefore natural that primitive man when he investigates the insides of animals feels that he is probing the secrets of the ages. When Xerxes made his army march between the two halves of the son of Pythios for good luck, both the vicarious sacrifice and the birth symbolism seem to have been combined in one act.[1]

The sacrifice of vegetation-deities was probably, as Westermarck believes, another rite of vicarious atonement. The Corn-God was the incestuous son who fertilized his own mother, the Earth-Goddess. The primitive husbandmen assisted at this crime and enjoyed it by proxy. But it reanimated their own unconscious incestuous and parricidal wishes. Therefore they killed an incarnation of the Vegetation-God, for their own sin, as well as his.

To this group of direct or vicarious suicide belong the various self-mutilations that from time immemorial have always been practised by the devout of all religions. Of these the most fundamental seems to be castration, which Rose classes with suicide as 'two closely related acts'.[2] It was practised by the priests of Cybele, at Atun by the peasantry of Gaul;[3] even St. Paul seems to recommend it,[4] and a modern Russian sect has literally followed his advice.[5] Origen too is said to have emasculated himself, and according to Eustathius the Egyptian priests were eunuchs who had sacrificed their virility as a firstfruit to the gods.[6]

Other forms of sacrifice that seem to be related to self-castration are circumcision and subincision in

---

[1] The magic circle which is so common a feature of magical rites may be supposed to give protection because it symbolizes the womb.
[2] Rose, *Encyclopedia of Religion and Ethics*, xii. 22.
[3] Frazer, *Golden Bough*, ii. 145. [4] 1 Corinthians, vii. 8-9, 27-40.
[5] Frazer, *Golden Bough*, ii. 270. [6] *Ib.* v. 270.

legends of self-inflicted initiation rites, the offering of finger joints,[1] the self-inflicted wounds of the priests of Cybele, and among women, the offering of virginity, or of hair which was sometimes a legitimate substitute. Hair is a frequent offering to gods or goddesses, to the dead, and to rivers.

Suicide and mutilation is psychologically akin to a gift. Every gift is in a sense a part of the self and the pleasure in giving is mildly masochistic. Although the impulse to give seems to originate in urethral and anal tendencies, it is also in part an inverted form of the impulse to take. There is a lively empathy with the imagined feelings of the recipient, and this combined with the pain of loss seems to make up the peculiar feelings of giving. In children the inversion from taking to giving can often be observed. First the little boy wants to take all the toys of his younger brother. Later under the influence of his parents, who disapprove of this selfishness, he comes to feel pleasure in giving things to his rival; but that this pleasure is not unmixed with pain is shown by the frequent tears for the lost possessions he now obstinately insists in giving away. The gifts to the gods which have formed so large a part of sacrifice must surely be accompanied by similarly mixed feelings. The offerings of first-born, of firstfruits, of virility, or of virginity, and the self-mutilations, are all sacrifices of psychological parts of the self and find their culmination in the act of religious suicide.

4. *The Unconscious Fantasy of the Father killing Himself*

The unconscious fantasy of the murder of the father by the father, that is of the suicide of the father, is formed by projecting the murderous impulse on to him, without altering its object. The same man is often both son and father, so that myths and practices that

---

[1] *Ib.* iv. 219—Sollas, *Ancient Hunters*, 347 *sq.*—In one recorded rite, one of the testicles was removed. Frazer, *Belief in Immortality*, iii. 146.

represent the suicide of the father to part of the community represent the suicide of the son to the principal victim.

The temporary Indian kings were expected to commit suicide, and Frazer records many examples of legendary divine monarchs who were said to have burnt themselves on a funeral pyre. Such were Sardanapalus, Hercules, and Croesus. It seems uncertain, however, whether the rule of royal suicide was as common as it seems. Subsequent tradition would be likely to shift the guilt of regicide from the people to the king himself; for, like the skilful murderer, tradition often passes off as suicide what was in reality murder. But there is no doubt that temporary divine kings have periodically destroyed themselves, and such a practice may have been common. To themselves their suicide would satisfy their own hatred of their own fathers with whom they identified themselves; and such a motive must have made it easier for them to conform to the custom that prescribed their death. But to their people they were fathers, not sons, and their suicide may have been forced upon them by their subjects, who thus avoided the trouble and the guilt of killing them.

As in the direct deicidal rites such practices were probably rationalized as agricultural prophylactics. In other words, they temporarily relieved the people of unconscious destructive tendencies which threatened to turn against themselves, and which gave rise, in consequence, to vague forebodings.

5. *The Unconscious Fantasy of the Mother killing the Father*

Sometimes the original object of the hostile tendencies is unaltered, but the tendencies are unowned and projected on to the mother. This situation is a common subject of fantasy. Thus, for example, there is a type of story in which the queen conspires against the king, but puts the blame on the prince, who is punished, or nearly punished, in her stead. Often the hero, who in the deeper layers of his mind is aware of the real culprit, accepts the fate which is apparently so unfair.

It is not easy to distinguish sacrifices that represent this fantasy from those that represent the killing of the son by the mother. The Meriahs of India, Osiris, Attis, and Adonis seem to have been son gods. But they may have represented the father to some of their worshippers, even if they were vicarious selves to others. The story of Ombure and Ngurangurane in which the mother assists the son to kill the father, as well as that of Duncan and Lady Macbeth, or of Agamemnon and Clytemnestra, illustrate the same motive. It is one of the fundamental variants of the Oedipus complex.

6. *The Unconscious Fantasy of the Father killing the Mother*

There is a common motive in myth and fairy tale in which a woman is persecuted by a monster. The woman is usually a symbol of the mother and the monster a symbol of the father. Such fantasies are formed by projecting those aggressive sexual impulses upon the father that every child possesses but soon disowns. Thus the child of two and a half quoted in Part I. who wanted to run over his mother with a steam roller, cut her up, take her clothes off, and eat her up for lunch, will soon disown these tendencies and, by projecting them, build the common fantasy of the lady in distress.

But if, for any reason the child's unconscious fails to learn the distinction between the sexes and confuses his mother with his father, such a fantasy may become the carrier of the destructive impulses that were originally directed to his father. Then the mother-substitute will become a composite symbol of mother and father and the object both of the aggressive sexual, and of the destructive, impulses. But these impulses will remain unowned and projected upon a father symbol. In this way may be developed a post-Oedipus fantasy of the killing of the mother by the father which will be consciously expressed in a symbolic form. Those who possessed this complex would interpret any sacrifice of a female victim by a priest or a god in accordance with their peculiarities.

But it seems unlikely that this meaning was ever very general. The same rite can have different meanings to the different members of the group. Probably female victims offered to gods symbolized sisters rather than mothers to the majority. Of course the sister may stand for the mother, but she may also stand for the female double of the self.

7. *The Unconscious Fantasy of being killed by the Father*

The fantasy of being killed by the father is the complete reversal of the fantasy of killing the father. Object and subject have changed places. The hostility is projected on to the father and its object is replaced by the self.

The meaning of a sacrifice may be one thing to the sacrificer and another to the victim. And the spectators can identify themselves with either rôle, or with both at once. Thus the sacrifice of Isaac does not represent to Jacob the unconscious fantasy of being killed by the father. To the sacrificing father the meaning is both parricidal and suicidal. Parricidal because the son is to the unconscious a reincarnation of the father. Suicidal because the son is also a part of the self. To Isaac, however, the sacrifice is the realization of the inverted Oedipus fantasy, in which the killing is done, not by himself, but by his father, and in which he, not his father, is the victim. The spectator can identify himself with either rôle. If he is sadistic he will play the part of the father; if masochistic that of the son.

The initiation ceremony in which the youths are symbolically killed and castrated by the older generation is psychologically akin to the sacrifice of sons.

Something has already been said about its meaning to the older generation. To the youths, even if they are not voluntary sufferers, such rites probably have some masochistic compensation. For their effect in working off the sense of guilt must be similar to acts of expiation. The demand for punishment, especially among Eastern peoples, is often a great embarrassment to magistrates, who are inundated with false confessions. The sense of guilt is the fear of an inverted destructive impulse. It may be satisfied by punishment inflicted by others. And for this reason punishment is often desired. Even the extreme bellicosity of primitive peoples may be in part due to the same need. In Shaw's *Methuselah* Cain says that his conscience does not trouble him ; but he admits that instead he is compelled to expose his body in combat to all comers.

Thus expiatory sacrifices to a god probably have a masochistic compensation in the satisfaction of the fantasy of being killed by the father. The offerer, to some extent, probably identifies the sacrificer with the father and himself with his offering. He unconsciously interprets the sacrifice as a punishment, a punishment from God, and at the same time derives masochistic satisfaction in the act, ' For whom the Lord loveth he chasteneth and scourgeth every son whom he receiveth '[1] and ' Blessed is the man whom thou chasteneth, O Lord.'[2]

8. *The Unconscious Fantasy of the Mother killing Herself*

In the fantasy of the suicide of the mother neither the original object nor subject appear. Both the son as subject, and the father as object, are replaced by the mother. Such a presentation seems ill-suited to represent the original Oedipus desires. Nevertheless it sometimes occurs as a further development of the fan-

---

[1] Heb. xii. 6.   [2] Ps. xciv. 12.

tasy either of the suicide of the self or of the murder of the mother.

In the fantasy of suicide destructive urges are inverted. But, in so far as there is a masochistic compensation, aggressive sexual impulses also are turned against the self. The self becomes not only the object of the destructive impulse and a symbol of the hated father, but also the object of the aggressive erotic desires and a symbol of the mother. Thus the son (or daughter) who fantasies his own suicide often introjects his mother so that for him the fantasy of the suicide of the mother may be the fantasy of suicide by proxy.

But the idea of the mother's suicide may also be derived from the idea of killing her, for, as in the fantasy of the father killing himself, the destructive impulse may be disowned and attributed to its own victim.

Perhaps the unconscious wish for the mother's suicide, however it is derived, was satisfied in the worshippers of goddesses who, like Dido and Semiramis, perished voluntarily in the flames. Perhaps also the same wish was responsible for the acquiescence of sons (and daughters) at the suicide of their mothers on their fathers' funeral pyres.

9. *The Unconscious Fantasy of being killed by the Mother*

In the fantasy of the murder of the son by the mother, the son, as object of the destructive impulse, is ultimately a symbol of the father, and the mother, as subject, is ultimately a symbol of the son. But, since this fantasy is often derived from the inverted fantasy of the murder of the son by the father, the mother can also stand for the father. And not only is the destructive impulse inverted, not only does the fantasy represent the inverted Oedipus complex, the desire to be killed by the father; it represents also the masochistic reunion of son and mother.

In Japan human sacrifices were made to the earth

goddess, in India boys were offered to Anna Kuari, and children were sacrificed to Hera Acarca at Corinth. Holocausts were offered to Artemis, so was Iphigenia, and the flogging of the Spartan youths at her sanctuary may have been a weakened form of sacrifice. Aphrodite demanded the sacrifice of chastity of her daughters, and human sacrifices were offered to Ge. And these all seem to have been examples of sons and daughters who returned in death to the great mother from whence they came, or who, at least, suffered at her commands.

Possibly Osiris, Attis, and Adonis were victims of this type, who were once offered to Isis, Cybele, and Astarte. The sacrifice of such gods was connected with fertility rites. Typical is the legend of the reconception of the slaughtered son by his mother who eats something that represents him. Typical is also the legend that the son rules henceforth in the underworld, which we know from myth as well as from analysis is a symbol of the womb. And there can be little doubt that the death of the lover of the dread goddess symbolized his return to the womb, from whence he was believed to be reborn.

Rank, for whom the shock of birth is the origin and unconscious meaning of every fear, would see in a death that symbolized the return to the womb an adequate motive for the dread that seems always to have been associated with the Great Mother. But those who attach a greater importance to the Oedipus complex will suspect that some father Imago is the main cause of this fear. If I am right he is to be found in the dual personality of the goddess, who can appear either as a Gorgon and a Fury or as a Madonna.

When, therefore, the goddess is threatening and terrible she is no longer the merciful mother, but the jealous father, who is ultimately the projection of the son's own parricidal wishes. The fact that the goddess seems often to have had phallic attributes helps to support this view. Her common symbol is the snake, the snake that devours and destroys its victims. She is herself terrible, an object of nameless dread. She devours in the flames or castrates her victims. She demands life and virility. She was perhaps evolved at an epoch in which society was only possible through the deification of women, and the transference to them of the feelings that were originally directed to the father and which if they had still been directed to the male ruler would have destroyed the state in perpetual revolution. If the erotic and the destructive urges that were originally divided and attached to different objects were not united and turned against the goddess, the state might have perpetually collapsed like the Cyclopean family, in which the primeval father was slain as soon as he was old, and in which his death was followed by a period of anarchy until one of his sons was strong enough to take his place and to suffer in time the same fate. The progress that demands continuity and stability would have been impossible.

So may the Great Mother have been evolved. As a representative of the father she was sometimes slain and sometimes demanded victims, according to whether the destructive impulses were retained or projected. As a representative of the mother, either her violent death or her fatal embrace, alike symbolized to the unconscious its dearest wish.

CHAPTER V

RATIONALIZATION AND OVERDETERMINATION

ANY situation which is desired, or feared, or both, is associated with earlier events which excited, often with more justice, the same affects. In analysis these are recalled and shown to have partially determined the emotional character of the present. Thus we say that the present event symbolizes the past, or that the past event is the meaning of the present.

Assuming that the Unconscious exists and is a receptacle for all the forgotten and repudiated ideas and desires of our whole lives, any given present event has a whole hierarchy of different meanings in the different strata of our minds. It is the symbol of all these meanings and is mistaken for them by the several layers of the unconscious. Thus the same event has many interpretations. It is the symbol of many earlier or repressed situations which were desired or feared.

In the last two chapters I have tried to give interpretations of sacrificial rites at the Oedipus and at the post-Oedipus level. In this I shall try to fill up the gaps by giving some account of the meanings of such rites at the pre-Oedipus and the conscious level, that is, at the levels before and after those that have already been considered.

Interpretations other than those that at the moment attract the attention of a psycho-analyst he calls over-determinations or rationalizations according to whether they are in a lower or a higher stratum of the mind to that he is considering. The Oedipus and the post-Oedipus levels are generally supposed to be the most important, and since I believe that complexes at these levels are at least the necessary conditions for sacrificial rites, I have dealt with them first, and have regarded what goes on at the pre-Oedipus and the conscious levels, respectively, as overdeterminations and rationalizations. But, since some have thought that one of these other levels is more important, it is desirable to give an account of them here. This chapter, then, will deal briefly on the one hand with the views of analysts who have speculated upon the early stages of the development of human impulses and on the other with those of pre-analytical anthropologists.

Overdeterminations

It may be that all instincts and their derivatives are themselves derived from an ultimate tendency of the organism to return to the last state of equilibrium from which it was disturbed. For Rank the final situation that we above all desire is the return to the womb from whence we came, the Nirvana, the Paradise of the Golden Age. Everything we seek, from the love of the normal man to the suicide of the melancholic, is a substitute for this situation. The desire for it forms the deepest layer of the unconscious. But this situation that is above all others desired is also above all others feared; for the shock of birth stands between us and our fantasied return. And this same fear even pursues the symbols of this situation, so that we are compelled to seek ever more circuitous routes towards our goal. Thus to the birth trauma we owe our lives, our culture, and our progress. Such is Rank's theory; or rather such is the theory that Rank finds sufficient to explain alike our achievements and our ills.

The child that burns his fingers dreads the fire; for the sight of the flame sets off the avoidance mechanism that was first elicited by the pain. But this reaction may be overdone, and the child may henceforth avoid all bright objects, whether they are hot or cold. Thus the original evoking situation of an avoidance mechanism is itself avoided, and with it much that even irrelevantly resembles it.

If a situation not only involved the greatest of all

traumas, but was also the object of the most fundamental desire, the organism would continually seek, and as continually avoid, it. And this ambivalence would be transferred to all that resembled it; for the desire would ever seek associated ends only to be blocked by the same fear. Unable on account of the avoidance mechanism to seek it directly, the desire would pursue ever more distantly associated ends, which would be likely to be in turn avoided before their harmless nature had been proved by experience.

If Rank is right, the prenatal life, removed as far as possible from stimulus, is such a situation that is above all others desired and above all others feared and avoided. And all our aims in life are but substitutes for this one that is not only physically impossible, but inseparably associated with the trauma of birth. If this end were merely physically impossible compensation could be found in Plato's Eros that in love reunites what was divided. But it is not only impossible, but dreaded. And this dread spreads over all substitutes and forces man to ever wider sublimations, to greater achievements, or to new diseases, that each in turn disappoint his real desire. For it is this trauma of birth that stands between him and the direct road to the death and the absence of all sensation which he really seeks, and that converts the death urge into the life urge from which there is no escape. If, therefore, Rank's theory is correct, every urge is ultimately reducible to the urge to return to the mother and every fear to the shock of birth. The incest desire, which had been observed but inadequately explained, is the desire to return to the womb. And the incest taboo, which Freudians reduced to the fear of the father, is the fear of the maternal vagina. For the first impediment to a fantasied return is the trauma of birth, and the fear of the father, who is the new impediment, is displaced from the fear of this trauma.

If, then, behind the Oedipus complex stands the trauma of birth, sacrifice, like all sublimated activities, must be ultimately a symbolic attempt to break through the trauma and return from whence we came. Thus the last type of sacrifice we have considered, the killing of the son by the mother, may be in reality the prototype. It symbolizes most nearly the return to the womb. For the son god is killed and perhaps eaten by his mother and reborn by her, or he lives as the ruler of the Underworld, which is itself a symbol of the womb. And, as in the rites for the dead, so in initiation ceremonies, the same motive appears, death, or the return to the womb, and rebirth. But it is difficult to trace the eating of a father-symbol to the same source.

Perhaps we may accept the positive conclusions of Rank's theory, many of which were anticipated by Freud, and at the same time feel that he underestimates later events and especially the Oedipus complex. The trauma of birth may be the ultimate anxiety experience of mankind, but it does not follow that it could maintain its importance if it were not revived in the trauma of weaning, in the trauma of the education in cleanliness, in the threat of castration and in the Oedipus complex. Even that dread of mother-symbols, that seems best to support Rank's compact theory, is perhaps due to the combination of two incompatible beliefs, which have been found to play an important part in the development of neuroses. These are: the belief of the child that the mother has a penis, and his knowledge that she has not. The knowledge is associated with the trauma of the threat of castration and is in consequence repressed.[1] The false belief that takes its place converts the mother into a father-substitute and so again into an object of dread. Thus the unconscious revival of either belief revives the dread of castration. The belief that the woman has no penis suggests the possibility of castration. The denial of this belief in a higher stratum turns the mother into a father symbol, and attracts to her that penis envy which, when projected

---

[1] Freud, ' Some Psychological Consequences of the Physiological Difference between the Sexes ', *International Journal of Psycho-Analysis*, viii. 137 ; also ' Fetishism ', *International Journal of Psycho-Analysis*, ix. 161-6.

and inverted, becomes the dreaded desire to emasculate the self.

In the mystic drama where New Guinea novices are swallowed, circumcised, and ejected by the monster Balum ; in the sacrifices of Carthaginian children to Moloch ; in the myth of the Maori hero who was bitten in two by his ancestress Hine-nui-te-po, into whose mouth he had to crawl before he could win immortality for mankind ; and in the legends of the seeking of immortality by a dangerous journey to a Hades in the bowels of the earth ; in all these there is a symbolic return to the womb. And this symbolic return is realized in the fantasy of those who listen to the legend or the myth, or who witness and execute the sacrifice or drama ; and even by their victims.

But the doom which is inevitably associated with this desire seems less directly the repetition of the trauma of birth than the symbolic realization of the castration fear. Thus, though certain fantasies and rites may be pleasurable and have survived because they recall the dimly remembered state of prenatal bliss, it seems likely that their terror is derived mainly from that fear of castration which became acute when the incestuous aim was first discovered as a substitute for the loss of the protecting womb.

But perhaps even this concession to the Rankian view is premature. It is still difficult to decide whether there is a fundamental desire to return to the womb from which, by the substitution of similar ends, all other desires have been derived ; or whether fantasies which seem to have this content are not substitutes for a forgotten, or undiscovered, genital and incestuous aim. In short, we do not know whether the desire for incest, by substituting a part for the whole, is a symbol of a desire to return to the prenatal state, or whether the fantasy of returning to this condition, by the substitution of the whole for a part, is a symbolic incest. If the prenatal aim is really fundamental it ought to be possible to show that the oral and the anal stages of libidinal development, as well as the genital stage, can be plausibly derived from it. This deduction has not, so far as I am aware, been attempted. Upon its success must depend, to some extent, our belief in the desire to be de-born.

Of the later pre-Oedipean impulses our knowledge is far more secure. Analysts, we know, have divided the development of the sexual impulse into three main stages, the oral, the anal, and the genital. Through each of these first two stages the individual should pass. But each is a point at which he may remain fixed, or to which he may return, if the Oedipus complex, which culminates in the genital phase, inhibits, or represses, the normal growth. Characteristic of each stage are a set of sublimations and reaction formations which determine for the analyst the libidinal age of those with whom he comes in contact. But the character of the individual who has returned to an early stage is not the same as that of him who has never left it. For a position once gained leaves its mark even on those who have been forced to evacuate it. Thus the habitual reactions of neurotic, or pervert, individuals are often, in matter, oral or anal derivatives, while their form retains the Oedipean structure of the genital level. It seems likely that the same is true of the rites and customs of primitive and ancient peoples.

It is obvious that in all those forms of sacrifice in which the victim is eaten, oral elements play a part. And in order to reconstruct, as far as possible, the history of this part it will be desirable to acquaint ourselves with the observations and theories of analysts on the origin and development of oral erotism.[1] But first it will be necessary to say something about the relation of eroticism to libido.[2]

Sexual hunger, or libido, is probably the psychical correlate of the mechanical or chemical action of

[1] For analytical views on oral erotism, see Starke, *International Journal of Psycho-Analysis*, ii. 179 ; Glover, vi., Part 2 ; Abraham, vi., Part 3. Freud, *Drei Abhandlungen zur Sexualtheorie*, 5. Aufl. 45, 62.
[2] Freud, *Drei Abhandlungen*, 5. Aufl. 74.

certain substances, such as the seminal fluid, upon the receptors of the glands that contain them, or upon those of the blood-vessels into which they are discharged. Some, or all, of these substances seem to be partially active from infancy, since libido is already present at this period. But only at the time of puberty is their action complete. And, we may suppose, that only from this period can this action be periodically terminated by an orgasm.

The orgasm, however, does not occur merely when the sex fluids have accumulated to a certain point. It requires an elaborate mechanism which secures, or should secure, its occurrence only at appropriate moments. For this purpose certain zones have acquired the property that their stimulus, like the scratch that relieves the itch only to increase it, augments the sexual tension until this is terminated with the complete orgasm. Such zones are misnamed erotogenic, for they do not create desire in the absence of the stimulus of the sex fluids; they only relieve and increase it when it is already there. They are snares which Nature has placed in the individual for her ends. Contact with them first gives pleasure, that is, it decreases a need. But this pleasure is immediately followed by an increased need to which relief is sought in the same manner. And in this way the rhythmical process of tumescence brings the tension to the critical point at which it finally discharges. But before puberty the orgasm is impossible and the stimulus of erotogenic zones can only increase a sexual need without securing it a final relief.

Such zones, however, are not limited to the region of the genitals. In fact, it is probable that any part of the skin can become erotogenic. But the zones which appear to be the most important are the lips, the anus, and the genitals. These seem to develop their erotogenicity in this order, and to give rise in turn to the three stages of libidinal evolution, the oral, the anal, and the genital.

Taste receptors bear to hunger much the same relation as erotogenic zones to libido. The appropriate stimulus of either increases need, and this arrangement was probably evolved by selection, since it secures that the need should usually only become urgent in situations where it is likely to be relieved to the advantage of the race. This resemblance of erotogenic zones to taste receptors suggests that it may be desirable to generalize the concept and devote a word to qualify a zone the stimulus of which increases any periodic natural want. I would propose the English adjective 'need-increasing,' or, if it is preferred, some Greco-Latin equivalent.

The same zone may be 'need-increasing' to more than one need. And to this fact is perhaps due the early development of oral eroticism. For the same stimulus of sucking that increases hunger seems to awaken a dormant sexual need, to which complete satisfaction is as yet impossible, but which is rhythmically relieved and increased by the act of sucking. Hence sucking becomes a persistent unsatisfiable activity, independent of hunger, and the main preoccupation of the infant. Like Sisyphus, he cannot abandon an attempt because he cannot complete it. But when he is a grown man on the genital level of development his libido, increased by the stimulus of kissing, will no longer secure the endless repetition of this oral act; for it will be relieved in the act of coitus. To arrive, however, unhindered at the genital level of libidinal development is rare, especially for the savage. Often he is a mass of inhibitions, so that a great part of his libido finds no final outlet, but returns to, or persists in, infantile aims which increase more than they relieve it. But the pregenital aims of the inhibited adult are only partly the same as those of the child. For they are substitutes for half-discovered or forgotten genital aims as well as repetitions of the pregenital desires of infancy. Thus, in primitive peoples, as in neurotics, we should expect to find many activities in which, though the form is derived from the Oedipus complex, the content is pregenital and perhaps pre-Oedipean.

Such a condition seems to be well illustrated in the primitive totem sacrament, in which the clan destroys by eating an animal which is a symbol of a father who was both loved and hated. For the same act at once satisfies the hate by obliterating its object and the love by orally incorporating it. In this act the love and hate which have for so long developed independently regress to their common source in the second oral phase when the child first learns that the object from which he derives his sustenance and pleasure is not under his sole control. The world is henceforth divided into the me and not-me. And the ambivalence that commenced with this knowledge is perhaps ultimately the expression of the desire to obliterate the not-me and to reunite it with the me. If so, it is a product of that insecurity which is the lasting scar of life's first great disappointments. For in the beginning that which fulfils hope is me and that which disappoints is not-me ; and this is the first distinction between image and sensation, between the internal and the external world.

Next after the oral phase analysts distinguish an anal phase of libidinal development.[1] The anal like the oral zone is erotogenic. Its stimulation both excites and relieves libidinal tension. Thus the functions of this zone soon become an important preoccupation of the child. And, perhaps because the loss of the objects that stimulate this zone terminates the pleasure without relieving the sexual component of the need, the child soon learns to resent parting from his anal products. Like the nipple or the finger that stimulates another zone their loss is a threat of aphanisis. It is resisted and feared ; that is, these objects become articles of value. But the child will give them up in exchange for something that he wants still more —for the love of his nurse or mother whom he has

[1] Freud, *Drei Abhandlungen*, 5. Aufl. 50 *sq*.

already learnt to value in the oral phase. Sometimes, if he performs when and as he should he is praised and petted ; and when he refuses to do so he is blamed. In this way he learns to make the first gift, which is really an exchange of faeces for love.[1] He is induced to give them up in order to regain attentions that he needs still more. And if he later becomes inhibited and reverts to the anal level he will ever after react to an estrangement to a loved object that is necessary to him with gifts. He will bring chocolates to soothe his outraged mistress, or victims to the altar of a jealous god.

If such views are correct, and they are founded upon actual analyses, those forms of sacrifice in which the idea of a gift is present must be determined largely by reversion to the anal level. But in spite of this reversion the form of some mode of reaction to the Oedipus complex is still retained. The victim, in so far as it is a gift, stands for the self in the place of the father. The destructive impulse is turned inwards and is akin more to suicide than parricide. Yet it is not purely self-destructive. It destroys a part only of the self in order that a lost love may be regained. That is, it operates in the manner of the anal gift.

The sacrifice of children, especially, seems often to be dictated by this regression. It is known that the love of dolls and the desire to have children is one of the earliest derivatives of the desire to retain the products of the anal function. And when primitive or ancient peoples have brought their children in sacrifice to a god or goddess in return for benefits to come they are only repeating the act of the infant who barters faeces for love.

---

[1] Perhaps largely for this reason the tender feeling of receiving love is ever after tinged with a mysterious sense of loss. That such a sense of loss is really included in the tender emotion of receiving love is shown in Shand's admirable analysis of gratitude. True, he thinks that the sense of loss is sympathy with the loss to the person who receives gratitude for love. But we must have felt loss in giving before we can attribute it to others. Stout, *Groundwork of Psychology*, ch. xvi., by A. F. Shand; Ernest Jones, *Papers*, 2nd ed., 684; Freud, *Drei Abhandlungen zur Sexualtheorie*, 5. Aufl. 52 ; Abraham, ' Contributions to the theory of the Anal Character ', *International Journal of Psycho-Analysis*, iv. 406.

Sometimes, indeed, the reversion seems to be complete. Thus the Tongans, at the funeral of their sacred kings, held a singular rite, which seems to have no other explanation. 'While the conches were sounding and the voices of the singers broke the silence of night, about sixty men assembled before the grave, where they awaited further orders. When the chanting was over, and the notes of the conches had ceased to sound, one of the women mourners came forward, and sitting down outside the graveyard, addressed the men thus : "Men ! ye are gathered here to perform the duty imposed on you ; bear up, and let not your exertions be wanting to accomplish the work." With these words she retired into the burial-ground. The men now approached the mound in the dark, and, in the words of Mariner, or of his editor, performed their devotions to Cloacina, after which they withdrew.'[1] When we remember the extraordinary regard which such savages usually possess for their excreta, which is, with other bodily products, hidden to prevent its misuse by a sorcerer, it is less difficult to appreciate to what extent they are fixed at the anal level, and to understand how they can devote their faeces as an offering to the divine dead. For, though they may have rationalized their custom, it can hardly have had a different unconscious purpose.

Rationalizations

Sacrifices have usually been classified according to the conscious motives of those who practised them. To the psycho-analyst such motives are rationalizations. But they are not necessarily unimportant. If a symbolic action cannot be rationalized, the unconscious may have to try some other form of self-expression. And, further, the avowed meaning is often itself but a distorted version of the unconscious purpose.

The *Encyclopaedia Britannica* (11th ed.) gives a

[1] Frazer, *Belief in Immortality*, ii. 143.

classification of sacrifices according to the conscious, or at least semi-conscious, motives of the sacrificers which may form a basis for a short discussion of these motives.

(i) *Communal Sacrifice.*—In this sacrifice the victim which is sacred, or divine, is consumed by the community. Its purpose is to establish, or re-establish, kinship with the god (Robertson Smith), or to incorporate the sanctity which has been imparted to the victim.

Here the conscious purpose is part only of the unconscious purpose. Unconsciously the sacrificers desire to destroy and to become their fathers. Consciously they destroy a god; but they do not desire to destroy him; they regard his death as a sad necessity. But they are aware that they desire to incorporate the virtues of the god, or at least to identify themselves with him in kinship.

(ii) *Deificatory Sacrifice.*—This type of sacrifice is said to provide a tutelary deity, or to prolong or strengthen the life of a god already in existence. ' In Burma, as in many other countries, those who die a violent death are held to haunt the place where they met their fate; consequently when a town is built living men are interred beneath the ramparts and the pillars of the gates. . . . Gods may be sacrificed (in the theriomorphic form) to themselves as a means of renewing the life of the god.'[1] These two types of deificatory sacrifice seem to be psychologically distinct, so that we will consider them separately.

It is difficult to believe that the desire to convert the soul of a victim into a guardian angel can have been an original motive for any sacrifice. Westermarck thinks that such rites were once expiatory, and this seems the reasonable view. If it is right, the unconscious motive must have been inverted hostile feelings which were diverted from the self to a vicarious object. Such feelings are apt to arise before wars or other un-

---

[1] Robertson Smith, ' Sacrifice ', *Encyclopaedia Britannica*, 11th ed.

dertakings that symbolize the attack upon the father, and are apt to express themselves in rites of expiation. Similarly, I suppose that primitive man regarded any building, like the tower of Babel, as a challenge to some spirit, and felt compelled to expiate his act. But, since the unconscious hostility was originally directed against this spirit and was diverted from him to a vicarious substitute for the self, it is natural that the victim and the spirit to whom it was offered should have been confounded. In this way might develop the belief that the spirit and the ghost of the victim were one, and the rationalization that the guardian was created by sacrifice.

The second type of deificatory sacrifice, in which a god is sacrificed to himself in order to prolong his life, is typical of the attempt of a puzzled and disappointed love to attribute to itself an act of unconsciously motivated hate. The worshippers desire their god to live for ever, yet they destroy him. Therefore they say that they destroy him in order that he may live for ever. It is not wonderful that Frazer has found it difficult to show that the acts of such peoples are rational according to their lights.

(iii) *Mortuary Sacrifice.*—There are four avowed purposes for this type of sacrifice mentioned in the *Encyclopaedia Britannica*. These are '(*a*) to provide a guide to the other world ; (*b*) to provide the dead with servants or retinue suitable to his rank ; (*c*) to send messengers to keep the dead informed of the things of this world ; (*d*) to strengthen the dead by the blood or life of a living being, in the same way that food is offered to them or blood rituals enjoined on mourners.'

In an age when life was cheap some of these motives might have been alone sufficient to perpetuate customary sacrifices ; but, if I am right, such motives did not originate the rites they purport to explain. After the murder of Ombure by his son Ngurangurane, Ngurangurane offered sacrifices to his father which at once repeated and expiated the crime. Primitive people do not regard death as an accident ; it is for them always the work of some evil spirit or wizard. And this wizard is the projection of the mourner's own unconscious. Therefore the mourner himself deserves to die. Sometimes he does die, but more often he finds a substitute. In other words, after the death of a loved relation the unconscious ambivalence becomes more intense. Love will not accept the fact of death, and hate, which is thus thwarted, becomes more urgent. It cannot find its first object. Therefore, it turns upon the murderer, who by his act often introjects his victim. But this murderer, who is an evil spirit, is the projection of the mourner's own unconscious, so that the mourner is himself in danger from his own unconscious hate. He may save himself by a vicarious expiation. But this whole process is unconscious, so that the sacrificer explains his act in terms of the current rationalization. Often neither the rationalization nor the unconscious motive would be a sufficient condition for mortuary rites. Both are necessary. Without the unconscious motive there would be no conflict to work off in action. Without the rationalization this conflict might have to find some other solution. In an age that is without gods or superstitions the only outlet is often the neurosis.

(iv) *Piacular Sacrifice.*—Here a victim, which is perhaps an avowed substitute for the sacrificer, is offered to save him from the wrath of a god. This type of sacrifice differs from the mortuary and from one form of the deificatory rite in that the motive is more conscious. The offerer is aware, or almost aware, that the victim is a substitute for himself. Unconscious only is the fact that the wrath of the god, that is so much feared, is the projection of the worshipper's own hate of the father who is symbolized by the god. This hate is conscious but disowned.

(v) *Cathartic Sacrifice.*—This type of sacrifice was supposed to eliminate sin and disease, or excessive holiness. Here, as everywhere in primitive thought, three concepts that are to us incompatible appear as almost identical. To remove sin, two goats were taken; one, after the sins of the tribe were confessed over it, was driven into the wilderness; the other was slain as a sin offering. To cure leprosy, two birds were taken; one was let loose to carry away the disease; the other was sacrificed. To eliminate an excessive holiness, dangerous to the cattle associated with Rhudra, a bull was sacrificed to him.

What is taboo, or sinful, is to sit in the throne of Zeus and brandish his lightning, to eat or touch the food of the chief, to possess his wives, to touch the property of God, in short to become, or to usurp the place of, the father. It is perhaps bold to generalize from so few examples, but we may admit as an hypothesis, which we have not the space to prove, that the fundamental sin is to covet the place of an Imago. And this view is in accordance with the findings of psychoanalysis. But from analysis we know further that it is dangerous to introject someone who is hated; for to do so is to turn the hate against the self. Thus sin is dangerous because in it the self identifies himself with the father and attracts to himself his own envy. Thus the breaker of taboo feels that he has within him something that has possessed him and from which he must at all costs free himself before he is destroyed. And thus also uncleanliness and excessive holiness are identical and alike fatal; for they are the result of dangerous introjections.

This analysis of the danger of sin is supported by the study of melancholics who are often convinced that they have committed the unforgivable offence and that they are damned without hope of salvation. Psycho-analysis. has shown that they hate, and often destroy, themselves, because they unconsciously believe themselves to be a former object of intensely ambivalent feelings. They have introjected their fathers, sometimes their mothers, without having previously reconciled themselves with them.

If this interpretation of the destroying power of sin is once accepted it should not be hard to understand the mechanism of cathartic rites. A ceremony is performed to suggest to the sinner that the devil he has introjected is reprojected on to some new symbol. In the cathartic sacrifice the substitute is killed. In other rites it is simply driven away. In the best-known Jewish ceremonies both forms were combined: two goats were taken; one was slain and the other driven into the wilderness. But it was only the goat that was driven away that bore the sins of the people. Thus there was a sort of double purification. First the sins were transferred to one goat. And then, perhaps because this goat was still too nearly identified with the people, or with a son god, another was taken to die in its place.

Those who partook in such rites were aware only that there was something within them that attracted a remorseless and undying hate, and that this something must be removed or they would surely perish. They did not know that this hate was their own hate of their fathers, nor that it had turned upon them because they had gratified in unconscious fantasy their desire to be its object.

(vi) *Honorific Sacrifice.*—In this type of sacrifice gifts are not offered because the god is thought to need them, but because the worshippers desire to honour him and to show their gratitude. This, according to Iranaeus, should be the sole motive of the Christian who offers the first fruits to God.[1] The desire to honour and to express gratitude is complex. It is perhaps mildly masochistic, the destruction of a part of the self for love. But I do not suggest that it is morbid; for there is perhaps an element of masochism in all love. All human relationships are to some extent ambivalent, and where love protects its object, a certain amount of aggressiveness is likely to be turned against the self.

[1] Hatch, ' The Idea of Sacrifice in the Christian Church ', *Encyclopaedia Britannica*, 11th ed.

Thus in love there is a loss to the self—a loss that is masochistically enjoyed. And love readily expresses itself in gifts.[1] But to the unconscious the gift is often the most valuable part of the self, so that it can symbolize self-destruction or self-mutilation. I do not suggest that all honorific sacrifices are rationalizations of unconscious inverted impulses. Often the rationalized motive and custom would be alone sufficient. But there is little doubt that to the deeply religious the gift symbolizes the inverted act of complete self-abnegation.

Sacrifice of the Vegetation-Spirit.—A discussion of the rationalizations of sacrifice, however short, would be incomplete without some mention of the killing of vegetation spirits. Such rites have become prominent in recent times through the work of Frazer. They are distinct from communal sacrifices ; for the victim is a son god rather than a father god, and he is not necessarily eaten. Because they were supposed to assist agriculture Frazer has correctly classified them as magical, but I think that Westermarck is also right in believing that they were piacular.

The earth from which all plants sprang was the Great Mother Goddess of primitive religion, and the vegetation which she brought forth, and from whose seed she was fertilized, was her divine, and incestuous, son. Thus guilty forebodings awoke in the minds of the primitive cultivators when they assisted in that act of the Vegetation-Spirit which awoke their own unconscious wishes. Unless the sinner were slain the crops would surely fail, or some other evil would fall upon them, and, mainly for this reason, they took a victim who personified the Son God and caused him to die, for their sins as well as his. Thus began the sacrifice of deities, like Attis, Adonis, and Osiris, whose cults contributed to the interpretation of the death of Christ.

In conclusion, an attempt may be made to appor-

[1] See section on Overdetermination.

tion the responsibility for sacrificial rites between three factors. These are the innate dispositions of man, the early experience of the child, and the example and sanction of cultural contact or tradition.

The innate disposition is the disposition to incestuous wishes and the disposition to hate any object that thwarts desire. The early experience is the experience that develops a child's Oedipus complex. And the example and sanction of cultural contact or tradition is the example and sanction of existing sacrificial rites.

Without an innate disposition it is unlikely that the Oedipus complex would be general, and if it were not general it would not return symbolically in social acts. Without an infancy that developed this complex, and perpetuated it in the Unconscious, the example of a custom would not long be followed. And without the example and sanction of an existing custom repression might not permit the expression of an unconscious ambivalence in any form of sacrificial rite. But, where tradition or cultural contact provides an example of symbolic parricide, repression is reduced in a given direction and the form of expression of the unconscious ambivalence determined.

Thus I believe that while the energy necessary for sacrificial rites is derived from the Oedipus complex, which is the product of innate disposition and early experience, the direction in which this energy will find an outlet is determined by the example of existing cults. To determine a given rite all three factors would seem severally necessary and collectively sufficient.

ABSTRACT

Part I

THE ORIGIN AND DEVELOPMENT OF THE OEDIPUS COMPLEX

I. *The Unconscious*

It is logically possible, and it is convenient, to assume the existence of unconscious thoughts. But it is compatible with pyscho-analytic theory to substitute for such thoughts the concept of inhibited potential thoughts.

II. *Incest and Parricide*

Interpretation of neurotic symptoms, dreams, and literary productions disclose unconscious incestuous and parricidal desires, which may be due to the long infancy of the human child. Such impulses have been realized occasionally in history and probably habitually in primeval times.

III. *Origin and Maintenance of Repression*

External competition enforces internal co-operation. Love of mothers may have been transferred to threatened hunting grounds and to protecting fathers. Hate of fathers may have been transferred to new foes. Love of fathers once acquired would survive the conditions that provoked it. Sons who have loved their fathers transfer these feelings to their sons, who reciprocate this affection and in turn transfer it to the next generation. But it is probable that repression has not become innate, and that it would be lost if the transference series were broken.

IV. and V. *Ambivalence and Inferiority; The Resolution of Ambivalence*

The ambivalence of love and unconscious hate may produce a sense of impotence, which is terminated either by the death of the father and his introjection, by an inversion towards him, or by a compromise between these two solutions.

VI. *The Return of the Oedipus Complex*

The Oedipus situation of childhood may return with new actors. The rôle of the father may be played by substitutes, such as the chief, the totem, or the god.

Part II

THE MEANING OF SACRIFICE

I. *The Distribution of Sacrifice*

Sacrifice has occurred in many forms among all the peoples of the world. (In China, Japan, etc., and among primitive peoples.) To avoid the selection of examples that fit a preconceived theory, it is desirable at first to arrange them according to the peoples that practised them, rather than according to any supposed similarities between the rites themselves. But in describing the sacrifices of primitive peoples as a whole, it is necessary to introduce some inherent classification. Thus sacrifices may be divided into four types according to the rôle played by a supernatural being: Sacrifices of him, sacrifices to him, sacrifices for him, and miscellaneous rites of destruction.

II. *The Theories of Sacrifice*

For Tylor sacrifice is a gift made to the soul of a person or object, or to the spirit of a personified cause. For Robertson Smith it is a communion which establishes or re-establishes the kinship between the worshipper and his god. Frazer sees in it a form of imitative magic, in which, for example, the sacrificer kills the corn spirit incarnate in a victim to preserve it from decay. Westermarck stresses the idea of the substitution of a victim for the worshipper who has incurred the wrath of the gods. Hubert and Mauss think that the victim is an intermediary between the worshipper and the dangerous forces of the supernatural world. Loisy sees in the various types of sacrifice different combinations of the ritual gift and the magical and symbolic rite of destruction either to acquire something desirable or to eliminate an ill. Common to all these theories is the attempt to reconstruct the conscious purpose that originally provoked the rite. But Freud, for the first time introducing the concept of the unconscious and fresh from the discovery of parricidal tendencies, sees in the sacrifice of the totem animal the unconscious repetition of a primeval crime.

III. *The Essence of Sacrifice*

Those who are acquainted with psycho-analysis cannot doubt that in some sense sacrifice is related to parricide. But the words repetition and commemoration used by Freud either give no adequate explanation of the motive for this repetition, or they imply a racial mind and the inheritance of acquired memory. This assumption is dangerous, since it is not supported by biology. It is, further, unnecessary if a psycho-analytic explanation of sacrifice is possible without it. Such an explanation would seem to be already implicit in Freud's writings; for sacrifice may be regarded, less as the result of a primeval crime, than as the symbolic expression of an unconscious desire for parricide which each individual has himself acquired.

IV. *The Modes of Sacrifice*

The above theory of sacrifice so far applies only to the slaughter of obvious father-substitutes such as totems and divine kings. But by a process of projection and substitution the original parricidal desires may easily be directed towards, or attributed to, other members of the family. Thus, starting from the triangular family of father, mother, and son, nine variants of the Oedipus fantasy of killing the father occur. And it is probable that each of these has been expressed symbolically in sacrifice.

V. *Rationalization and Overdetermination*

The same act may satisfy different impulses at different levels of the mind. Meanings of sacrifice in levels below and above the Oedipus level can be called respectively Overdeterminations and Rationalizations. Among such Overdeterminations of sacrifice may be mentioned an apparent desire to return to the prenatal state, together with the oral and anal pregenital impulses of infancy. Rationalizations, too, may have contributed to perpetuate sacrificial rites, and such motives have been discovered in abundance by pre-psychoanalytical anthropologists. Finally, it is desirable to apportion the responsibility for varieties of sacrifice between the three factors: innate disposition, early environment, and cultural contact or tradition. Probably each is necessary, but none alone sufficient.

INDEX

Abraham—
  on inbreeding, 26-7
  on Amenhotep IV., 65
  on oral eroticism, 244
  on the anal character, 248
Abraham and Isaac, the legend of, compared with the sacrifice of Thessalian kings, 112
Abu Nerus, a deputy Pharaoh, 86
Acosta, on sacrifice in Mexico, 141
Acropolis, Aglauros' jump from, 117
Adonis—
  phallic attributes of, 60
  a Semitic god, 91
  his development from victim to recipient of sacrifice, 93
  his rites compared with rites of Gonds, 97
  as the lover of Aphrodite, 116
  his legend compared with the legend of Persephone, 117
  his sacrifice as a son-god, 233
  sacrifice of, 237
  analysis of sacrifice of, 255
Aelian, on impregnation of Jewish maid by serpent, 62
Aesculapius, worshipped as a serpent, 62
Agamemnon and Clytemnestra, their legend illustrates fantasy of son and mother killing father, 233
Agdestis—
  a double of Attis, 119
  Attis reborn from, 125, 210
Aglauros, worshipped in Cyprus, 117
Agrionia, a festival of Dionysus, 124
Ahriman, sacrifices made to, 102
Akikuyu, rites of circumcision and rebirth among, 161
Aknaton, his belief in an impersonal god, 65
Alcibiades, accusations of incest against, 25
Alexander—
  on weaning and education of sphincters, 41

Alexander (contd.)—
  on dread of castration, 43
Alexander the Great, supposed to be the child of a serpent, 62
Alkathous, his sacrifice of his son, 121
Altar—
  of earth in China, 73
  ancestral tablet kept on, in China, 75
  burnt offerings on, at Chinese feasts of dead, 76
  in Japanese house, 78
  sacrifice of virility at, of Cybele, 102
  Cronus-Israel sacrificed son on, 109
  King Lycaeon sacrificed child on, to Zeus, 110
  barley cakes laid on, at Bouphonia, 111
  Kings of Thessaly sacrifice sons on, of Laphystian Zeus, 112
  flagellation of Spartan youths before, of Artemis, 114
  Ancient, to Faunalia Rustica, 132
  Mexican gods sacrificed on stone, 141-6
  Beduin sacrifice of camel on, 149
Ambarvalia, procession of victims at, 131
Ambivalence—
  towards father, 37 ff., 188-9, 193
  resolution of, 49 ff.
  unconscious, 252, 256
  in mortuary sacrifice, 252
Amenhotep, IV., 65
Anal eroticism, 20
  impulse to give partly derived from, 231, 247
Ancestor worship—
  in China, 73 ff.
  at Parentalia, 134-5
Animism, 165
Anna Kurari—
  human sacrifice to, 98
  boys sacrificed to, 237

262 INDEX

Anwyl—
  on concealment of children from their fathers, 318
  on human sacrifice caused by economic pressure, 141
Apepi—
  destruction of, 90-91
  hatred of, 215
Aphrodite—
  her connection with sacred stones, 60
  the similarity of her cult with that of Hera, 112
  rites of, 116
  sacrifice of chastity to, 125, 237
Apollo—
  katharmata sacrificed to, 114
  festivals of, 120-22
  attributes of, 122
  sacrifice of a god in rites of, 125
Ares, slaughter of Adonis by, 117
Aristomenes, legend that he was begotten by a snake, 62
Armenia, sacrifice of virginity in, 116
Artemis—
  her affinity with totems, 113
  -Agrotera, goat sacrifice to, 113
  -Brauronia, 113-14
  a goddess of childbirth, 116
  sacrifices of and to, 125, 224
  holocausts offered to, 237
Ashurbanipal, his sacrifice to Sennacherib, 97
Astarte—
  phallic emblems of, 6
  a Semitic goddess, 91
  compared with Artemis, 113
  compared with Demeter, 117
  son-sacrifice to, 237
Athens, Ge worshipped at, 117
Atkinson, on behaviour of primeval man, 32, 189
Attis—
  phallic attributes of, 60
  as a Semitic god, 91
  his development from victim to recipient of sacrifice, 93
  his rites compared with rites in India, 97
  his legend compared with legend of Persephone, 117
  the commemoration of his death and resurrection, 118
  blood given to, 125

Attis (*contd.*)—
  conception of, 210
  as Father-god, 221
  his sacrifice as a son-god, 233, 237
  the interpretation of the sacrifice of, 255
Augustus, the legend that he was the son of the serpent of Apollo, 62

Ball, Dyer, on human sacrifice, 77
Balum, New Guinea initiation ceremonies of, 243
Bantu, representation of ancestors by phallic symbols among, 63
Barbar Archipelago, phallic symbols erected at feasts in, 61
Baudelaire, incestuous fixation of, 25
Beardless One, ride of, in Persian feast, 103
Bechuanas, purification after manslaughter among, 162
Birth-trauma—
  a cause of later anxiety, 41
  in funeral rites and suicide, 228-229
  its connection with the sacrifice of son-gods, 240-41
  rebirth, symbolized in rites, 163
Blood—
  of victim used in Chinese contracts, 78
  temples and royal ornaments consecrated with, 79
  offered to gods of nature in China, 80
  offered on graves in Japan, 81
  of black dog used to procure rain, 81
  of bear drunk by Ainos, 83
  human, scattered on fields in India, 98
  of victims sucked by Kali, 99
  from woman's breast offered to Kali, 101
  of wolf offered to Ahriman, 102
  offered to Cybele, 109
  offered to Attis, 126
  of winning horse in race at Regia, 132
  youths smeared with, in Lupercalia, 134

INDEX

Blood (*contd.*)—
  boundary stones sprinkled with, in Terminalia, 135
  of Christians drunk by Slavonic priest, 136
  offered to Mexican maize-goddess, 144-5
  poured on ground in Australia, 148
  sacrifices of, 154-7
  used in expiation, 184
  poured over statue of Ombure, 226
Blood feud, compared to human sacrifice, 181
Blood offering, made by Dieri men to corpses, 160
Bloodless sacrifice, 157
Bona-Dea—
  fertility sacrifice to, 128
  temple dedicated to, 130
Boniface, apostle to Germans, 140
Botocidos, enemies eaten by, 197
Bouphonia—
  sacrifice of ox at, 111
  compared with Poplifugia, 131
Breasted, on Egyptian kings feasting on gods, 89
Brückner—
  on Slav harvest festivals, 136
  on Slav funeral, 137
Buddha, The, an example of the conquest of desire, 195
Buddhist monks, the suicide by burning of, 228
Burrows, on snake symbolism in Crete, 95

Cannibalism—
  the eating of defeated enemies among Slavs, 138-9
  its practice to cause conception, 210
Castration—
  fear of, 40 ff.
  its relation to Oedipus complex, 45
  self inflicted, 91, 230
  of Siva by Kali, 101
  of the Beardless One, 104
  of Cronus, 105-6
  symbolized in initiation rites, 107, 218
  its relation to sacrifice, 109
  in rites of Cybele, 119

Castration (*contd.*)—
  associated with rites of goddesses, 223-4
  threat of, 242
Celts, children forbidden to approach father armed among, 31
Ceres, Roman fertility rites of, 128
Cerialia, burning brands fastened to foxes at, 128-9
Christ—
  legend that he was begotten by a serpent, 62
  his connection with Semitic son-gods, 91
  the redemption of world by, 184
  his commemoration in the communion, 190
  the interpretation of the sacrifice of, 255
Cinteotl, sacrifice and festival of, 144-5
Circumcision—
  as a sacrifice, 155, 230
  to ensure rebirth, 161
  as a substitute for castration, 161
Clotha, incestuous marriage of, 25
Compulsive repetition, 189-90
Conflict—
  between love and hate, 65
  Spinoza's solution of, 67-8
Conklin, on foundling fantasy, 56
Continuity, of adult mind with that of child, 16-17
Corn Spirit, sacrifice of, 175
Crawley, on formation of primeval family, 32
Croesus, his suicide by fire, 232
Cronus—
  myth of, 105-9
  in myth of Dionysus, 122
  sacrifice of, 124
Cybele—
  a Semitic goddess, 91
  sacrifice of virility at altar of, 102, 125, 155, 230
  compared with Artemis, 103
  her ritual, 118
  sacrifice of son-gods to, 237
Cyclopean family, 238

Darwin, cited in support of theory of primeval parricide, 32, 186
Daly, on Kali, 100

INDEX

Dead—
  offerings to, 159
  their reincarnation in snakes, 63 n. 2
  ceremonies for, in China, 75-6
  ceremonies for, in Egypt, 87-8
  driven away after feast of all souls in Japan, 82
Delphi, Ge worshipped at, 117
Demeter, drama of, 117
Descartes, *Meditations* of, 67
Destruction of self, unconscious fantasy of, 224-31
Dido—
  sacrifice of, 94
  symbolism of sacrifice of, 236
Dieri—
  fire made on graves by, 159
  blood offered to ancestor by, 160
Dies parentales, sacrifice to family ghosts on, 133
Dionysus, myth and cult of, 122-5
Distortion, in Slav myth of origin of funeral rites, 197-8
Domitian, suspicious nature of, 219
Don Carlos, incest motive in, 24
Dostoevsky, illustration of introjection in novel of, 55
Dream—
  as disguised expression of unconscious thought, 17
  as wish fulfilment, 57
  phallic symbolism in, 63
Duncan, his murder by Lady Macbeth symbolizes murder of father by mother, 232
Duruy, on consolidation of society through war, 33

East and Jones, on inbreeding and outbreeding, 26
Eleusinian mysteries, drama of Demeter in, 117
Encyclopaedia Britannica, classification of sacrifice, in, 249
Ergamenes, his refusal to commit suicide, 153
Erechtheus, his cult fused with that of Poseidon, 120
Eros, Plato's conception of, 241
Erotic impulses—
  oral and genital, 21, 43
  child to his mother, 22
  inversion of, 228-9

Euripides, Dionysiac rites in 'Bacchae' of, 123
Eustathius, on self-castration of Egyptian priests, 230
Ewe Negroes, first-fruits offered by, 152
Exogamy, institution of, 186, 191, 203

Farnell—
  on identification of Cronus and Moloch, 106
  on King Lycaeon, 110
  on ritual of Bouphonia, 112
  on Hera, 112
  on ritual of Artemis, 113-15
  on conical stone as symbol of Aphrodite, 116
  on ritual of Ge, 117
  on the Thesmophoria, 117
  on Eleusinian mysteries, 118
  on rites of Poseidon, 120
  on rites of Apollo, 122
  on rites of Dionysus, 123-25
Father Imago, projection of, into animal, 188
Faunalia Rustica, Roman farmers propitiatory sacrifice at, 132-3
Fear—
  its relation to unconscious wishes, 42
  of loss of mother, 43
  of castration, 44
Ferenczi—
  on Ice Age and the origin of repression, 33
  his Lamarckianism, 190
Feriae Latinae, a festival uniting the Latin race, 130
Fertility rites—
  at festival of Dionysus, 122-5
  struggle for horses' head in Roman, 132
  eating phallic symbol in, 110
First-fruits, feast of, in Japan, 80
Finow, mourning at death of, 156
Firmicus Maternus, on Dionysiac rites of Cretans, 123
Flagellation, of Spartan ephebi at altar of Artemis, 114
Flaminica Dialis, at festival of drowning rush images, 131
Florenz—
  on sacrifice in Japan, 79

INDEX

Florenz (*contd.*)—
  on human sacrifice, 80
Flügel—
  Study of the Family, 26
  on guilt, 205
Fordicidia, fertility sacrifice at, 128
Foutin, St., an ithyphallic saint, 62
Fowler, on Roman festivals, 126, 127-35
Franke, on Chinese rites, 73-8
Frazer—
  on Nyakang, 58-9
  on totemic gods of Egypt, 60
  on conception by snakes, 63
  on images carried through fire, 74
  on drowning of maiden in Yellow River, 77
  on Chinese man-eaters, 78
  on sacrifice for rain in Japan, 81
  on punishment of god for drought, 82
  on Ainos bear sacrifice, 83
  on myth of Osiris, 84
  on sacrifice of geese and gazelles as enemies of Osiris, 85
  on feast of Sed, 86-7
  on myth of Ra and Isis, 88
  on flight of Egyptian embalmer, 89
  on sacrifice to rivers, 89
  on ceremony of sun-god, 90
  on cult of mother and slain son, 91, 94
  on personification of gods by Semitic and Sumerian kings, 92
  on ritual of Attis, 92
  on sacrifice of first-born, 93
  on legends of Dido and Semiramis, 95
  on human sacrifice in India, 98
  on parallel between Kali and Astarte, 101
  on eunuchs dedicated to an Indian goddess, 102
  on Persian burial customs, 103
  on Beardless One, 104
  on legend of Cronus, 106, 109
  on sacrifice of sons to prolong life, 108
  on legend of Zeus, 110, 112
  on Bouphonia, 111

Frazer (*contd.*)—
  on ritual of Artemis, 113
  on rites of Aphrodite, 116
  on myth of Demeter, 117
  on spring festival of Attis and Cybele, 118-19
  on myth of Dionysus, 133
  on ritual combats, 126
  on sacrifice in Rome, 127-35
  on sacrifice of Slavonic kings, 138
  on sacrifice among Germans, 139
  on sacrifice among Celts, 140-41
  on sacrifice in Mexico, 141-6
  on sacrifice among primitive peoples, 147-64
  his theory of sacrifice, 172-8
  his theory compared with that of Hubert and Mauss, 179
  his theory criticised, 181
  on multiple origin of sacrifice, 182
  on expiatory rites and transference of evil, 184
  on magical destruction of enemies, 198
  on origin of Olympic games, 200
  on sacrifice of kings, 216
  on initiation rites, 218
  on suicide of Chinese monks, 228
  on self-mutilation, 230
  on royal suicide, 232
  his account of Tongan funeral rites illustrate anal overdeterminations in sacrifice, 249
  on magical sacrifice of vegetation spirits, 255
Freud—
  on satisfaction of needs, 15-16
  on parents' preference for child of opposite sex, 22
  on unconscious wishes, 24 *n.* 1, 30 *n.* 1
  on hetero-sexual impulse, 34
  on taboo surrounding kings, 35
  on postponed obedience, 39
  on effect of birth, weaning, and education of sphincters, 41
  on education of infants, 42, 44
  on unconscious father substitutes, 49
  on inversion of impulses, 51
  on formation of super-ego, 53
  on effect of death of leader, 54

INDEX

Freud (*contd.*)—
  on anxiety reaction to unconscious wish, 55
  on dreams as wish fulfilments, 57
  on fetishism, 96, 223-4, 242
  on totem sacrifice, 148
  his theory of sacrifice, 185-7
  on primeval parricide, 188
  on the compulsion to repeat, 189
  his reconstruction of primeval parricide, 191, 193
  on inheritance of psychical dispositions, 192
  on origin of totem feast, 194, 214
  on hate, 195
  his theory of the taboo of totems, 196
  on the destruction of toys symbolizing killing of rival, 199
  on the reaction after sacrifice, 200
  on the covenant to share guilt, 203
  his analysis of sadism, 206
  on oral eroticism, 244
  on anal eroticism, 244, 247-8
Funeral rites—
  of Persians, 103
  dead buried or burnt in, in Mesopotamia, 97
  Slavonic, 136
  Teutonic, 139
  sacrifices at, 181
  Loisy's theory of, 183
  mutilation of corpse in, 187
  compared with totem sacrifice, 198
  suicide on tombs at, 227-9
  Tongan, anal character of, 249

Gait, on sacrifice to Kali, 99-101
Gaulish peasantry, self-castration practised by, 230
Ge, rites of, 116-17, 237
Genital impulse, development of, in women, 209
Gilganiesh, his transformation into a god, 60
Glover, on oral eroticism, 244
Gompertz, on geographical cause of lack of centralized religion in Greece, 105
Gonds, their sacrifice of Brahman boys, 97

Gray, on castration of adulterers, 40
Great Mother Goddess—
  as Isis, 87
  among Semites, 91-6
  as Kali, 97-101
  Hera a possible example of, 113
  compared with Artemis, 114
  Aphrodite a form of, 116
  as Rhea-Cybele, 118
  as Bona Dea, 130
  sacrifice of, as father symbol, 221-4
  evolution of, 236-8
  a personification of earth, 255
  symbols of, 96, 116, 118, 237
Greek games, as funeral rites, 127
Gregory III. exhorts Germans to abstain from horse flesh, 140
Groot, de, on killing and eating of first-born, 78
Gubernatis, on origin of Cerialia, 129
Gunn and Jarmerik, their killing of the king of the Slavs, 138
Guilt, a result of inversion, 205

Hair, sacrifice of, 90, 231
Haman and Vashti, an example of dying god and his consort, 104
Hamlet—
  incest motive in drama of, 24
  his unconscious conflict, 37
  the neurotic failure of, 47
Hartland—
  on ithyphallic statues, 61
  on cult of St. Foutin, 62
Hatch, on Christian sacrifice, 254
Havelock Ellis, on sadism and masochism, 206
Heliogabalus, his sacrifice at stone of Emesa, 60
Hera—
  a goddess of marriage and childbirth, 112-13
  -Acarca, children sacrificed to, 237
Hercules, his suicide by fire, 232
Hermann, on Oedipus and castration complex in apes, 32
Hermes, represented by a phallus, 61
Herodotus, on Persian religion, 102

INDEX

Hierapolis, Aphrodite demanded sacrifice of virginity at, 115
Hine-nui-te-po—
  a New Zealand goddess of death, 155
  legend of, a symbolic return to the womb, 243
Homo Neanderthalensis, displacement of, by men, 33
Hopkins, on the apotheosis of kings, 60
Horace, his description of Fournalis Rustica, 132
Horus, myth of, 84-8
Hubert and Mauss, their theory of sacrifice, 178-80
Huligamma, eunuchs dedicated to, 102
Hunting, sacrifice to, 176

Id, the, 201
  the attitude in melancholia of, 224
Ides—
  of May, vestal virgins cast rushes into river on, 131
  of October, horse race and sacrifice on, 132
Imago—
  as a substitute for the real father, 193
  totem feast frees from, 196
  introjection of, by women, 209
  the danger of introjection of, 253
  despot's fear of, 218-19
Incest—
  prevalence of, 25-6
  attitude of poets towards, 25
  attitude of sophists towards, 26
  avoidance of, not a natural instinct, 26
  taboo, 26-7
  relation of, to parricide, 27 ff., 34 ff.
  innate tendency towards, 192, 256
  birth-trauma a cause of taboo of, 241
Incestuous tendencies, in children, 20 ff.
India—
  stones used to procure fertility in, 63
  fertility rites in, 97-8

Indian kings, suicide by, 232
Inhibition—
  due to fear, 39
  due to love, 46
  caused by father, 50
Initiation—
  as symbolic parricide, 218
  psychological similarity of, to sacrifice of sons, 234
Introjection—
  of father, 49-50, 55
  distinguished from identification, 52
  of parental inhibitions, 67
  of totem god, 201
  in cathartic sacrifice, 253
Inversion—
  of destructive impulse, 203
  of sexual impulses, 220
  of acquisitive impulse, 231
Ipalnemohuani, a Mexican sun-god, 174
Iphigenia, the sacrifice of, 115, 237
Iranaeus, on Christian sacrifice, 254
Isaac, sacrifice of, illustrates inverted Oedipus fantasy, 234
Isis—
  her search for the lost phallus of Osiris, 61
  myth of, 84-9
  compared with Cybele, 91
  son sacrificed to, 237
Israel, the sacrifice of his son in time of war, 109
Istar, identified with Aphrodite, 116

Jacob, his sacrifice of Isaac illustrates inverted Oedipus fantasy, 234
James, William, his description of shame, 38
Janet, on unconscious thought, 16
Japan—
  ithyphallic Shinto gods in, 61
  sources of the religion of, 79
  youths sacrificed to earth goddess in, 237
Javeh, a humanized totem, 59
Jeoud, the sacrifice of his son, 109
Jones, Ernest—
  on inbreeding, 26

INDEX

Jones, Ernest (contd.)—
  on the earth as a mother symbol, 34
  on transference of affection from father to son, 35
  on mother rite and sexual ignorance of savages, 36
  on castration fear in mediaeval superstition, 40
  on anal erotic character traits, 42, 248
  on *aphanisis*, 43
  on Hamlet, 47
  on displacement of conflict with father to uncle, 107
  on development of female sexuality, 209
Juno, Dionysus destroyed by, 123

Kali—
  human sacrifices to, 99
  identified with Kesai Khati, 100
Kant, on the categorical imperative, 67
Kartharmata, criminals as, sacrificed to Apollo, 114
Khai-mah, state of, first-born sons devoured in, 77
Konow, on sacrifice in India, 97
Kore, double of Demeter, 118
Kufu, builder of Great Pyramid, 88

Lang, Andrew, on sacrifice in Mexico, 143
Leukos, parachutes of feathers fastened to victims at, 121
Levy-Bruhl, on funeral rites, 197
Lewis, on Spinoza, 66
Libido, evolution of, 244-5
Loisy—
  his essay on sacrifice, 72
  on rites to recall ghosts in China, 75
  on taboo of name of deceased, 75
  on offerings to dead in China, 76, 77
  on sacrifice to nature spirits, 78
  on sacrifice for condemned men, 78
  on the fate of perjurers, 78
  on sacrifice in Japan, 80
  on purification of Mikado, 81
  on similarity between cults of gods and cults of the dead in Egypt, 85

Loisy (contd.)—
  on king sacrificed as Osiris, 89
  on sacrifice in Mesopotamia, 97
  on Indian sacrifices, 101
  on Persian sacrifice, 102
  on Slavonic sacrifice, 136
  on Germanic sacrifice, 139
  on Celtic sacrifice, 140
  his theory of sacrifice, 182-5
Lupercalia, a fertility rite, 134
Lycaeon, his sacrifice to Zeus, his metamorphosis into a wolf, 110
Lykurgos—
  scourges Maenads, 124
  killed by Bacchanals, 153

McDougall, on instinct of display, 38, 39
McKenna, Stephen, his novel *Midas and Son*, 48
Maenads, their place in the rites of Dionysus, 123-5
Malinowski, on absence of Oedipus complex among Trobrianders, 36
Mallan and Kurmi, purification from cholera among, 101
Mamurius Veturius, driven out at new year, 127
Mana, in Hubert and Mauss' theory of sacrifice, 179
Mannhardt, his explanation of horse sacrifice, 132
Marduck and Istar, Babylonian vegetation deities, 104
Mariner, on Tongan customs, 155, 249
Mars, sacrifice of winning horse to, 132
Masculine and feminine, concepts of, their importance in Chinese thought, 74
Masochism, result of inverted hate, 205-6
Masochistic compensation—
  in women, 210
  in sacrifice of self, 234-5
Masturbation of children, 20, 23
Mata, a smallpox goddess, 156
Matricide, unconscious fantasy of, 219-24
Maui, myth of, 155
Medea, associated with Hera and child sacrifice, 112

INDEX

Melancholia—
  inverted hate in, 207
  attitude of Id to Ego in, 224
Meriahs, sacrifice of, 233
Mikado—
  sacrifice of, 80
  an incarnation of sun-goddess, 81
  human sacrifice offered at grave of, 81
Moloch—
  children sacrificed to, 93
  identified with Cronus, 106
  children sacrificed to, symbolize return to womb, 243
Moore, on sacrifice received by proxy, 78
Mordecai and Esther, personifications of new god and goddess of vegetation, 104
Mortuary offerings—
  of wives and servants in China, 79
  in Egypt, 84-5
  of food and clothing in Mesopotamia, 97
Musset, A. de, incestuous inclinations, of, 25
Mutilation—
  of circumcision to ensure rebirth, 161
  of self, 231
Mykonos, Ge worshipped at, 117
Mythra, sacrificed as bull, 102

Nero, allegations of incestuous relations with Agrippina against, 25
New South Wales, first-born eaten in, 164
Ngurangurane—
  his expiatory sacrifice to Ombure, 207, 251
  legend of, 225
Nias, people of, their worship of sacred stones, 61
Nilus, his account of Beduin totem sacrifice, 149, 215
Nogi, his suicide at funeral of Mikado, 227
North American Indians, destruction of person by injuring model among, 198
Nyakang—
  mysterious death and resurrection of, 58, 60

Nyakang (contd.)—
  execution of, 152

Oedipus complex—
  incest motive in, 22, 29
  manifest in dreams, 30
  behaviour of apes as evidence for, 32
  inhibition of, 37
  its relation to castration fear, 45
  inhibition of, due to love, 46
  ambivalence towards father in, 48
  direct solution of, 49
  inverted solution of, 51, 227, 234-8
  mixed solution of, 52-4
  return of, 57-8, 196
  Freud's theory of, 186
  in sacrifice, 194, 256
  female development of, 207-11
  variants of, 213 ff.
  level of, pre-, 240-44
  level of, post-, 213
Ombure—
  fan legend of, 225
  in illustration of son and mother killing father, 233
  sacrifice to, 251
Oral-eroticism, 20
  -stage, in women, 208-9
  -phase, concept of external world developed in second, 247
Orestes, piacular element in sacrifice of, 115
Origen, self-castration of, 230
Osiris—
  probably once a king, 58
  mysterious death of, 60
  myth of, 84-9
  sacrifice of, compared with sacrifices in India, 97
  legend of, compared with legend of Persephone, 117
  rites for dead derived from sacrifice of, 126
  as sacrificed son-god, 233
  his sacrifice as a symbolic return to womb, 236
  interpretation of his sacrifice, 255
Ovambo, rites of first fruits among, 158

INDEX

Over-determinations—
  due to birth-trauma, 240-44
  oral, 244-7
  anal, 247-8
Ovid, on origin of Cerialia, 129

Pacification, of hostile dead, Roman festival of, 131
Pales, festival of, 129
Paley, his contributions to scepticism, 67
Parilia, purification of sheep and shepherds at, 129
Parricide, *see* Oedipus complex—
  children's unconscious desire to commit, 28 ff.
  prevalence among primitive people, 32
  symbolic repetition of, 186
  primeval, 188-9
  its association with totemism, 190
  deicide a commemoration of, 192
  symbolized in sacrifice of kings, 216
  analysis of fantasy of, 214-19
Paul, St.—
  Spinoza's epigraph from, 66
  his recommendation of castration, 230
Pausanias, on origin of Priapus, 61
Pentheus, an incarnation of Dionysus, 124
Pepi, possibly related to Apepi, 91
Persephone—
  myth of, 117
  the mother of Dionysus, 122
Perseus and Gorgon—
  myth of, compared with myth of Osiris and Isis, 88
  symbolism of myth of, 222
Petrie, on Sed feast, 86
Phallic-attributes—
  of gods, 60-61
  of father substitutes, 62-3
  as projections of self, 63
  of Kali, 100
  -symbols, in dreams, 53
  -emblems, used in rites of Artemis, 116
  in Dionysiac festivals, 125
Pharaoh—
  burial rites of, 84
  as chief priest, 85
  apotheosis of, at Sed festival, 86
  originally sacrificed, 86

Philipson, on Spinoza, 66
Philo of Byblus, on Semitic king's sacrifice of his son, 109
Phocaea, human victim burnt to Artemis at, 115
Plato, his theory of the origin of love, 241
Pluto, his rape of Persephone, 217
Poets, incestuous tendencies of, 25
Poplifugia, flight after sacrifice at, 131
Poseidon, sacrifices to, 120
Preller, on connection between *robigo* and Cerialia, 129
Priapus, his introduction to Greece from Lampsacus, 61
Propitiation, of ghost in Central Australia, 156
Puberty rites—
  similarity of, with rites of Dread Mother, 100
  symbolize castration and death, 107
Purification—
  by fire of sheep at Parilia, 129
  rites of, 162-3, 184
  Loisy's theory of, 185
Pythios, son of, sacrificed by Xerxes, 103, 230

Quetzalcoatl, man sacrificed in character of, 142

Ra—
  his name stolen by Isis, 87
  magical injury of Apepi in aid of, 90
Rank—
  his theory of birth-trauma, 22, 240-44, 223, 228, 230, 237
  on incest motive in literature, 24
  on incest motive in history, 25-6, 40
  on inbreeding of neurotics, 27
  on conflict between sons and fathers, 28, 30
  on the stepmother motive, 31
  on origin of castration fear, 41
Regifugium, 135
Reik—
  on couvade and initiation ceremonies, 35, 36, 100, 107
  on development of Jehovah from totem to god, 60
  on demons as degraded gods, 91

INDEX

Reik (contd.)—
  his Lamarckianism, 109
Reinach—
  on Celtic education, 31
  on survival of Snake-goddess in Greek furies, 96
  his interpretation of Mythraic legend, 102
  on totemic origin of Greek gods, 114
  on traces of totemism among the Germans, 140
Rhea, *see* Cybele—
  her marriage with her brother, 105
  as mother of Zeus, 110
Rhode, on rites of destruction, 197
Rhudra, cathartic sacrifice to, 253
Robertson Smith—
  on the flagellation of Spartan youths, 11-15
  on totemic sacrifice, 148-9
  his theory of sacrifice, 168-72, 177, 184, 203, 250
  his theory compared with Frazer's, 172
  compared with Hubert and Maus', 79
Robigalia, 129-30
Roheim—
  on primeval parricide, 32
  on totem as brother, 59
  on sacrifice of Dionysus, 125
  on rites to prevent resurrection of ghosts, 139
  on animals as father symbols, 188-9, 193
  on piacular sacrifice, 207
  on cannibalism as a method of conception, 210
  on Ngurangurane, 226
Rohleder, on inbreeding, 25
Roman festivals, 118, 126-35
Romans, their belief in reincarnation in snakes, 63
Romulus, his connection with Poplifugia, 132
Roscoe, on slaying of first-born, 164
Rose—
  on absence of matrilineal descent in Greece, 106
  on ritual combat, 126
  on self-castration, 230
Rousseau, 25

Russians, their suicide by fire or starvation, 228

Sacrifice—
  in China, 73-9
  in Japan, 79-83
  in Egypt, 83-91
  among Semites, 91-7
  in India, 97-102
  in Persia, 102-5
  in Greece, 105-26
  in Rome, 126-35
  among Slavs, 135-9
  among Germans, 139-40
  among Celts, 140-41
  in Mexico, 141-6
  among primitive peoples, 146-64
  theories of—
    Tyler, 165-8
    Robertson Smith, 168-72
    Frazer, 172-8
    Hubert and Maus, 178-80
    Westermarck, 180-82
    Loisy, 182-5
    Freud, 185-7
  of supernatural beings, 147-54, 194-207
  to supernatural beings, 154-60
  for supernatural beings, 160-61
  in rites of destruction, 161-4
  cathartic, 252-4
  communal, 250
  consecratory, 184
  contractual, 78, 103, 183
  deificatory, 250-51
  divinatory, 80, 97, 183, 229
  expiatory, 18 ff., 204-7
  foundation, 101, 163, 181
  in fertility rites, 78, 87, 92, 97-8, 109, 175, 255
  gift, 166-8, 248
  honorific, 167, 177, 254
  mortuary, 75, 139, 251-2, *see also* funeral rites
  piacular, 114-15, 135, 169-71, 176-8, 252
  propitiatory, 84, 139, 156, 158, 202-7
  purificatory, 79, 81, 97, 101, 103, 128, 135
  reincarnation through, 173
  rejuvenation by, 174-5, 80, 85, 97
  seasonal, 183, *see also* Sacrifice in fertility rites
  totemic, 217, *see also* Totemism

INDEX

Sadism, a form of vicarious expiation, 205-6
Salamis, man sacrificed to Aphrodite in, 116
Sand, George, her relation with de Musset, 25
Sardanapalus, suicide of, 232
Saturnalia, 133
Saussaye, de la, his *Lehrbuch der Religionsgeschichte*, 72 ff.
Scapegoat, 107, 128, 254
Scipio, the elder, supposed to have been the son of a snake, 62
Sed festival, 85-7
Seligman, Brenda, on 'Incest and Descent', 27
Semele, in myth of Dionysus, 123
Semiramis—
  a form of Istar, 95, 104
  her identity with Aphrodite, 116
  her suicide, 235
Sennacherib, rebel sacrificed to, 97
Set, his destruction of Osiris, 84
Sexual impulse—
  stages of development of, 20 ff., 240 ff.
  inhibition of, 39
  inferiority, 38
Shand, his analysis of gratitude, 248
Shaw, his *Methuselah*, 136
Siculus Flaccus, on Roman boundary rites, 135
Siegfried and Brunhilde, their legend a condensation of Oedipus fantasy, 222
Sisyphus, 246
Slavonic harvest festival, 235
Sollas, on offering of finger-joints, 231
Sophists, their attitude to incest, 26
Sovij, the myth of, 137, 197
Spencer, on the worship of plants and animals, 59
Spinoza, the philosophy of, 65
Ssŭ-ma Ch'ien, on human sacrifice for rain, 77
Starke, on oral eroticism, 244
Stendhal, incestuous tendencies of, 25
Stout, *see* Shand
Sublimation—
  superiority in sexual, 51

Sublimation (*contd.*)—
  feminine, 53
Super-ego—
  formation of, 53, 67
  prohibitions of, 55
  of Kant, 67
  repression, by, 67
  reconstruction of, 67
Svantovit, Slav god of harvest, 136
Sympathetic magic, 198-9

Taboo, *see* Incest
  of totem, 195-6
  purification of breaker of, 253
Tacitus, on rites connected with sacred stones, 60
Tammuz, his transformation into a god, 60
Tang, volunteers himself as sacrifice for rain, 77
Tari-Pennu, human sacrifices to, 98
Tarquin, his commemoration in Regifugium, 135
Tellus, pregnant cows offered to, 128
Terminalia, boundary rites at, 134-5
Tezcatlipoca, man sacrificed in character of, 142-3, 153
Thargalia, human sacrifice at, 121
Theseus and Queen of Amazons, their legend a condensation of Oedipus fantasy, 222
Thesmophoria, 117
Tibet, image offered for sick in, 158
Tonquin, first-born son devoured in, 77
Totem—
  original worship of, 58-9
  bear, sacrificed by Ainos, 83
  introjection by eating of, 102
  Mythra originally a, 102
  Artemis originally a, 113
  killed by Slavs, 138
  of clan, as father Imago, 193-5
  slaughter of, a satisfaction of direct and inverted hate, 207
  as father symbol, phallic symbol, and fetish, 215
Totemic communion—
  sacrifice of kings derived from, 110-11
  in rites of Artemis, 115
  traces of, among Germans, 140

INDEX

Totemic communion (*contd.*)—
  among Australians and Beduins, 148-9
  development of, 168-9
  Freud's theory of, 187
  of primal parricides, 189
  as symbolic parricide, 190-94
Tradjas, animal sacrifices among, 156
Trilles, on totemism among Fans, 207, 226
Tubilustrium, 128
Tylor—
  his theory of sacrifice, 165-8, 177, 183
  on animism, 173
  his theory compared with that of Hubert and Maus, 179
  his theory compared with that of Loisy, 184

Uganda, first-born son strangled in, 164
Unconscious—
  discussion of, 18 ff., 239
  acceptance of father substitutes, 49
  hate as motive of totem feast, 194
  fantasy of killing the father, 214-19
  of killing the mother, 219-24
  of suicide, 224-31
  of the father's suicide, 231-2
  of the mother killing the father, 232-3
  of the father killing the mother, 233-4
  of being killed by the father, 234-5
  of the mother's suicide, 235-6
  of being killed by the mother, 236-8
  desire to return to the womb, 240
  perpetuation of Oedipus complex in, 256
Unis, his feast on gods, 217
Urethral tendencies, generous impulses derived from, 231

Vestals—
  present at fertility rites of Fordicidia, 128

Vestals (*contd.*)—
  rush images cast into river by, 131
Vicarious atonement, sacrifice of vegetation deities as, 230
Vicarious expiation, analysis of, 202-7
Virginity, as an offering, 83-4, 231
Viti Levu, circumcision for recovery of sick in, 155
Vitzilopochtli, his sacrifice, 142, 152
Volcanalia, fishes burnt at, 132
Votive offerings, to Kali, 101

Wajagga, uncircumcised child sacrificed to river among, 89
Weigall, on Aknaton, 65
Westermarck—
  on sacrifice of Meriah to earth-goddess, 98
  on eating of victim in Mexico, 142
  on vicarious sacrifice, 163, 176, 180-82, 204, 230, 250, 255
  on motives for cannibalism, 197
Whipping, in fertility rites, 124, 127, 130, 134
Whydah, king's son killed because he was supposed to be his grandfather in, 164
Wollunqua, a snake totem, 149

Xerxes, his sacrifice of the son of Pythios, 102, 230

Yabim, initiation ceremonies among, 154
Yellow River, marriage of maiden to, 77

Zacharis, his exhortation to Germans to abstain from horse-flesh, 140
Zeus—
  rites of, 109-12, 114
  in myth of Persephone, 117
  in myth of Dionysus, 122-3
  his development from victim to recipient of sacrifice, 125
  his possessions tabooed, 253
Zulliger, on the covenant to share guilt in sacrifice, 204